Hippocrene U.S.A. Guide to
CHICAGOLAND &
Beyond

D0169402

Hippocrene U.S.A. Guide to

CHICAGOLAND & Beyond

Nature and History within 200 Miles

Gerald L. Gutek
and
Patricia A. Gutek

HIPPOCRENE BOOKS
New York

For information, address
HIPPOCRENE BOOKS, INC.
171 Madison Avenue
New York, NY 10016

Library of Congress Cataloging-in-Publication Data available

ISBN 0-87052-036-9

Printed in the United States of America.

Contents

MAPS

Introduction

"What should we do this weekend?" is one of the questions most frequently asked by family members and friends. Too often the response is, "There's nothing to do!" That answer implies that there is nothing new to do, that you've seen every museum, visited every historic building, viewed every scenic nature area, taken advantage of every recreational facility in the entire Chicago area.

The authors of this guidebook believe that's not true, that there are plenty of fascinating historic and natural outings still to be explored by every Chicago resident or visitor. Your choices of what to do this weekend are many, varied and satisfying. Our goal is to tell you about them, to whet your appetite for fresh experiences, to help you discover additional "old favorites" to which you will return over and over. We believe this travel guide will provide you with many new suggestions for day or weekend outings.

Chicago is a great city, full of energy, lively people, questionable weather, a wonderful lake shore, excellent ethnic restaurants; in all, a livable city, appreciated and loved by its residents, underrated by non-residents. Even life-long Chicagoans regularly stumble on or hear about new places to go and things to do in this rich and varied environment.

Chicago is a Midwestern city, part of America's heartland. It is located in Illinois, a state known for prairies and Abraham Lincoln. Nearby Michigan and adjacent Wisconsin are vacation meccas because of their many lakes and rural scenery. Another bordering state, Indiana, is considered to be the epitome of Americana. Stressed-out, weary Chicagoans have only short distances to travel for refreshing, slow-paced rustic settings in which to unwind.

There are many guidebooks on Chicago and the Midwest, each with a particular orientation. There are guides to restaurants, inns, bicycle trails, architecture, discount shopping, and neighborhoods. Since no one guide could cover everything about a great metropolitan area and its environs, authors focus on their areas of expertise. This book is a guide to historical and natural sites because those are our specialties, the kinds of things we know, like and have always sought out. The destinations reflect our personal bias towards beautiful natural areas and fascinating historical sites, especially those suitable for families with children. We feel qualified to make good choices since we are both natives of and life-long residents of Illinois. Pat is a native Chicagoan while Gerald is from Streator, a small town ninety miles from Chicago. We are both nature lovers. Our experience as historical travel writers has led us to little-known, but interesting discoveries. We are also family-oriented, having raised two daughters, Jennifer and Laura. We, too, were constantly seeking "something to do" with our girls on the weekends.

We have chosen natural and historical sites that are located either in the immediate Chicago area or within two hundred miles of the city. Some are suitable for a day's outing while others would involve a reasonable amount of driving, thus occupying an entire weekend. Destinations include state parks, presidential homes, botanical gardens, outdoor museums, historic houses,

museums and much more. We have visited and enjoyed each of these sites.

The name of each site featured in this guide is followed by a description which includes its history,
buildings, size, and unique attributes so that you have
a clear picture of what to expect. National Historic
Landmarks (NHL) and those sites listed in the National Register of Historic Places (NR) are marked ac-
cordingly. Practical information includes the hours
and months of operation, admission charges, address,
phone number, facilities, location, and directions. Ac-
commodations—B&Bs, motels, campgrounds,
lodges—are provided for destinations that would lend
themselves to overnight stays. Appendices list Chicago-area hotels and motels for those coming from out
of town.

Maps not only indicate where sites are in relation to
Chicago, but will help you combine visits to sites in
the same area. Photographs may help you visualize
sites you have chosen to visit. We hope this travel
guide will be used frequently as a research tool in
helping Chicagoans, Midwesterners, and visitors from
all over decide what outing to take this weekend.

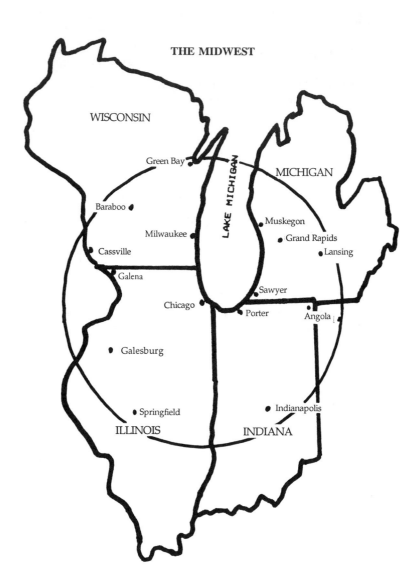

THE MIDWEST

WISCONSIN

Green Bay

MICHIGAN

LAKE MICHIGAN

Baraboo

Muskegon

Milwaukee

Grand Rapids

Cassville

Lansing

Galena

Sawyer

Chicago

Porter

Angola

Galesburg

Springfield

Indianapolis

ILLINOIS

INDIANA

PART 1

Chicago and Suburbs

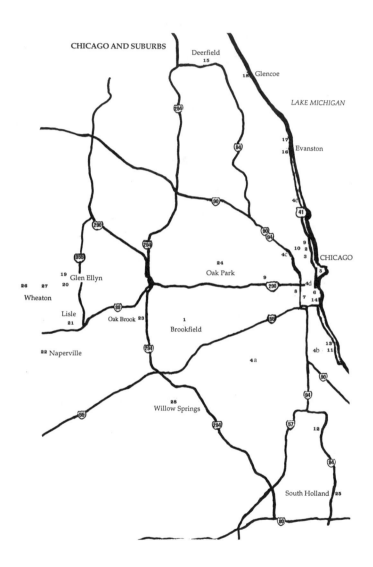

CHICAGO AND SUBURBS

Deerfield
15

18 Glencoe

LAKE MICHIGAN

294

84

17
16 Evanston

4c

41

90

80
84

9
10 2
4c 3

CHICAGO

290

24
Oak Park

5

19 Glen Ellyn
26 27 20
Wheaton

9
290 4d

8
7 6
14

355

294

Lisle
21

88

Oak Brook 23

1
Brookfield

55

13
4b 11

22 Naperville

294

4 a

90

84

55

28
Willow Springs

294

57

12

84

South Holland 25

80

1. BROOKFIELD:
BROOKFIELD ZOO/CHICAGO ZOOLOGICAL SOCIETY

User-friendly, world-class Brookfield Zoo has been delighting generations of Chicagoans since 1934. With over 2,000 animals, including 153 mammal species, 124 bird species, and 132 types of reptiles and amphibians, it is a leader in breeding in captivity. Its 204 spacious and well-landscaped acres dotted with lush

Chicago and Suburbs

1. Brookfield: Brookfield Zoo/Chicago Zoological Society
2. Chicago: Chicago Academy of Sciences
3. Chicago: Chicago Historical Society
4. Chicago: Ethnic Museums
   a. Balzekas Museum of Lithuanian Culture
   b. DuSable Museum of African American History
   c. Polish Museum of America
   d. Spertus Museum of Judaica
   e. Swedish American Museum Center
5. Chicago: Chicago Children's Museum
6. Chicago: Field Museum of Natural History
7. Chicago: Glessner and Clarke Houses
8. Chicago: Jane Addams' Hull-House Museum
9. Chicago: Lincoln Park and Garfield Park Conservatories
10. Chicago: Lincoln Park Zoo
11. Chicago: Museum of Science and Industry
12. Chicago: Historic Pullman
13. Chicago: Robie House
14. Chicago: John G. Shedd Aquarium
15. Deerfield: Edward L. Ryerson Conservation Area
16. Evanston: Charles Gates Dawes House
17. Evanston: Grosse Point Lighthouse Park
18. Glencoe: Chicago Botanic Garden
19. Glen Ellyn: Stacy's Tavern
20. Glen Ellyn: Willowbrook Forest Preserve and Wildlife Haven
21. Lisle: Morton Arboretum
22. Naperville: Naper Settlement
23. Oak Brook: Fullersburg Woods Forest Preserve and Nature Center; Old Graue Mill and Museum
24. Oak Park: Frank Lloyd Wright Home and Studio
25. South Holland: Sand Ridge Nature Center
26. Wheaton: Cantigny
27. Wheaton: Illinois Prairie Path
28. Willow Springs: Little Red Schoolhouse Nature Center

flower gardens make this zoo a place both children and adults visit over and over again.

Brookfield is a vital facility which frequently updates its exhibits. Although in the past, animals were exhibited in large buildings with barred cages lining the walls, Brookfield now places most animals in naturalistic settings. For instance, the Fragile Kingdom consists of the Fragile Desert, which is a simulated African desert with desert plants, mongoose, jackals, small cats, foxes, mole rats, hedgehogs and jerboas; and the Fragile Forest, which simulates an Asian forest inhabited by reptiles, otters, and leopards.

The Seven Seas Panorama is the site of popular dolphin shows. A new facility completed in 1987, the theater has 2,000 seats for viewing dolphins in a 110-foot-long performance pool. Outside, at the Seven Seas Seascape, harbor seals and California sea lions can be viewed frolicking in their Pacific Northwest shore setting. Dolphin shows are given daily, from June through Labor Day at 11:30 a.m. and 1, 2:30, and 3:45 p.m. with an additional show at 5 p.m. on Sundays and holidays. From September through May, shows are held at 11:30 a.m. and 2:30 p.m. on weekdays with additional shows at 1 and 4 p.m. on weekends and holidays.

To enter Tropic World is to enter the hot, steamy rain forests of South America, Asia and Africa, complete with thunderstorms, pools, waterfalls, lush vegetation and 50-foot trees. Residents include giant gorillas, golden lion tamarins, monkeys, orangutans, siamangs, gibbons, macaques, otters, mandrills, pygmy hippos, sloths, tapirs, anteaters, and vultures.

Baboon Island is an old favorite of children, who never tire of watching the antics of the active, fun-loving, human-like creatures. At the Bear Grottos, visitors can see huge polar and kodiak bears who lie on the rocky ledges or laze in their pools; they are fed at 3 p.m. daily. Slow-moving giraffes, who extend their heads over the fences and are sometimes accompanied by very tall babies, can be viewed at the Giraffe House. The Pachyderm House is home to huge but lovable elephants who, along with their trainers, during the summer perform for an audience. Demonstrations are given outside the Pachyderm House at 11:30 a.m. and 2:30 p.m. on Tuesday, Friday-Sunday and holidays, and at 2:30 p.m. only, on Wednesday and Thursday. At 4 p.m., watch the feeding at the Aquatic Bird House.

The Children's Zoo is a separate area with wild and domestic animals that children may see up close, and even touch. During the summer, Seabury Arena is the site of special shows of trained animals—horses, dogs, birds, even pigs—at 2 and 3 p.m. In the Pet and Learn Circle, zookeepers introduce an animal to the children and explain its special characteristics. Children are encouraged to pet their new friend, which might be a boa constrictor, a tortoise or a duckling. The hatchery is a good place to see baby chicks and ducklings. Domestic animals in the Children's Zoo include horses, cattle, goats, pigs, llamas, ducks, and geese. Cow and goat milking demonstrations are given at 11 a.m. and 1 p.m. daily.

Brookfield is a large zoo with a lot to see and a lot of walking. You can take a narrated ride through the zoo on the Motor Safari from early spring through late fall; stations are at North Gate, Tonga Hut, South Gate and Safari Stop. During cold weather, from November through March, the zoo offers free tours on the Snowball Express, heated buses. Bring strollers for small children and think seriously about renting a chair for anyone who tires easily. Available at both the North and South gates, adult strollers rent for $5.00, child strollers for $4.00, and wagons for $6.00.

ADDRESS: First Avenue and 31st Street, Brookfield, IL 60513
TELEPHONE: 708-485-0263
HOURS: Daily, Memorial Day to Labor Day, 9:30 a.m. to 6
p.m.; rest of year, 10 a.m. to 5 p.m.
ADMISSION: Zoo: adults $3.50, children 3-11 and seniors
$1.50; Tuesdays and Thursdays are free. Parking: $4.00;
Dolphin Shows: adults $2.00, children and seniors $1.50;
Children's Zoo: adults $1.00, children and seniors $0.50;
Motor Safari: adults $2.00, children and seniors $0.50
FACILITIES: Zoo with more than 2,000 animals; 204 acres;
Children's Zoo; Seven Seas Dolphin Show; Tropic World;
Fragile Kingdom; multi-image show in Discovery Center;
restaurants; concession stands; gift shops; book store; Mo-
tor Safari; Snowball Express; chair, wagon, and stroller
rentals; handicapped accessible.
LOCATION: Brookfield is a western suburb, 14 miles from
downtown Chicago
DIRECTIONS: From I-290, Eisenhower Expressway, take First
Avenue, exit 20, south to 31st Street; or from I-55, the
Stevenson Expressway, take First Avenue, exit 282, north to
31st Street; or from I-294, Tri-State Expressway, take Ogden
Avenue, exit 28, east to First Avenue, north on First Avenue
to 31st Street

2. CHICAGO:

CHICAGO ACADEMY OF SCIENCES

Great for kids, the Chicago Academy of Sciences is
easily overlooked in a city of great science museums.
Not only is it interesting, but the majority of its exhibits are particularly well placed for viewing by little
people. Life-size dioramas and the many hands-on exhibits are also geared to children. The Chicago Academy of Sciences is a museum large enough to spend a

whole afternoon in, yet small enough not to result in cranky, overtired kids and parents.

Don't get us wrong. This isn't a children's science fair. The Academy of Sciences is a highly respected natural science museum. Founded in 1857, it was the first science museum in the city, and has been housed in an imposing neo-classical building in Lincoln Park since 1894. The natural history of the Chicago and Great Lakes area is its specialty.

On the second-floor of the museum are large dioramas which reproduce the terrain, plants and animals that inhabited the Great Lakes in past eras. You'll see dunes, prairies, woodlands, bogs and marshes, birds, bears, moose, foxes, wolves, deer, and flying squirrels, along with native flowers and trees.

A large diorama in the middle of the floor on the natural communities of the Great Lakes contains life-size explorers and Indians. In the center of this display are small exhibits on native birds, including owls, hawks, blackbirds, woodpeckers, sandpipers, warblers, hawks, doves, wrens, falcons, and gulls.

The second floor ceiling simulates a night sky with diagrams of stars. If you enter the Atwood Celestial Sphere, a mini-planetarium, you'll gaze at Chicago's night sky.

On the third floor are the South Gallery, used for changing exhibits on environmental issues; the Children's Gallery with puzzles, live animals, books, games and discovery boxes; and the Dinosaur Corner with lots of hands-on exhibits and games like Dino Trivia. Nature videos are shown in the small Conservation Theatre.

Upcoming exhibits will focus on the rain forest and on portraits by Alex Rakosy of plankton, the tiny aquatic organisms at the base of nature's food chain. The museum offers a regular schedule of lectures, family programs, children's workshops and field trips on topics such as prairie wildlife, cave environments and glaciers.

Tired and hungry museum-goers can get refreshed at the newly refurbished Cafe Brauer which is located across the street from the back (Stockton Drive side) of the museum.

ADDRESS: 2001 N. Clark Street, Chicago, IL 60614
TELEPHONE: 312-549-0606, 312-871-2668 (24-hour information)
HOURS: Daily, 10 a.m. to 5 p.m.; closed Christmas day
ADMISSION: Adults $1.00, children 6-17 and seniors $0.50; Mondays are free
FACILITIES: Museum shop; handicapped accessible; family and children's workshops; lecture series; field trips; birthday parties for children 4-12
LOCATION: In Lincoln Park, on the near north side along Lake Michigan; museum is at Clark Street and Armitage Avenue (2000 North)
DIRECTIONS: Lake Shore Drive, U.S. 41, to North Avenue exit, west a very short distance to Clark Street, Clark north two blocks; or from the Kennedy Expressway, I-94, take North Avenue, exit 48B, east to Clark Street, north on Clark; Public transportation: CTA buses are 22-Clark, 36-Broadway, 73-Armitage, 151-Sheridan and 156-LaSalle

3. CHICAGO:

CHICAGO HISTORICAL SOCIETY

A day wandering through the galleries of the Chicago Historical Society is an enjoyable way to soak up history. One of Chicago's finest museums, its collections, exhibits and programs are of the highest quality. The Historical Society has more than 20,000,000 artifacts in its collections which are organized into Library; Archives and Manuscripts; Architectural, Decorative and Industrial Arts; Paintings and Sculpture; Prints and Photographs; and Special Collections.

Founded in 1856, just nineteen years after the city of Chicago was incorporated, the Chicago Historical Society is a storehouse and museum of American, Illinois and Chicago history. In 1932, the Society moved to its present Lincoln Park site where additions were built in 1971 and 1988. Unfortunately, during the most recent construction, an accident flooded the building, damaging thousands of documents and artifacts.

Chicago history is the focus of exhibits in the second floor galleries. Beginning in 1803 with the founding of Fort Dearborn which was designed to secure Lake Michigan for the Americans against the British who still controlled the territory, they depict the story of Chicago's growth to the present day. Ethnic groups that settled in Chicago are identified, and maps indicate where they lived. Early Chicago sports are detailed. Chicago architecture, especially the work of architectural giants like Louis Sullivan and Frank Lloyd Wright, are displayed using drawings and diagrams. Radio programs broadcast from Chicago, including Don McNeil's "Breakfast Club," "First Nighter" (a program of plays), and jazz music can be heard in a special booth.

The Illinois Pioneer Life Gallery focuses on domestic life in Chicago in the 1840s. Demonstrations of spinning, weaving, dyeing, quilting, candle-dipping, flax processing, and printing are given.

We the People: Creating a New Nation, 1765-1820 is an outstanding exhibit which chronicles the efforts of both common people and the founding fathers to create a democratic nation. The first published editions of the Declaration of Independence, the Constitution, and the Bill of Rights are displayed, along with letters, diaries, prints, paintings and other objects from the Society's collections.

A House Divided: America in the Age of Lincoln begins in 1820, where We the People left off. The Society's extensive antebellum, Lincoln, and Civil War holdings are used to illustrate the issues facing the United States during this tumultuous period. The exhibition explores the institution of slavery, the fierce sectionalism of free and slave economies in the rapidly expanding country, and the overwhelming destruction caused by the Civil War.

The Society's Education and Public Program Center offers a variety of activities, including neighborhood walking tours, bus tours to historic sites outside Chicago, student and teacher workshops, public workshops, in-service teacher training, and films.

The Museum Store has a good selection of books on Chicago and Illinois, along with gift items. The Society Cafe is open Monday through Saturday from 11 a.m. to 3 p.m. and Sunday from 9:30 a.m. to 3 p.m.

ADDRESS: Clark Street at North Avenue, Chicago, IL 60614
TELEPHONE: 312-642-4600
HOURS: Monday-Saturday, 9:30 a.m. to 4:30 p.m.; Sunday, noon to 5 p.m.
ADMISSION: Adults $3.00, students 17-22 and seniors $2.00, children 6-17 $1.00; Mondays are free
FACILITIES: Hands-On History Gallery; Chicago History Galleries; American History Wing; Library and Archives; traveling exhibitions; lectures; films; workshops and family programs; craft demonstrations; museum store; cafe; handicapped accessible
LOCATION: Clark Street at North Avenue, at the south end of Lincoln Park
DIRECTIONS: Lake Shore Drive, U.S. 41, to Division Street (1200 North) exit, west to Clark Street, north on Clark to North Avenue (1600 North)

4. CHICAGO:
ETHNIC MUSEUMS
a. BALZEKAS MUSEUM OF LITHUANIAN CULTURE

Lithuanian art, culture, tradition and history are preserved at the Balzekas Museum, which was founded in 1966 and 20 years later moved to expanded facilities. The three-story building houses permanent exhibits on folk art, numismatics, philately, textiles, and memorabilia associated with Chicago's Lithuanian community.

The major exhibit, Lithuania Through the Ages, focuses on Lithuania's long history with displays of maps, prints, medieval arms and armor, coins, photographs, and books. There are exhibits on the medieval era, when Lithuania was a large nation with territory that extended from the Baltic Sea into what is today's Poland and the Soviet Union. Lithuania was then incorporated as a subject part of the Russian empire of the tsars. After World War I, Lithuania declared its independence and again became a free nation. Many of the photographs, documents, and books exhibited illustrate the years of Lithuanian independence from 1919 to 1939. In 1939, Lithuania was forcibly seized by the Soviet Union and became a republic in the Soviet state system.

Lithuanians, both those in Lithuania and those of Lithuanian descent in the United States, never accepted the incorporation of their homeland into the Soviet Union. In 1991, Lithuania declared its independence, and once again became an independent nation. A new exhibit in the Balzekas Museum focuses on the Lithuanian struggle for freedom.

The Women's Guild Room features Lithuanian costumes, amber jewelry, handwoven textiles, dolls, folk art and wooden eggs. There is also an exhibit on outstanding Lithuanian women. The art gallery exhibits paintings, graphics and sculptures by Lithuanian artists.

The Research and Reference Library includes 20,000 books, periodicals, autographs, manuscripts, and photo and artist archives. The Rare Maps Exhibit is outstanding, both in terms of the ancient maps' aesthetic beauty, and the visual presentation of Europe's historical development.

Children will delight in the hands-on exhibits in the Children's Museum of Immigrant History. Fantasy comes alive in Castle Quest, entered via a drawbridge. Kids can don medieval costumes, build a castle with blocks, or play with a knight jigsaw puzzle. Puppet shows can be staged by boys and girls at Puppet Palace which has puppets, books and tapes. A dollhouse made of wooden logs with a straw roof shelters both people and animals.

Workshops for children and adults perpetuate holiday traditions by teaching how to make straw Christmas ornaments and decorated Easter eggs.

ADDRESS: 6500 S. Pulaski Road, Chicago, IL 60629
TELEPHONE: 312-582-6500
HOURS: Daily, 10 a.m. to 4 p.m.; open until 8 p.m. on Friday; closed Christmas and New Year's days
ADMISSION: Adults $4.00, seniors and students $3.00, children $1.00
FACILITIES: Exhibits on Lithuanian art and culture; audio-visual room; Children's Museum of Immigrant History; li-

brary; lectures; adult and children's workshops; gift shop; handicapped accessible

LOCATION: On Chicago's southwest side, just southeast of Midway Airport, near Marquette Park

DIRECTIONS: Stevenson Expressway, I-55, to Pulaski, exit 287, south on Pulaski to 6500 South

4b. DUSABLE MUSEUM OF AFRICAN AMERICAN HISTORY

DuSable Museum of African American History was founded in 1961 and its growth parallels the blossoming of black consciousness. The private collection of black art donated by Dr. Margaret Burroughs formed the basis of the DuSable Museum. Now considered one of the finest African American museums in the country, it is dedicated to exploring the experience of American blacks. In addition to its concentration on history, art and music are also emphasized.

Located in Washington Park which was designed by landscape architect, Frederick Law Olmsted in 1873, the museum is housed in the former Washington Park Administration building designed in 1910 by D. H. Burnham & Co. The museum is named for Jean Baptiste Point DuSable, a French-speaking black fur trader from Haiti whose trading post, built on the Chicago River around 1781, was the first permanent settlement in Chicago. Thus DuSable was Chicago's first settler.

African American history and culture are presented through a variety of artifacts from Africa and the United States. Included are paintings, murals, sculpture, masks, dolls, textiles, jewelry and musical instruments. Particular topics explored in exhibits include the experiences of Africans brought to America as slaves. Generations in Struggle is a display featuring a timeline from 1700 to the present which notes significant events in African American history. Segregation and leaders of the civil rights movement are highlighted in another exhibit. A series of paintings focuses on blacks in Illinois.

The museum has a library and archives. Programs are presented regularly and include lectures, films, creative performances, arts and crafts festivals, book fairs, and poetry readings.

ADDRESS: 740 East 56th Place, Chicago, IL 60637
TELEPHONE: 312-947-0600
HOURS: Monday-Friday, 9 a.m. to 5 p.m.; Saturday-Sunday and holidays, noon to 5 p.m.
ADMISSION: Adults $2.00, seniors and students $1.00, children under 13 $0.50; Thursdays are free
FACILITIES: Museum of African American history and culture; guided tours; lectures; films; handicapped accessible; gift shop; archives; classes
LOCATION: On Chicago's southeast side, in Washington Park
DIRECTIONS: Dan Ryan Expressway, I-90/94, to Garfield Boulevard, exit 57B, east to Cottage Grove; or Lake Shore Drive, U.S. 41, south to 55th Street, west to Cottage Grove

4c. POLISH MUSEUM OF AMERICA

The Polish Museum of America provides insights into the history and culture of Poland for both Polish-Americans and the general public. Founded in 1935, the museum bills itself as the oldest and largest ethnic museum in America. Individuals wanting to learn more about their Polish roots should head directly here. Its outstanding library and archives house more than 60,000 volumes of historical and contemporary books and manuscripts, some of which date to the sixteenth century. The museum focuses both on the history of the Eastern European country and the American experiences of Polish immigrants and their descendants.

Those not of Polish ancestry will still enjoy the abundance of Polish artwork, artifacts and memorabilia in this well-conceived museum. Exhibits in its Great Hall include folk art, militaria, old prints and maps, flags of Polish duchies, and regional costumes.

Polish and Polish-American paintings, sculptures, drawings and lithographs, including World War II refugee relief posters and a stained glass window displayed at the 1939 New York World's Fair, are exhibited in the art gallery. Special subject rooms include the Room of Polish Royalty and the Maritime Room.

Specific exhibits focus on the lives of famous Poles such as Copernicus, Madame Sklodowska-Curie, Chopin, Modjeska, Pulaski, Kosciuszko, and Paderewski. The Paderewski exhibit contains a reconstruction of his bedroom at New York's Buckingham Hotel. Traveling exhibits on Polish art and culture, lectures on Polish history, concerts of Polish music, and Polish movies are presented regularly.

ADDRESS: 984 N. Milwaukee Avenue, Chicago, IL 60622
TELEPHONE: 312-384-3352
HOURS: Daily, noon to 5 p.m.
ADMISSION: Free
FACILITIES: Polish and Polish-American art, culture and history museum; library; special events including concerts, movies, lectures
LOCATION: On Chicago's near northwest side, just off the Kennedy Expressway, at Milwaukee Avenue and Augusta Boulevard

DIRECTIONS: Take I-90/94, Kennedy Expressway, to Milwaukee Avenue, exit 49B

4d. SPERTUS MUSEUM OF JUDAICA

The largest Jewish museum in the Midwest, Spertus Museum of Judaica was established in 1966 by Spertus College of Judaica. This ethnocultural museum presents the heritage, customs and art forms of Jewish people from countries all over the world.

The permanent collection contains contemporary and ancient art, and artifacts related to Jewish history. Religious ceremonial objects, textiles, costumes, jewelry, coins, archaeological artifacts, paintings, sculpture and graphics are exhibited. The Ann C. Field Gallery of Contemporary Art displays the work of contemporary Jewish artists.

Especially for children, the Paul and Gabriella Rosenbaum Artifact Center is a hands-on gallery focusing on the archaeology and history of the ancient Middle East. This delightful interactive center provides children with costumes, puppets, and a simulated camel ride. Youngsters can get the feel of an archaeological dig at the Kipper Archaeological Tell, visit the Iron Age Marketplace, and reenact biblical stories.

The Bernard and Rochelle Zell Holocaust Memorial focuses on the historical background of the German Jews who were the victims of Hitler and Naziism from 1939 to 1945 through artifacts, photographs and literature. Six pillars at the entrance to the memorial record the names of Holocaust victims whose families live in the Chicago area.

ADDRESS: 618 S. Michigan Avenue, Chicago, IL 60605
TELEPHONE: 312-922-9012
HOURS: Sunday-Thursday, 10 a.m. to 5 p.m.; Friday 10 a.m. to
3 p.m.; closed Saturday; Artifact Center: Sunday-Thursday,
1:30-4:30 p.m.
ADMISSION: Adults $3.50, children, seniors and students
$2.00
FACILITIES: Museum of Judaic artifacts and art; contemporary
art gallery; Holocaust Memorial; children's Artifact Center
LOCATION: In the south loop area of downtown Chicago,
south Michigan Avenue at Harrison
DIRECTIONS: Lake Shore Drive, U.S. 41, to Balbo Drive (700
South) west to Michigan Avenue

4e. SWEDISH AMERICAN MUSEUM CENTER

Preserving the cultural heritage of Swedish people
in America was the motivation for founding the Swedish American Museum in 1976. Swedes settled on the
north side of Chicago as early as 1840. At first, Swede
Town was on the near north side in the area bounded
by Grand Avenue, Wells Street, Division Street and the
Chicago River. By the 1870s, many Swedish families
had relocated to Lake View and, by the turn of the
century, many called the Edgewater community,
around Foster and Clark, home. Known as Andersonville, it was the last of Chicago's three Swedish neighborhoods. Now, it is occupied by many other ethnic
groups too.

Starting small, the Swedish American Museum
moved to a 24,000-square-foot facility in 1988. The
king of Sweden, His Majesty Carl XVI Gustaf, was
present at the museum's dedication. The new facility

contains the Svea Library, a repository of books, manuscripts and photographs. Permanent exhibits of Swedish artifacts include costumes, folk art, handcrafted textiles, embroidery, wooden carvings, dolls, prints and traveling exhibits of art work by Swedish Americans. Artifacts used by Swedish immigrants are displayed, along with exhibits on life in the early Chicago Swedish community.

Educational programs and Swedish holidays are a particular focus of the Swedish American Museum. Classes are presented on genealogy, arts and crafts, and the Swedish language. Holiday celebrations at the museum include Midsummer in June, Leif Erickson Day, Lucia in mid-December, and Christmas.

The Raoul Wallenberg Room is named for the heroic Swedish diplomat who saved thousands of Hungarian Jews from Nazi concentration camps.

ADDRESS: 5211 N. Clark Street, Chicago, IL 60640-2101
TELEPHONE: 312-728-8111
HOURS: Tuesday-Friday, 11 a.m. to 4 p.m.; Saturday 11-Sunday, a.m. to 3 p.m.
ADMISSION: Adults $1.00, children $0.50
FACILITIES: Museum of Swedish-American history and culture; workshops; cultural programs; Svea Library; Raoul Wallenberg Room; museum store; wheelchair accessible
LOCATION: In Andersonville, on Chicago's north side, at Foster and Clark
DIRECTIONS: Lake Shore Drive, U.S. 41, north to Foster Avenue exit, west to Clark; Public transportation: CTA buses are 22-Clark and 92-Foster

5. CHICAGO:
CHICAGO CHILDREN'S MUSEUM

Chicago Children's Museum is not a collection of children's toys, clothes and furniture as are most children's museums. Rather, Chicago Children's views itself as a laboratory for teaching and learning, firmly endorsing the philosophy of learning by doing. The museum's goals are to trigger creativity, sensory learning and problem solving in children through interactive exhibits and workshops.

This does not mean that a visit to this museum isn't fun. Quite the contrary. Just listening to the squeals and laughter of kids playing with bubbles, or exploring the Three Bears House dispels that notion. In this museum, all the usual "Do Not Touch" signs have been replaced with signs that read, "Do Touch."

Both permanent exhibits and special programs are geared toward satisfying children's curiosity and encouraging self-expression. A permanent exhibit called City Hospital is designed to alleviate the mystery and fear that surround visits to doctors and hospitals. Children can try a wheelchair obstacle course, or put a plaster cast on themselves or a teddy bear.

Chicago's architecture is the subject of an exhibit called Amazing Chicago. Scaled to children's size, the model of urban Chicago can be walked through. Children can enter the post office, the TV station, an architect's office and the Art Institute.

Some exhibits are geared specifically to preschoolers. In the Touchy Business exhibit, kids can crawl through the tactile tunnel and feel its many textures, explore the old-fashioned Three Bears House, or travel to imaginary lands on a Fantasy Vehicle.

The museum also maintains a regular schedule of

special programs, particularly on weekends, in which workshop leaders share their area of expertise. Topics have included African Stories and Songs, Family Mystery Hours, Western Adventures for Cowgirls and Cowboys, and a Woodworking Series for Young Carpenters.

To encourage creativity at home, the museum maintains a Recycle Arts Center filled with material donated by area businesses which can be used for arts and crafts projects. A bag may be purchased for children to fill with the items they like.

ADDRESS: North Pier Chicago, 435 East Illinois Street, #370, Chicago, IL 60611

TELEPHONE: 312-527-1000

HOURS: Summer: Tuesday-Sunday, 10 a.m. to 4:30 p.m.; rest of year: Tuesday-Friday, 12:30-4:30 p.m.; Saturday and Sunday, 10 a.m. to 4:30 p.m.; also Thursday evenings, 5-8 p.m.; preschool exhibit only, Wednesday-Friday, 10 a.m. to 12:30 p.m.; closed Mondays

ADMISSION: Adults $3.00, seniors and children $2.00; Thursday evenings are free

FACILITIES: Children's museum with interactive exhibits; museum shop; workshops

LOCATION: On Chicago's near north side, close to lakefront at Illinois Street, (500 North), just west of Lake Shore Drive, in North Pier

DIRECTIONS: Lake Shore Drive, U.S. 41, to Grand Avenue exit, Illinois is the first street south of Grand; parking is available in lots adjacent to North Pier and in the Navy Pier parking lot; Public transportation: CTA buses are 29, 56, 65 and 66.

6. CHICAGO:

FIELD MUSEUM OF NATURAL HISTORY

One of Chicago's great museums, great tourist attractions, great assets, the Field Museum of Natural History is the kind of place that families go back to again and again. Because it's so big, feet and bodies tire out before interest wanes. And, in addition to the multitude of permanent exhibits, the Field frequently has spectacular special exhibits that require return trips.

The Field Museum was founded in 1893 at the close of the World's Columbian Exposition in Chicago. A one-million-dollar donation from Marshall Field enabled the organizers to purchase collections from Columbian exhibitors. Since 1921, the museum has been at its lakefront location. Designed by Daniel H. Burnham and Edward R. Graham of the D. H. Burnham & Co. architectural firm, the massive, white Georgia marble building is in the Greek Ionic style.

The Field Museum is considered one of the four great natural history museums in the world. Specializing in anthropology, zoology, botany and geology, collections include 19,000,000 artifacts and specimens. Especially important are the museum's collections of Egyptian mummies, dinosaurs, Indian artifacts and gemstones. There are 1,000,000 square feet of exhibition, research and storage space on three floors, and 32 permanent exhibits.

The impressive scale of the three-story-high main hall creates a dramatic first impression. Called Stanley Field Hall, the immense atrium houses the gigantic skeleton of an albertosaurus and statues of African elephants, and is surrounded by Greek columns and balconies.

Four hundred taxidermied mammals and 1,200 mounted bird specimens, collected around the turn of the century and including endagered and extinct species, are the basis for a modern permanent exhibit called "Into the Wild: Animals, Trails & Tails." Focusing on conservation and evolution, it features a Nature Walk, the Field Guide to North American Birds, the World of Birds and the World of Mammals.

Inside Ancient Egypt is a permanent exhibit which provides a new setting for the Field's extraordinary collection of mummies and Egyptology. Visitors enter a recreated, life-size Egyptian tomb, the tomb of the royal son, Unis-Ankh. The burial chambers below are accessed by a 35-foot burial shaft. You can get a close-up look at the unbelievable mummies, both adult and children, and the artifacts that were buried with them.

Second floor galleries focus on Dinosaurs; Fossil Shells and Plants; Plants of the World; Useful Plants; China; Tibet; Ancient China; Families at Work: Strategies for Rearing Young; and the spectacular Gems exhibit.

Also on the second floor is the Field's permanent exhibit, an extravaganza called Traveling the Pacific. Many aspects of the Pacific islands are covered, from island formation to plants and animals, canoe building, early settlers, cultural changes, art and rituals. The 17,000-square-foot exhibit includes a recreated lava flow modeled on Hawaii's active volcano, a lava theater with lots of special effects, and 100-year-old lava samples. To introduce visitors to a Pacific island environment, the Field has recreated an island in which they can wander from the windswept ocean-front beach, through a mid-island forest, to the peaceful lagoon-side beach. To enhance the island experience, beachwalkers hear bird calls, pounding surf and leaves rustling in the ocean breeze.

Interactive exhibits geared to children include the Pawnee Earth Lodge, a life-size replica of a traditional Pawnee Indian dwelling; Place for Wonder, a room filled with a large variety of touchable displays; and Sizes, where kids can try on William "Refrigerator" Perry's football shoulder pads or a size 76 pair of Levi jeans.

Don't miss the excellent book and gift shop, the best one we've seen for educational toys, games and books. The adult selection, including travel books, is very good.

ADDRESS: Roosevelt Road at Lake Shore Drive, Chicago, IL 60605-2496

TELEPHONE: 312-922-9410

HOURS: Daily, 9 a.m. to 5 p.m.; closed Thanksgiving, Christmas and New Year's days

ADMISSION: Adults $3.00, children 2-17, seniors and students $2.00, families $10.00; Thursdays are free

FACILITIES: World-class science museum with 32 permanent exhibits; interactive exhibits for children; changing exhibits; museum stores; restaurant; workshops; handicapped accessible

LOCATION: In Chicago's south loop, in Grant Park on the lakefront, on Lake Shore Drive

DIRECTIONS: Take Lake Shore Drive, U.S. 41, to Roosevelt Road (1200 South); parking is available at Field Museum's north and east lot and at the Soldier Field lot on 14th Street; Public transportation: CTA bus 146-Marine/Michigan and CTA Culture Bus

7. CHICAGO:

JOHN J. GLESSNER HOUSE and HENRY B. CLARKE HOUSE

You might think that you have to go East to see restored early-to-mid-nineteenth century mansions. No, just south of downtown Chicago, the Chicago Architecture Foundation offers tours of two such houses: the Henry B. Clarke House, and the Glessner House. They are located in the Prairie Avenue Historic District, once Chicago's most elegant street.

Built in 1836, the Clarke House is the oldest house in Chicago. This charming white-frame Greek Revival house has survived more than 150 years, three Chicago locations, a move over elevated train lines on a freezing winter night, and a nearly devastating fire during restoration.

The city of Chicago originally grew up around Fort Dearborn, which was erected in 1803, burned by Indians in 1812, and rebuilt in 1816. Chicago was incorporated as a town with a population of 550 in 1833. That year, the local Indians sold their land and moved west, and a permanent settlement was soon established. In 1837 Chicago, with a population of 4,000, became a city.

Most new arrivals were from the East, as was Henry B. Clarke who came from upstate New York in 1835. Clarke purchased 20 rural acres on the shore of Lake Michigan, south of the Fort Dearborn area, along the Michigan City road. A year later, Clarke had a Greek Revival home built. Prior to the completion of the interior, the financial panic of May 1837 resulted in serious financial losses for Clarke's wholesale hardware business. Clarke turned to farming, fishing, and hunting deer to support his family, using the unfinished portion of the first floor as a slaughterhouse for game. He served as Chicago's city clerk in 1846-47.

After Clarke's death from cholera in 1849 his widow, Caroline, began selling off parcels of the property. She earned enough money to have the interior of the house finished in the 1850s; she also added a cupola. The Clarke family, which included six children, remained in the house until 1872.

The next owners, the Chrimes family, moved the house from its original location at 16th Street and Michigan Avenue to 45th Street and Wabash Avenue in 1872. It remained there until it was purchased by the City of Chicago in 1977 and moved to its present location in the Prairie Avenue Historic District. This move, which was televised, met with many difficulties, including below-freezing weather, overhead wires, expressways, and elevated train tracks.

The Clarke House has been carefully restored by the Chicago Architecture Foundation and furnished with original American furniture by the Colonial Dames of America. Noted for its symmetry, the house has a center entry and an interior hallway which leads to the back entrance. There are two triple-hung windows on each side of the front and back entrances, and a portico with columns adorns the front of the house. Inside, rooms open to the center hallway. There is an 1840s parlor, a small office, and an 1850s sitting room which was occupied by Alice Barnard, a teacher who boarded with the Clarke family. It is now furnished as a sick room. On the other side is a more formal 1850s dining room and a parlor. Upstairs there are six bedrooms; the kitchen is in the basement.

The Glessner House, which was built in 1886, represents a breakthrough in architectural style. Its architect, Henry H. Richardson, who was from Brookline, Massachusetts, was primarily a designer of public buildings. He pioneered a prototype of the later Prairie School of Louis Sullivan and Frank Lloyd Wright. The Richardsonian style featured the use of native materials such as the rough granite stones from southern Illinois on the exterior walls of the Glessner House, facing 18th and Prairie streets.

The massive stone Glessner House has a fort-like exterior and encloses a courtyard. Built for the city, it evokes feelings of security with its formidable exterior; the windows facing the streets are narrow slits. The enclosed courtyard is designed for family privacy. The side of the house facing the courtyard looks like an English country manor, quite different from its appearance on the street side. Courtyard walls are of common brick with limestone trim and have many large windows.

Also influenced by the English manor, the interior has dark panelled walls and beamed ceilings. Furnishings, most of which are original to the house, are of the Arts and Crafts era. The four-story building has an irregular floor plan with an interior staircase from the entrance level up to the main floor, curved walls, a library, a main floor master bedroom with dressing rooms and bathrooms, a modern kitchen, three stairways to the upper floors, and a schoolroom on the bottom floor. Prints and china collected by the Glessners decorate the house. The large collection of prints is especially impressive.

ADDRESS: 1800 S. Prairie Avenue, Chicago, IL 60616
TELEPHONE: 312-326-1393
HOURS: April-October: tours are given at noon, 1, and 2 p.m., Wednesday-Friday, and at 11 a.m., noon, 1, 2, and 3 p.m. on Saturday and Sunday; November-March: tours are given at noon, 1 and 2 p.m. Wednesday and Friday-Sunday; closed holidays

ADMISSION: Both houses: adults $6.00, seniors $4.00; one house: adults $4.00, seniors $2.00; free tours on Wednesday
FACILITIES: Tours of two historic houses; Clarke House is wheelchair accessible; book store; NR
LOCATION: The Prairie Avenue Historic District is in the South loop area, north of McCormick Place, between Roosevelt and Cermak roads, east of Michigan Avenue
DIRECTIONS: From the loop, take Michigan Avenue south to 18th Street, east on 18th to Prairie Avenue; or from Lake Shore Drive, U.S. 41, exit at 22nd Street/Cermak Road, west on Cermak Road to Indiana Avenue, north on Indiana to 18th Street, east on 18th to Prairie; or from the Dan Ryan Expressway, I-90/94, take 18th Street, exit 52C, east to Prairie Avenue; Public transportation: CTA buses 1, 3, and 4 stop at 18th and Michigan Avenue

8. CHICAGO:

JANE ADDAMS' HULL-HOUSE MUSEUM

Chicago, a city with strong ethnic identities, grew and prospered on the influx and labor of European immigrants. Strangers in a strange land, these foreigners sought a sense of psychological security by living together in ethnic ghettos. They looked in vain for government aid in their adjustment to America. Jane Addams founded Hull-House as a settlement house devoted to the education and social adjustment of Chicago's foreign-born newcomers.

When Hull-House was chartered in 1889, immigrants constituted about half of Chicago's population. Prior to 1890, the great majority came from northern and western Europe. In the next three decades, almost 10,000,000 southern and eastern Europeans immigrated to the United States. They were drawn to post-

Civil War America by the jobs created by rapid industrialization.

Hull-House was a multi-purpose settlement house
dedicated to serving the needs of both adults and children. Addams envisioned it as a linking agency, a
bridge builder, between Old World experiences and
the challenges of acclimation to the New World environment. The neighborhood was occupied by Italians,
Russian and Polish Jews, Irish, Germans, Greeks and
Bohemians.

Facilities at Hull-House, all of which were open to
the public, included an art gallery, libraries, public
baths, a playground, a gymnasium, a little theatre, a
public kitchen, the Labor Museum, and a swimming
pool. Services available included day care, kindergar-
ten, an employment bureau, music and art classes,
citizenship preparation classes, college extension
courses, and Boy Scouts.

Jane Addams and the other Hull-House residents
championed many social reforms. They were active in
the formation of labor unions, lobbied for strong child
labor laws and compulsory education laws, were instrumental in establishing the first juvenile court in the
nation, advocated women's suffrage, and helped
found the National Association for the Advancement
of Colored People and the American Civil Liberties
Union.

Jane Addams' social work in Chicago attracted national attention and she was the first American woman
recipient of the Nobel Peace Prize. She was born in
Cedarville, Illinois, in 1860, the year Abraham Lincoln
was elected president. Brought up in an upper middle-
class family, she was educated at Rockford Female
Seminary. On a post-college trip to Europe, Addams
was profoundly impressed with the work of the Reverend Samuel A. Barnett, the founder of Toynbee Hall,

a settlement house in the slums of London. Jane decided to do similar work with Chicago's recent immigrants. She and her Rockford Female Seminary classmate, Ellen Gates Starr, established Hull's House on Chicago's west side. They were joined by other women who believed in their cause.

The mansion known as Hull-House was built by Charles J. Hull on a large estate in 1856. Although it was spared by the devastating Chicago fire of 1871, this part of the city became industrial, causing Hull to move away in 1880. In 1889, when Jane Addams rented the house, retaining its original name, it was a rundown building in a city slum.

As the work of Hull's House grew, so did its property, eventually becoming a 13-building complex occupying an entire city block. Additional buildings were the Butler Art Gallery; the Coffee House and Gymnasium; the Children's Building; the Jane Club; which was a cooperative living venture for working girls; the Men's Club; the Women's Club; the Resident's Dining Hall; the Boy's Club; and the Mary Crane Nursery.

The Hull-House site fell victim to the University of Illinois' controversial decision in 1961 to raze the area for their Chicago campus. Eleven of its buildings were demolished in 1963. The two original buildings that remain are the Hull Mansion, built in 1856, and the Residents' Dining Hall, built in 1905. They have been restored and are maintained by the University of Illinois. The nineteenth-century buildings are in stark contrast to the tall, modern structures that comprise the campus of the University of Illinois at Chicago.

The Hull Mansion, an impressive brick two-story rectangular house in the Italian Villa style, has a first-story porch on all four sides, tall arched windows, and a cupola. A National Historic Landmark, it is on the National Register of Historic Places. Hull Mansion has many of Jane Addams' personal possessions. Addams lived and worked in the building until her death in 1935.

On the first floor of the Hull Mansion is a reception room with exhibits of documents and memorabilia, double parlors and the Octagon Room, a settlement office filled with photographs. On the second floor, there is a sitting room-office with Addams' own furnishings. The Hull Mansion has some floor-to-ceiling windows, carved woodwork, and reproduction gas-to-electric ceiling fixtures. A small courtyard of flowering trees and shrubs lies between it and the Residents' Dining Hall. The Dining Hall displays Near West Side: Gateway to Neighborhood History, an exhibit which consists of more than 250 photographs, newspaper clippings, maps, broadsides, documents, artifacts and memorabilia. Other exhibits include a scale model of the 13-building Hull-House complex, original street signs, and large photographs of neighborhood scenes.

ADDRESS: Polk and Halsted Streets, P.O. Box 4348, Chicago, IL 60680
TELEPHONE: 312-413-5353
HOURS: Monday-Friday, 10 a.m. to 4 p.m.; Sunday, noon to 5 p.m., closed Saturday
ADMISSION: Free
FACILITIES: Two buildings; tours; slide program; parking in a university lot across the street; NHL; NR
LOCATION: On Chicago's near west side, on the campus of the University of Illinois at Chicago, south of Greektown, east of the old Italian neighborhood
DIRECTIONS: Take the Eisenhower Expressway, I-290, exit at Racine, go east to Halsted Street, south to campus; or the Dan Ryan Expressway, I-90/94, exit at Taylor Street, west to campus

9. CHICAGO:
LINCOLN PARK CONSERVATORY and GARFIELD PARK CONSERVATORY

Pink and white azaleas blooming in Chicago in mid-February. A gardening miracle? No, its the Chicago Park District's annual Azalea and Camellia Show held at both the Garfield Park and Lincoln Park conservatories. Wandering through their Southern flower gardens is the perfect cure for the mid-winter blahs. At these top-flight conservatories are artfully arranged bushes and pots of colorful azaleas and camellias, interspersed with spring crocuses, daffodils and tulips.

The Azalea and Camellia Show is only one of four annual shows at the Chicago conservatories. Each November, the spectacular Chrysanthemum Show features hundreds of thousands of chrysanthemums in colors ranging from pastels to deep autumn golds. The Christmas Flower Show, which begins in December, emphasizes the traditional Christmas flower, the poinsettia, in hues from vivid red to pure white. In April, the Spring and Easter Flower Show presents bounties of Easter lilies, colorful varieties of tulips, narcissi, hyacinths, muscari, cinerarias, hydrangeas, primroses, and bleeding hearts. During the seasons that Chicago's outdoor gardens are dormant, these four floral shows provide visitors with extraordinary floral exhibits. Shows usually last two to three weeks, giving ample time for visits and revisits.

Even when there isn't a floral show, the two large conservatories provide year-round displays of exotic plants and trees in their greenhouses. The Lincoln Park Conservatory, built in 1892, consists of four huge glass buildings. The largest area is the Palm House, which has palms, rubber trees, and fig trees from tropical lands along with an outstanding display of orchids. The Fernery presents a wide variety of ferns, while the Cactus House displays a collection of cactus plants in a Southwest desert setting.

The Garfield Park Conservatory, even larger than the Lincoln Park Conservatory, is considered to be one of the world's finest public botanical gardens under glass. Its collection includes over five thousand varieties and species of plants. Three hundred thousand plants are grown in its greenhouses annually. Like at Lincoln Park, there is a Palm House; Fernery; Cactus House; and Show House in addition to an Aroid House with tropical vines and plants; and the Warm and Economic Houses which display tropical fruits, citrus trees and spice plants.

Outdoor gardens bloom during the summer months at both Lincoln Park and Garfield Park. Lincoln Park's Main Garden, just south of the conservatory, has eight formal beds on a seven-acre site and is planted with 25,000 bedding plants. Grandmother's Garden has been blooming since 1893 and contains 30,000 perennials along with the 10,000 annuals that are planted each year.

Garfield Park's formal gardens cover four acres. Over 25,000 annuals are planted in 56 flower beds arranged in a geometrical pattern. There are also two huge lily pools which contain 50 varieties of waterlilies, and a Garden for the Blind.

Besides the conservatory and gardens, there are other attractions in Lincoln Park, such as the Lincoln Park Zoo, the Chicago Historical Society, the Chicago Academy of Sciences and the recently renovated Cafe Brauer for a snack. The Lincoln Park neighborhood is known for its profusion of "in" restaurants, some of them ethnic.

ADDRESS: Lincoln Park: 2400 Stockton Drive, Chicago, IL 60614; Garfield Park: 300 N. Central Park Boulevard, Chicago, IL 60624
TELEPHONE: Lincoln Park: 312-294-4770; Garfield Park: 312-533-1281
HOURS: Daily, 9 a.m. to 5 p.m.; during major shows, Saturday-Thursday, 10 a.m. to 6 p.m. and Friday, 9 a.m. to 9 p.m.
ADMISSION: Free
FACILITIES: Large conservatories with Palm Houses, Ferneries, and Cactus Houses; four major flower shows annually: the Chrysanthemum Show in November, the Christmas Show in December and January, the Azalea and Camellia Show in February and March, and the Spring and Easter Show in March and April; outdoor flower gardens
LOCATION: Lincoln Park is along Lake Michigan on Chicago's near north side; the conservatory is on Stockton Drive (67 West), just south of Fullerton Parkway (2400 North); Garfield Park, on the west side of Chicago, is bounded by Independence Boulevard (3800 West), Homan Avenue (3400 West), Kinzie Street (400 North), Van Buren Street (400 South), and is bisected by the Lake Street elevated; the conservatory is north of Lake Street
DIRECTIONS: Lincoln Park: Lake Shore Drive, U.S. 41, to Fullerton exit, west one block to Stockton, south on Stockton; Public Transportation: CTA buses: 151-Sheridan, 156-LaSalle, 22-Clark, 36-Broadway and 73-Armitage. Garfield Park: Eisenhower Expressway, I-290, to Independence Boulevard exit, north to Lake Street, east on Lake Street to Central Park, north on Central Park; Public transportation: CTA buses: 16-Lake Street and 82-Kimball/Homan; CTA rapid transit: B trains on Lake Street/Dan Ryan to Homan Avenue station

10. CHICAGO:
LINCOLN PARK ZOO

A day at the zoo is a traditional family summer outing, full of memories and repeated with each new generation. Chicago is doubly blessed with two outstanding zoos that have international reputations for their collections, breeding techniques and research. What it means for you and me are two great places to spend an interesting day outside, and a sure-fire successful excursion with the kids. And, Lincoln Park Zoo is free.

Founded in 1868, Lincoln Park Zoo is one of the oldest zoos in the United States. Today, it is completely modern, with over 2,000 animals exhibited in habitats replicating their natural environments. The zoo's 35 acres are in an exciting, crowded, urban neighborhood whose residents use the zoo and lakefront Lincoln Park as their backyard and playground.

The Children's Zoo is a popular destination for younger children who tire easily. Its five acres are really a mini-zoo in which children get a close look at a variety of animals. During warm weather, zoo staff members bring animals to the Animal Arena, where they usually allow the children to pet or hold the animals.

Foxes, hedgehogs, ferrets and snakes reside in the Children's Zoo's main building. Outside, in the Animal Gardens, are river otters, a bobcat, deer, prairie dogs, raccoons, porcupines, ducks, owls and hawks. African pygmy goats may be petted and fed. Kids can see newborns in the zoo nursery and watch the animals' food being prepared in the kitchen. In Kids' Corner: A Discovery Place, children can play with discovery boxes, a walk-through mural and other hands-on activities.

The Farm-in-the-Zoo, an agricultural oasis in the city, opened in 1964 and has recently been renovated, though it retains its rural flavor with red barns and white fences. Exhibits introduce the world of Midwest farming to urban kids through demonstrations of milking, egg candling, meat grading, butter making, cider pressing, horse shoeing, and sheep shearing. Farm animals include chickens, cows, pigs and horses.

The Great Ape House is a modern habitat housing chimpanzees, orangutans, and 26 gorillas living in three family groups. Lincoln Park has the largest and finest gorilla collection in captivity and has successfully bred gorillas.

The new Regenstein Birds of Prey Habitat features three outdoor aviaries which have been planted with trees and shrubs to recreate the natural environment of its eagles, vultures, African secretary birds, great grey owls and snowy owls.

The ever-popular elephants reside in a naturalistic outdoor habitat, the Large Mammal Area. Other residents include rhinos, bears, wolves, and hippos. Lions now reside in renovated quarters.

Amusing penguins swim along realistic ice formations in the Penguin and Seabird House. In the Polar Bear Habitat is the largest polar bear pool in the United States; it has an underwater viewing window.

Food is an essential ingredient of a zoo visit and Lincoln Park Zoo has a variety of hot dog, popcorn and ice cream stands in addition to the Landmark Cafe and the North Garden Cafe. Stop for a bite at the recently renovated 1903 Cafe Brauer.

ADDRESS: 2200 North Cannon Drive, Chicago, IL 60614
TELEPHONE: 312-294-4660 and 312-294-4662

HOURS: Zoo: daily, 9 a.m. to 5 p.m.; Large Mammal Area, Great Ape House and Antelope/Zebra Area: 10 a.m. to 5 p.m.; Farm-in-the-Zoo: 10 a.m. to 4:30 p.m.
ADMISSION: Free
FACILITIES: Zoo with over 1,600 mammals, reptiles and birds; Farm-in-the Zoo; Children's Zoo; special events; Landmark Cafe, North Garden Cafe, Cafe Brauer; gift shops; stroller rentals; reference library; handicapped accessble
LOCATION: In Lincoln Park, on Chicago's near north side, just off Lake Michigan, at Fullerton Street and Lake Shore Drive
DIRECTIONS: Lake Shore Drive, U.S. 41, to Fullerton Avenue exit, west to zoo

11. CHICAGO:
MUSEUM OF SCIENCE AND INDUSTRY

In the current movement among museums to create interactive exhibits for children, the Museum of Science and Industry could have written the book. Kids have been pushing buttons, pulling levers, turning cranks, touching objects, talking into things and generally interacting with exhibits for as long as we can remember, and that's a pretty long time. In fact, the founder, Julius Rosenwald, envisioned a participatory science and technology museum in 1926.

The Museum of Science and Industry, one of Chicago's major museums and top tourist attractions, is the nation's oldest and largest museum of contemporary science and technology. Opened in 1933, it is housed in a classical Greek building that was formerly the Palace of Fine Arts for the 1893 World's Columbian Exposition. There are more than 2,000 exhibits in 75 exhibit halls covering 400,000 square feet. In other words, this is a big museum to which you will return again and again.

Attractions on the ground floor include Colleen Moore's Fairy Castle, the ultimate doll house; a collection of antique, modern and ethnic dolls; and the giant Foucault Pendulum. Transportation is an important theme on this floor, with displays on everything from nineteenth-century bicycles; classic, racing and antique cars; covered wagons; Victorian carriages; historic trains; the U-505, a German submarine captured during World War II which can now be toured, to the Apollo 8 and the Aurora 7 Mercury spacecrafts.

The spacecrafts are in the Henry Crown Space Center, a 1986 addition which focuses on space exploration. In a simulated space shuttle cabin, visitors can experience lift off and docking with the help of a 3-D movie. The Omnimax Theater presents specially made films on a 76-foot-diameter, five-story, tilted domed screen that surrounds the audience. Film subjects, which change every few months, have included Australia's Great Barrier Reef, shooting the rapids in the Grand Canyon, space flights, the human body, and beavers.

The entrance floor includes the perennial favorite, the coal mine. In this reproduction of a southern Illinois coal field operation, visitors descend 50 feet into a mine shaft to watch demonstrations of the mining process. Another popular exhibit is the model Santa Fe Railroad on 1,200 feet of track. Every gizmo a model railroader has ever dreamed of can be seen here.

Yesterday's Main Street is a full-sized replica of a 1910 Chicago cobblestone street complete with stores such as Marshall Field's. You can have your picture taken in costume at the Arcade Studio.

Other exhibit subjects include the post office, time, architecture, electricity, urban wastes, farming, newspapers, food, money, aviation, the circus and telephones. Kids love the Whispering Gallery, a room specially constructed to demonstrate sound, and across which whispers can be heard.

Children never fail to react, some with fascination, others with distaste, to the Prenatal Development exhibit on the balcony, with its sequence of preserved specimens of human embryos and fetuses. Other exhibits related to the human body are the Transparent Anatomical Manikin, Anatomical Models, Anatomical Sections: Windows into the Body, Learning and Learning Disabilities: Explorations of the Human Brain, Good Teeth, Conquest of Pain, and Sickle Cell Anemia. The balcony also houses the Curiosity Place, an exhibit on motion, light and sound for three-to five-year-old children and their parents, and the Kungsholm Puppet Opera.

The museum's annual Christmas Around the World exhibit features Christmas trees with traditional decorations from countries all over the world. Running from Thanksgiving to New Year's Day, the exhibit also has a full schedule of performances by ethnic singers and dancers.

ADDRESS: 57th Street and Lake Shore Drive, Chicago, IL 60637

TELEPHONE: 312-684-1414

HOURS: Daily, 9:30 a.m. to 5:30 p.m., from Memorial Day to Labor Day, and on weekends and holidays; 9:30 a.m. to 4 p.m., Monday-Friday, from Labor Day to Memorial Day; closed Christmas Day

ADMISSION: Museum: adults $5.00, seniors $4.00, children 5-11 $2.00, Thursdays are free; Omnimax Theatre: adults $5.00, seniors $4.00, children 5-11 $3.00; combination museum and Omnimax: adults $8.00, seniors $6.00, children 5-11 $4.00

FACILITIES: Science and technology museum with over 2,000 exhibits; coal mine tours; U-505 Submarine tour; Henry

Crown Space Center; Omnimax Theatre; seven dining facilities; museum stores; handicapped accessible
LOCATION: On Chicago's south side, along Lake Michigan in Jackson Park
DIRECTIONS: Lake Shore Drive, U.S. 41, to 57th Street exit, west half a block to Museum

12. CHICAGO:
HISTORIC PULLMAN

A nineteenth-century company town in Chicago? Yes, in the 1880s, George Pullman built a planned community for 30,000 people, the employees of his railroad car business and their families. It was located in the then-isolated southeast suburb of Calumet, which was incorporated into Chicago in 1889. The community was praised as the most perfectly planned town and criticized as a slave pen without equal. Today, Pullman's charm lies in the consistency of Victorian-era architecture in an entire neighborhood of well-planned streets, and its historical background.

George Pullman viewed the model town as an experiment in applying business experience to a community but he was equally interested in aesthetics. He hired an architect, 27-year-old Solon Spenser Beman, and a landscape designer, Nathan F. Barrett, to design the Pullman Palace Car Company town and industrial complex on 4,500 hundred acres of land on the west shore of Lake Calumet. When completed, the industrial section and the community were separated by Florence Boulevard and surrounded by acres of undeveloped land which formed a natural barrier around Pullman. The industrial section contained the Pullman Palace Car Company, the Allen Paper Wheel Company, the Union Foundry, a water tower, lumberyard and gas works.

On the community side of Florence Boulevard were company officers' residences, the Florence Hotel, a school, stables, Greenstone Church, Market Hall, the block-long Arcade Building which contained shops, a library, a theater, and doctors' offices, and the Casino building which housed the maintenance department and a large lodge hall. Buildings were solidly built of brick and stone. Trees were planted along the avenues and there were several parks with flower gardens and fountains. Streets were arranged in a gridiron pattern.

Housing included detached and semi-detached homes, two-to five-family row houses and three-story apartment houses. Rents varied from $4.50 to $75.00 per month. One-third of the dwelling units were single-family homes normally occupied by skilled workingmen, foremen, company officers, town merchants and professionals. Two-thirds of Pullman's families lived in row houses or tenements, buildings containing 12 to 48 apartments. By September 1884, over 1,400 housing units had been built and Pullman had a population of 8,500; in 1893, 12,600. The land and the buildings were owned by the Pullman Company; all of the residents were renters.

The founder of the Pullman Palace Car Company, George Pullman, developed a luxurious railroad sleeping car. The maiden voyage of the first sleeping car he built was in the train carrying the body of assassinated president Abraham Lincoln from Chicago to Springfield in May 1865.

In 1867, the Pullman Palace Car Company incorporated for the purchase, manufacturing, operation and leasing of railroad cars. Cars were leased to the railroads in exchange for the proceeds from ticket sales for the Pullman car over and above the regular train fare.

Believing that people would willingly pay for quality, the cost of the sleeper was initially an outrageous $2.00.

Pullman introduced the dining car, a real innovation, as previously trains had to stop for passengers to get off and eat. The company then moved into the daycoach business with the parlor car. Pullman cars were notable for fine workmanship and luxurious appointments.

Pullman's sleeping car, dining car, and parlor car business boomed with the rapid expansion of the railroads in the United States in the mid-nineteenth century. Between 1850 and 1860, rail mileage increased from 10,000 to 30,000. When the Pullman Company outgrew its facilities, the site for a new factory was selected in Chicago's Calumet region because land was cheap, taxes were low, iron and steel mills were nearby; and six railroads passed through Calumet. Over 4,000 acres were acquired in 1880.

Calumet's isolated location was ideal to test Pullman's theory that people were corrupted by living in bad environments—for example, urban tenements—and would become moral, frugal, and industrious if provided with good housing in an attractive community with many recreational facilities and no taverns. Improving workmen's living conditions contributed to good employee morale, which furthered business production and avoided labor problems.

Despite the benefits of good housing and an attractive neighborhood, the company town was paternalistic and undemocratic. Residents had no role in governing the town, and could never become property owners. It was the company's town. Pullman residents resented the total control that the company exerted over workers' lives, even to their behavior in their own homes which could adversely affect their jobs. George

Pullman's assumption that the company's interests were identical with its employees' was simply not true.

In 1893, the railroads, suffering from overexpansion and mismanagement, fell victim to economic depression. Pullman's contracts fell off, so the Pullman Palace Car Company reduced wages and laid off many workers. Changes in management and a shift from hourly wages to piece work angered workers. Rents in Pullman were not reduced and many fell behind in their payments.

Though workers were dissatisfied, they realized that a few individuals could not effectively fight a huge company. Labor organizers from American Railway locals began organizing in the shops. Pullman employees called a strike on May 10, 1894. In June, a sympathy strike by the American Railway Union disrupted railroad traffic across the nation. President Cleveland authorized the use of federal troops to quell disorder and keep the railroads operating. The strike was not successful, and the Pullman factory reopened in August with newly hired workers and many former employees who had left the union.

George Pullman died in 1897. Although he had tried to fight it, the courts ruled that ownership of residential property violated the Pullman Company charter. The company was ordered to divest itself of its residential property, which it did by 1909. The company town became an industrial community. Over time, the new owners added porches, shutters, and garages, changing the uniform appearance originally designed by Beman. Pullman's managerial employees moved to other neighborhoods, and property deteriorated in the neighborhood which was now occupied by recent immigrants from southern and eastern Europe. The school was demolished in 1913, the Arcade in 1926.

Industrial areas surrounded Pullman on three sides. By 1930, the community was a run-down, lower-working-class neighborhood. In 1960, Pullman residents fought a move to rezone the area for light industry. The last railroad car was made at the Pullman Standard plant in 1981.

Today, Pullman is listed in the National Register of Historic Places as a historic district. The neighborhood, on the southeast side of Chicago, is bounded on the north by 103rd Street, on the south by 115th Street, on the west by Cottage Grove Avenue and by railroad tracks on the east. Hundreds of structures designed by Beman remain and the area has become a fertile field for rehabbers. Exteriors are protected by the historic status, but interiors are undergoing many changes. Most of the buildings in Pullman are private residences and can be viewed from the outside only, except during the annual house tour each fall. Walking the streets however, you can observe the harmony of the Queen Anne and Gothic-style buildings.

The Historic Pullman Foundation, formed in 1973, which has been committed to acquisition, stabilization and restoration, owned the Hotel Florence. An exciting development occurred in December 1990, when Governor Thompson committed $2,000,000 to purchase both the Hotel Florence and the old rail car works for the Illinois Historic Preservation Agency. Agency plans are to fully refurbish the Florence Hotel and transform the car factory into a museum.

The Hotel Florence, 11111 S. Forrestville Avenue, is the highlight of a visit to Pullman. Named for one of George Pullman's daughters, the majestic hotel is a four-story, Queen Anne-style, brick building encircled with porches. There were 51 guest rooms, a dining room, a ladies' sitting parlor, a reading room, a billiard parlor and the only bar serving alcohol in town. On the second floor is the restored Pullman Suite, a bedroom, sitting room and bath, which was reserved for George Pullman. A typical hotel suite complete with Eastlake furniture has also been restored. Wooden artifacts from the Pullman home on Prairie Avenue are displayed on the second floor. The first floor of the hotel has a restaurant which is open for lunch daily and Sunday brunch.

The Historic Pullman Center, 614 E. 113th Street, is the home of the Historic Pullman Foundation. The building was originally a boarding house which was purchased and remodeled by the Freemasons in 1904. Now used as a visitors' center, an audio-visual program on the history of Pullman is shown here. The foundation conducts walking tours which begin at the center. The Greenstone Church, 11211 S. St. Lawrence Avenue, a non-denominational church, was built of serpentine rock quarried in Pennsylvania. The church is a blend of Gothic revival and Romanesque. The restored interior has the original organ, and a stained glass window of a rose has been restored.

ADDRESS: 11111 South Forrestville Avenue, Chicago, IL 60628

TELEPHONE: 312-785-8181

HOURS: Guided walking tours are given on the first Sunday of the month, May through October, at 12:30 and 1:30 p.m.

ADMISSION: Guided walking tours: adults $3.50, seniors $3.00, children $2.00

FACILITIES: Hotel Florence's restored suites and restaurant; Visitors' Center in Historic Pullman Center with audio-visual program and guided walking tours; restored Greenstone Church; historic district; annual fall house walk; NR

LOCATION: On Chicago's southeast side, about 12 miles south of downtown

DIRECTIONS: From Chicago, take the Dan Ryan Expressway, I-90/94, continuing on the Calumet Expressway, I-94, to 111th Street, exit 66A, west on 111th one-half mile to the historic district

13. CHICAGO:
ROBIE HOUSE

A classic of the Prairie style of architecture developed by Frank Lloyd Wright, the Robie House was built in 1909. It was described by the Chicago Architectural Landmarks Commission as Wright's "boldest example of a Prairie House design and one of the most significant buildings in the history of architecture."

The Hyde Park house was commissioned in 1908 by Frederick C. Robie, a 27-year-old manufacturer whose wife was a graduate of the University of Chicago. Robie had definite ideas about what he wanted in a house and they seemed to coincide with the Prairie school of design. Robie asked for natural lighting, a children's indoor playroom at about ground level, no long halls, no boxlike rooms, early morning sunlight in the living room, and a nursery separated from the bedrooms. Robie got all this and more for $59,500. The lot cost $14,500, the house, $35,000, and Wright-designed furniture, $10,000.

Wright and his associates had been planning, building and developing Prairie houses for over a decade. They were striving for harmony with the environment as well as a sense of shelter, strength, and security. Reflecting their flat prairie settings, Prairie houses were low, horizontal, two-story buildings with long stretches of plain cement walls, terraces, and broad overhanging eaves.

Prairie houses were urban creations, usually located in the city, not on the prairie. Family privacy in an urban setting was achieved by overhanging eaves which made it difficult to look in the windows, doorways not easily visible form the street and high brick walls at the edge of the property. The Robie House has been described as fortress-like. Inside, family togetherness was fostered by a central hearth regarded by Wright as the heart of the home, an open floor plan, natural lighting and low ceilings.

The Robie House has a southern exposure and was built on a 60 x 180 foot lot. The broad, central chimney of the Robie House acts as a masonry spindle anchoring the building to its site. The brickwork is of long narrow red Roman brick. The south side of the house has three rows of windows, two long ones on the ground and first floors and a shorter one on the smaller second floor. Using the latest technology, including structural steel and a cantilever roof, allowed the use of low overhanging eaves which shaded long balconies. The back portion of the house has an attached three-car garage, an extremely unique feature in 1909, as Mr. Robie built cars. Servants' quarters were above the garages.

Since Wright did not like either attics or basements, he usually started his houses at ground level on a concrete slab. The ground level of the Robie House contained a billiard room, children's playroom, wine cellar, heater and laundry. On the first floor are a living room and a dining room separated by a large brick fireplace, a kitchen, and a guest bedroom and bath which were built for Mrs. Robie's mother. The other bedrooms are on the second floor.

The guided tour of Robie House is limited to the entryway on the ground level and the living and dining room on the first floor. The living room and dining room form one large open space in a ship-like design with windows lining each end of the ship, Most of the living room furniture is not original though there is a reproduction love seat with attached tables.

A stairway from the ground floor separates the living and dining areas. The pointed end of the dining room, which got the morning sun, was used as a breakfast area. It has built-in china cabinets on each side. The original dining room furniture, which Wright designed, is displayed in the nearby David and Alfred Smart Galley, 5550 South Greenwood Avenue.

In addition to designing built-in furniture, free-standing furniture, art glass windows, and light fixtures, Wright designed the rugs for Robie House. Reproductions of the original rugs have recently been installed in the living room and dining room. The rugs have a tan background, with emblems in blue, brown, red and gray which represent an abstract pattern of the house.

The interior of the first floor is sunny and spacious with its row of art glass French doors running the entire length of the southern wall while a row of art glass casement windows line the north wall of the living room. The French doors lead out to a long balcony. When the Robie House was built, there were no buildings between it and the Midway to the south and the University of Chicago quadrangle to the west so there were fine views. Planter boxes were built into the tops of the balconies and indicated Wright's concern for blending nature into his designs.

Robie House was designated a National Historic Landmark in 1963. It was donated to the University of Chicago by William Zeckendorf and restored in 1967. It had not been used as a residence since 1926. The university accepted it on the condition that they could use it as office space. Much of the building is now occupied by the University of Chicago Alumni Association. Although the building has been well-maintained, it has not been completely restored to its original look. For instance, at the rear of the house an eight-foot brick wall with an iron gate leading to the garages was replaced by an owner with a low, three-foot wall without a gate, and it remains that way.

While in Hyde Park, you should also visit Rockefeller Memorial Chapel, 5850 S. Woodland Ave., kitty-corner from the Robie House, and the University of Chicago quadrangle, whose Gothic buildings were designed by Henry Ives Cobb. The quadrangle extends from 57th to 59th Streets, between South Ellis and University Avenues.

ADDRESS: 5757 South Woodlawn Avenue, Chicago, IL 60637
TELEPHONE: 312-702-8374
HOURS: Tours: daily at 12 noon; closed major holidays
ADMISSION: Adults: $3.00; seniors and children 10-18: $1.00
FACILITIES: Guided tours; NHL
LOCATION: In Hyde Park, the University of Chicago campus area; Chicago's southeast side near the lake front.
DIRECTIONS: South Lake Shore Drive, US 41, to 57th St. exit, west on 57th to Woodland (approximately one mile); or Dan Ryan Expressway, I-90/94, to Garfield Blvd./55th St., exit 57B, east on Garfield to Woodland Avenue; south on Woodland.

14. CHICAGO:
JOHN G. SHEDD AQUARIUM

It's called Chicago's ocean by the lake because over 6,000 aquatic animals live in the John G. Shedd Aquarium, located on the shore of Lake Michigan. The Aquarium has been a fixture of Chicago's lakefront for 60 years, and an extremely popular outing for families and school groups for several generations. Three galleries hold exotic saltwater fish, while another three contain freshwater species. The Coral Reef exhibit has sharks, sea turtles and eels which you can watch being fed by a diver. As if this isn't enough, the Aquarium has been engaged in a massive expansion project that doubles its size, making it the largest indoor marine mammal facility in the world.

Called the Oceanarium, the Shedd's four-level addition allows the Aquarium not just to display fish, but to house an entire marine environment. Aquatic mammals including Pacific black whales, beluga whales, sea otters, white-sided dolphins, penguins and seals are shown in natural habitats. The Oceanarium has re-creations of the rocky coastlines of the Pacific Northwest and southeast Alaska, five cold saltwater pools, nature trails and visitor seating. The North Trail follows a stream to a cove with sea otters and a tidal pool with starfish, sea anemones, crabs and mussels. On the South Trail is the Seal Cove and a pool with beluga whales. A 2,000,000 gallon pool is the home of Pacific white-sided dolphins and Pacific black whales. On the lower level are underwater viewing galleries and a penguin habitat which replicates Falkland Island rock formations.

The Shedd Aquarium, which opened in 1930, is a classic Greek-style building with a central rotunda that has dimly lit galleries leading from it. The rotunda's Coral Reef exhibit consists of a 90,000-gallon tank with 300 tropical fish in a re-created Caribbean coral reef habitat. Most visitors try to see one of the coral reef feedings, which are performed by divers daily at 11 a.m. and 2 p.m., and also at 3 p.m. on weekends and every day from May through August. Everyone holds their breath as a diver enters the shark-filled tank, but the divers always survive. The Shedd has a variety of educational activities, workshops and excursions.

ADDRESS: 1200 South Lake Shore Drive, Chicago, IL 60605
TELEPHONE: 312-939-2426; 312-939-2438

HOURS: Daily, March-October, 9 a.m. to 5 p.m.; November-February, 10 a.m. to 5 p.m.; closed Christmas and New Year's days
ADMISSION: Adults $3.00, children 6-17 and seniors, $2.00; Thursdays are free; Oceanarium: adults $7.00, children and seniors $5.00
FACILITIES: Indoor aquarium with 6,000 aquatic animals; Coral Reef exhibit; Oceanarium; films; restaurant; gift shop
LOCATION: Near downtown Chicago, on Lake Michigan, near Grant Park, 1200 South
DIRECTIONS: Lake Shore Drive, U.S. 41, to Roosevelt Road/12th Street

15. DEERFIELD:
EDWARD L. RYERSON CONSERVATION AREA

A walk in tranquil, unspoiled woods by a river in the highly developed northern suburbs? Yes, it is possible. On land primarily donated by the Ryerson family in the 1960s and 1970s, the Lake County Forest Preserve District manages a 550-acre plant and wildlife sanctuary of mature bottomland forest and farmland along the Des Plaines River. To be able to acquire prime suburban land for conservation purposes so recently is a credit to the generosity and environmental concern of the donors.

Formerly inhabited by Potowatomi Indians, the region's first white settler, Daniel Wright, built a cabin in 1834. In 1928, Edward and Nora Ryerson built a small log cabin near the Des Plaines River to use as a weekend retreat. When the Ryersons acquired another parcel of land north of their cabin, they developed a farm and built a home called Brushwood Farm.

Edward Ryerson, who was very interested in conservation, was involved in the formation of the Lake

County Forest Preserve District in 1958. Since the Ryersons wanted their land to remain in its natural state, they decided to donate it to the Lake County Forest Preserve.

The Ryersons' house, an attractive Greek Revival house built in 1942 using nineteenth-century bricks from an old woolen mill, now serves as the visitors' center and library. Their farm is a demonstration farm featuring an exhibit barn, animal barns, and cultivated fields.

To enjoy the river bank and forest scenery, take the hiking trails that run throughout the property. On the South Trail are at least 15 species of trees including shagbark hickory, bur oak, basswood, sugar maple, American elm, choke cherry, white ash, wild black cherry and black willow. On a spring walk, you'll see the native wildflowers in bloom including masses of white trillium, hepatica, anemone, toothwort, and marsh marigold. Both trees and flowers have numbered posts which correspond to information in booklets available at the visitors' center.

As you walk along the Des Plaines River, look for geese, ducks, and herons. There are two exhibit cabins. One focuses on the natural phenomena of Ryerson Woods while the other cabin contains information about natural and human history relating to the Des Plaines River

A 280-acre portion of the Ryerson conservation area is a dedicated Illinois Nature Preserve. To keep the property as near as possible to its natural condition, picnicking, pets and picking flowers are not allowed.

Each year a series of lectures and workshops about nature is given by nationally prominent speakers on three consecutive Sundays in May. Many nature workshops on subjects such as star gazing, winter walks, nature photography, maple syruping, bird-watching and animal tracking are offered for adults and children.

ADDRESS: 21950 North Riverwoods Road, Deerfield, IL 60015
TELEPHONE: 708-948-7750
HOURS: Daily, 8:30 a.m. to 5 p.m.
ADMISSION: Free
FACILITIES: 550 acres; visitors' center; hiking trails; exhibit cabins; annual nature symposium; nature workshops; cross-country skiing; demonstration farm
LOCATION: Deerfield is a northern suburb in southeastern Lake County, about 30 miles north of downtown Chicago
DIRECTIONS: From Chicago, take the Kennedy Expressway, I-90/94, or Tri-State Tollway, I-294, north to I-94, exit at Deerfield Road, west to Riverwoods Road, north on Riverwoods; from the north: I-94 to Half-Day Road exit, west on Half Day to Riverwoods Road, south to entrance

16. EVANSTON:
CHARLES GATES DAWES HOUSE

The Evanston Historical Society maintains, and is housed in, the Charles Gates Dawes mansion, an elegant lakefront house built in 1894. Dawes was the vice-president of the United States from 1925-29 under Calvin Coolidge, and comptroller of the currency under President William McKinley. He was a member of the Reparations Commission after World War I, and the author of the Dawes Plan which established a schedule for German World War I reparations payments. For that, Dawes was awarded the Nobel Peace Prize in 1925.

Dawes purchased his Evanston home in 1909 and lived in it until his death in 1951. On his widow's death in 1957, the house was left to Northwestern University with the wish that it be occupied by the Evanston Historical Society. The largest home open to the public in the Chicago area, the 28-room mansion has been beautifully restored to the style of the 1920s. Its rich appointments reflect the prominence of its residents and guests.

Designed by architect Henry Edwards Ficken in 1894, the Dawes House is a three-story, yellow brick French chateau-style house with corner towers. The interior features exceptional craftsmanship in the extensive wood paneling, 14 fireplaces, vaulted ceilings, stained glass windows, Tiffany lighting fixtures, wood-coffered ceilings, and a carved oak staircase. Much of the 1920s-period furniture belonged to the Dawes family.

The Evanston Historical Society houses its costume collection and research facilities on the third floor.

ADDRESS: 225 Greenwood Street, Evanston, IL 60201
TELEPHONE: 708-475-3410
HOURS: Monday-Tuesday and Thursday-Saturday, 1-5 p.m.; closed Wednesday and Sunday
ADMISSION: Adults $3.00, seniors and students $1.00
FACILITIES: 28-room mansion; research facilities; NR; NHL
LOCATION: Evanston is adjacent to Chicago's northern border, on Lake Michigan; the Dawes house is at Lake Michigan and Greenwood, one block north of Dempster (8800 North)
DIRECTIONS: From Chicago, take the Kennedy Expressway, I-90/94, north to the Edens Expressway, I-94, exit at Dempster, east on Dempster about 4 ½ miles to the lake, Greenwood is one street north of Dempster; or take Lake Shore Drive, U.S. 41, north until it ends at Hollywood, then follow Sheridan Road into Evanston to Greenwood

17. EVANSTON:
GROSSE POINT LIGHTHOUSE PARK

Have you toured lighthouses in Maine? If you can't resist a lighthouse in the East, try exploring the one closer to home that guided ships into Port Chicago. Since Chicago was a major Great Lakes passenger and freight shipping port during the nineteenth century, Lake Michigan's navigational hazards and violent storms made lighthouses a necessity.

A particularly bad maritime accident occurred on Lake Michigan just north of Chicago in September 1860, when a passenger steamer, the *Lady Elgin*, collided with the schooner *Augusta* during a storm. As the *Lady Elgin* began breaking up, passengers tried to swim to Evanston's shore. Although 30 persons were rescued, 300 drowned. Immediately after that tragedy, citizens of Evanston petitioned the federal government for a lighthouse, but the project was delayed by the Civil War.

Finally, Evanston's Grosse Point Lighthouse was built by the federal government in 1873, as was a 2 ½-story brick duplex for the lighthouse keeper and his assistants. In 1880, two small brick buildings for steam fog sirens were added to the site. The 90-foot concrete lighthouse was made originally from brick, glass and steel. Because of erosion damage, a 3 ½-inch concrete coating was added to the lighthouse in 1914.

The first beam at the lighthouse came from a three-wick kerosene lamp inside a beehive-shaped lens built in 1850 by Henri Lepaute of Paris, France. His name is etched in the brass bordering the glass. The original signal was a fixed white, broken by a 10-second red flash every three minutes. A gear mechanism powered by a weight on a cable rotated the red glass around the lens.

In 1922, the lighthouse was electrified, and in 1932 use of the fog signals was discontinued. Although Grosse Point Light Station had guided thousands of ships through Chicago's harbors, by the 1930s it had become obsolete. It was decommissioned in 1935.

The lighthouse property was turned over to the City of Evanston to be used for a park. Restoration of the lighthouse began in its centennial year, 1973. The Evanston Historical Society restored the lighthouse signal, which had fallen dark during the World War II years. Take a guided tour of the lighthouse and climb to the top of the tower. The original reflector and revolving mechanism are intact. The view of Lake Michigan is exceptional.

Also in Lighthouse Park is the Evanston Art Center, which is located in the Harley Lyman Clark House. The art center has four galleries, used for art classes, programs and exhibits. There is also a greenhouse, a wildflower garden, and a garden of plants native to Illinois. The park has playground equipment, a beach and a beachhouse, making it a great outing for both adults and kids.

ADDRESS: 2535 Sheridan Road, Evanston, IL 60201
TELEPHONE: 708-328-6961
HOURS: Lighthouse Park is open year-round; Grosse Point Lighthouse is open on weekends, June-September, with tours at 2, 3, and 4 p.m.
ADMISSION: Lighthouse tours: adults $1.50, children $0.75
FACILITIES: Six-acre park; guided tours of restored lighthouse; playground; beach house; NR
LOCATION: Evanston is adjacent to Chicago's northern border, on Lake Michigan; Lighthouse Park is in northeastern

Evanston, on Lake Michigan, just north of Northwestern University

DIRECTIONS: From Chicago, take Lake Shore Drive, U.S. 41, north until it ends at Hollywood, then follow Sheridan Road into Evanston

18. GLENCOE:
CHICAGO BOTANIC GARDEN

It's a respite from the city with the feel of the country. Flowers blooming all year round in greenhouses and a wide variety of outdoor gardens can be enjoyed at the especially fine Chicago Botanic Garden. This 300-acre site, owned by the Forest Preserve District of Cook County and managed by the Chicago Horticultural Society, was a low, marshy area along the Skokie River before development began in the mid-1960s. Now it is a showplace.

Designed by landscape architect John O. Simonds, the gardens are on islands, similar in style to the garden islands of Suchow and Yuan Ming Yuan near Beijing, China. Approximately 60 acres are landscaped while the remaining acreage consists of woodland, prairie, freshwater lakes and stream beds. One of the best ways to see all of the outdoor exhibits is to take the 45-minute, narrated tram ride.

The Fruit and Vegetable Garden and the Perennial Garden are demonstration gardens devoted to plants that can be grown in the Chicago climate. In the Plant Evaluation Garden, specimens not usually grown in the area are planted and evaluated for possible adaption to this climate. The Annual Trial Garden tests annuals for their performance in the Chicago environment.

One of the loveliest gardens is the Krasberg Rose Garden, named after rose gardener Bruce Krasberg of Winnetka. Over 5,000 rose bushes representing 100 varieties are displayed. The rose garden was designed by landscape architect Geoff Rausch. It features curving brick pathways leading to banked rose beds of hybrid teas, floribundas, grandifloras and miniatures grouped by color.

Three traditional Japanese gardens, called Sansho-En, "the Garden of Three Islands," are on islands in the lagoons, and contain a shoin building, a viewing arbor and a moss garden.

The circular Heritage Garden is based on the design of Europe's first scientific botanic garden, established in 1545 at the University of Padua, Italy. Professors of medicine were the principal botanists at that time and their physic gardens were used in training students in herbal medicine, as well as being a source of medicinal plants.

The Learning Garden for the Disabled is a demonstration area both for the disabled and for those who work with them. The senses of smell and touch are used to appreciate the Sensory Garden for the Visually Impaired. Most of the Botanic Garden is accessible to the handicapped.

The Naturalistic Garden is a good place to get landscaping ideas as native Illinois plants are arranged in woodland, prairie and bird gardens. In the Bulb Garden, thousands of colorful spring tulips, daffodils and other flowers bloom each year. Other gardens include the Viburnum Walk, Aquatic Garden, Waterfall Garden, Dwarf Conifer Garden, and Children's Vegetable Garden. An English Walled Garden is being planned.

Cyclists may ride on the bike path running through the garden which connects with a Cook County Forest Preserve path. Hikers can wind their way along the

nature trail and enjoy the wildflowers in the woodlands. Birds, geese and ducks inhabit the lagoons and
there are raccoon, fox and deer to be seen.

The Education Center contains an auditorium, exhibition hall, museum of botanical art, a garden shop,
classrooms and a library. There is a complex of 10
greenhouses with displays of arid, temperate and
tropical plants.

Continuing education classes and lectures on landscaping, plant care, indoor plants, flower arranging,
and crafts are offered in the Education Center. Of special interest are children's classes for preschoolers as
young as 3 and school-age children. Family programs
involving both parents and children are also offered
regularly.

ADDRESS: P.O. Box 400, Lake-Cook Road, Glencoe, IL 60022
TELEPHONE: 708-835-5440
HOURS: Daily, 8 a.m. to sunset; closed Christmas Day
ADMISSION: Parking fee: $3.00; tram rides: adults $3.00, chil-
    dren, seniors and members $1.50
FACILITIES: Gift shop; library; restaurant; auditorium; green-
    houses; gardens; seasonal exhibits; nature trail; bike path;
    picnic area; tram tour; handicapped accessible; continuing
    education classes; children's classes; family programs
LOCATION: Glencoe is about 12 miles north of Chicago on
    Lake Michigan; the Botanic Garden is on Lake-Cook Road,
    one-half mile east of the Edens Expressway and one-half
    mile west of Green Bay Road
DIRECTIONS: From Chicago, take the Kennedy Expressway,
    I-90/94, north to the Edens Expressway, I-94, continue for
    a short distance on U.S. 41 when I-94 and U.S. 41 separate
    to exit at Lake-Cook Road, east one-half mile to entrance

19. GLEN ELLYN:
STACY'S TAVERN

Glen Ellyn, a picturesque western suburb is the site of Stacy's Tavern, a historic inn that served farmers and traders traveling to Chicago on the St. Charles and Geneva roads from the mid-to-late-1800s. A great rarity in the Chicago area, it remains on its original site, and is open to the public. Careful restoration of the 1846 inn was undertaken by the Glen Ellyn Historical Society and the village of Glen Ellyn. The inn is listed on the National Register of Historic Places.

Stacy's Tavern, a two-story yellow frame structure in a simplified Greek Revival style, was built by a farmer from Massachusetts, Moses Stacy. It was operated by the Stacy family until 1889. The interior, which includes a taproom, kitchen, dining room and bedrooms, contains pre-1850 furniture, much of which was locally made. The simply furnished rooms have wooden floors and were heated by iron stoves. On the grounds are a smokehouse and a privy.

Downtown Glen Ellyn has a number of high-quality antiques stores.

ADDRESS: 557 Geneva Road, Glen Ellyn, IL 60137
TELEPHONE: 708-858-8696
HOURS: Wednesday and Sunday, 1:30-4:30 p.m. with last tour at 3:45 p.m., March through December
ADMISSION: Adults $1.00, seniors and children $0.50
FACILITIES: Restored 1846 tavern; NR
LOCATION: In the western suburb of Glen Ellyn, just west of the intersection of Main and Geneva Road
DIRECTIONS: From Chicago, take the Eisenhower Expressway, I-290, west to exit at Roosevelt Road, IL 38, west on

Roosevelt Road to Main Street in Glen Ellyn, Main Street
north to Geneva Road, west on Geneva Road

20. GLEN ELLYN:
WILLOWBROOK FOREST PRESERVE AND WILDLIFE HAVEN

Less than a zoo, more than a park, its natural setting
and animal exhibits make Willowbrook Forest Preserve a destination families will always enjoy. Since
1956, immature or injured native wildlife have been
lovingly cared for at the Willowbrook Wildlife Haven,
a wildlife rehabilitation and education center. Approximately 100 permanently disabled animals are on
display, and they are the main attraction for children.

At the wildlife clinic, windows allow visitors to see
the furry and feathered patients. During recovery, they
are put in an outside rehabilitation area to re-adapt to
outdoor life. This area is not open to the public because
the animals are learning to become independent of
people.

In addition to the wildlife being treated, animals
that have been restored to health can be seen at Willowbrook. For a variety of reasons, these animals cannot be released. Some were raised by humans as babies
and have lost their ability to forage in the wild. Others
have permanent handicaps. In the outdoor animal exhibit, visitors can see Gussie, the great horned owl,
herring and ring-billed gulls, turkey vultures, red fox,
red-tailed hawks, raccoons, a badger, a coyote, and
two impressive golden eagles.

The indoor exhibit has smaller animals such as fox
squirrels and chipmunks. It also includes native northern Illinois birds such as mourning doves, red-billed

woodpeckers, dark-eyed juncos, kestrels, northern orioles, cardinals, and cedar waxwings.

Willowbrook Nature Walk, a half-mile loop, is a good place to look for animals in the wild. The trail, which encompasses a diverse field plant and tree community, has a number of tracking boxes where the outline of animal prints can be seen.

The education center has a theater with slide programs and a room called Possum Hollow in which children can handle and interact with many of the exhibits.

ADDRESS: Park Boulevard at 22nd Street, Glen Ellyn, IL 60137
TELEPHONE: 708-790-4900, ext. 245
HOURS: Daily, 9 a.m. to 5 p.m.; closed Thanksgiving, Christmas Eve, Christmas and New Year's days
ADMISSION: Free
FACILITIES: 43 acres; nature trail; picnic area; wildlife exhibits; nature programs; audio-visual program
LOCATION: Glen Ellyn is a western suburb 23 miles west of downtown Chicago
DIRECTIONS: From Chicago, take the Eisenhower Expressway, I-290, west to Butterfield Road, IL 56, around Hillside, west on Butterfield to Park Boulevard in Glen Ellyn, north on Park to entrance

21. LISLE:
MORTON ARBORETUM

"A Living Museum of Woody Plants" is the way the 1,500-acre Morton Arboretum describes itself. Collections include vast numbers and varieties of trees, shrubs and vines, displayed in both formal and natural landscapes. This privately endowed outdoor museum has two purposes: to conduct practical research on woody plants in northern Illinois, and to engender love of and knowledge about trees.

Joy Morton, the founder of the Morton Salt Company, established the arboretum on his estate, Lisle Farms, in 1922. Morton hired Charles Sargent, director of the Arnold Arboretum in Boston, to develop a major arboretum. Joy Morton inherited his love of trees from his father, J. Sterling Morton, who had been the territorial governor of Nebraska, and secretary of agriculture under President Cleveland. The elder Morton, who had encouraged Nebraskans to plant trees, originated Arbor Day.

The Morton Arboretum may be toured by car along 12 miles of one-way roads. As pleasant as that may be, it misses the whole point, which is to walk in the woods. Hassled urbanites need to get out of their cars, and to get into nature. Children need the freedom to see growing things close up, to smell the flowers, and look for birds and rabbits. We can't think of a better or more convenient place to do this than at the arboretum.

Although there are 25 miles of walking trails, each one is usually a mile or less. Some paths lead through woodlands and larger plant collections, while others are near gardens and park-like areas. The Illinois Trees Nature Trail, three loops from one-half to three miles long, wanders through meadows and woodlands that are carpeted with wildflowers in spring. Big Rock Trail meanders through oak woodland for a mile. On the Evergreen Trail, you'll view a lake and conifers, while the Geographic Trail features almost a mile of plants from around the world.

The Morton Arboretum is especially known for the delicate beauty of its flowering trees in spring. Blooming crabapple, lilac, magnolia and cherry trees are exquisite in April and May. Fall, when the leaves change, is another especially colorful time.

The arboretum is a boon to Chicago-area gardeners. The research staff at Morton constantly evaluates plants, trees, vines and shrubs for their suitability to the environmental conditions of northern Illinois. The arboretum's man-made landscapes provide examples which home landscapers can emulate.

Before deciding on what to plant, gardeners can examine the collections at the arboretum. There are gardens of ground covers, hedges, dwarf shrubs, pines, perennials, roses, and wildflowers. There is even a Plant Clinic which can be called for aid in selecting plants for landscaping, or diagnosis of woody plant ailments. The Plant Clinic's number is 708-719-2424.

Classes are offered for adults, children and family groups. Topics include natural history, botanical art, nature photography, horticulture and landscaping.

ADDRESS: Lisle, IL 60532
TELEPHONE: 708-968-0074
HOURS: Daily, 9 a.m. to dusk (no later than 7 p.m.) during daylight saving time; 9 a.m. to 5 p.m. during standard time
ADMISSION: $3.00 per car, $2.00 per senior citizen car, $1.00 per car on Wednesdays
FACILITIES: 1,500 acres; walking trails; visitor center; book and gift shop; restaurant; theater; library; research center; classes; Plant Clinic
LOCATION: 17 miles west of Chicago, just north of Lisle at the intersection of IL 53 and I-88
DIRECTIONS: From Chicago, take the Eisenhower Expressway, I-290, or the Tri-State Tollway, I-294, west to the East-West Tollway, I-88, exit at IL 53, arboretum entrance is a half mile north; if traveling east on the East-West Tollway, I-88, exit at Wheaton-Naperville Road and take Warrenville Road east to IL 53.

22. NAPERVILLE:
NAPER SETTLEMENT

You don't have to go all the way to Williamsburg to get a taste of American history. A museum village just west of Chicago re-creates life in a small northern Illinois town during the last three-quarters of the nineteenth century. Naper Settlement is a 25-building outdoor museum on 12 acres of land in Naperville, a 150-year-old DuPage County town. Reached by the Chicago sprawl during the last couple of decades, Naperville is now one of the city's biggest and fastest growing suburbs.

Naperville is named for Joseph Naper, a sea captain who in 1831 was the first white settler in the area, then inhabited by Potawatomi Indians. Naper and his family were soon joined by other pioneers, and a town grew up on the prairie. There was a saw mill, a school, a trading post, a grist mill, a store, a hotel and private homes. In 1857, Naperville was incorporated as the first town in DuPage County.

Naper Settlement is an outdoor museum operated by the Naperville Heritage Society. Reflecting the time period from 1831 to 1900, the museum's historic buildings are original Naperville structures that have been relocated to the site. The first building acquired by the Society, and the one that gave the impetus for the museum village, was the 1864 Century Memorial Chapel. The Gothic Revival church was moved to its new site in two pieces in 1969. Originally Episcopal, it is now non-denominational. The picturesque church has restored stenciling and a baptismal font. Weddings are frequently held there.

The 1841 Evangelical Meeting House is used as the Visitor Center. Fort Payne is a reconstruction of an 1832 fort built by volunteer militiamen during the Black Hawk War, but never used. Children particularly like the fort's blockhouse and stockade. Other buildings include an 1843 Log House, a stage coach inn called the Paw Paw Station, the 1842 Murray House, a one-room schoolhouse, a blacksmith shop, doctor's office and a stonecutter's shop. The two-story brick Half-Way House, built in 1843, was located halfway between Aurora and Naperville. The 1860 Fire House has a restored pumper that was purchased by the city of Naperville in 1874 for $1,000.

Very different from the small log cabins is the 1883 Martin-Mitchell Mansion. On its original site, the two-and-a- half-story brick Victorian mansion was the home of George Martin II, who came from Scotland and founded a brick, tile and limestone business. The house reflects the lifestyle of a successful late-nineteenth-century businessman. Listed on the National Register of Historic Places, the house, called Pine Craig, has a handcrafted solid walnut staircase, both upstairs and downstairs parlors, five bedrooms, servants' quarters and marble fireplaces. The furnishings are Victorian and some belonged to the Martins. George's daughter, Caroline Martin-Mitchell, willed the house and 200 acres of land to the city of Naperville in 1936.

During December, Naper Settlement is decorated for Christmas. Candlelight strolls, Christmas concerts and holiday tours are offered. The Settlement has several other special events during its season.

ADDRESS: 201 W. Porter Avenue, Naperville, IL 60540
TELEPHONE: 708-420-6010
HOURS: Wednesday, Saturday and Sunday, 1:30-4:30 p.m.,

from first Sunday in May through last Sunday in October; also second and third weekends in December

ADMISSION: Adults $4.00, children 6-17 and seniors $2.00, families $10.00

FACILITIES: Re-created nineteenth century museum village; 25 historic buildings on 12 acres; Martin-Mitchell Mansion; museum store; special events; Christmas festival

LOCATION: In Naperville, a far western suburb, about 30 miles from downtown Chicago; Naper Settlement is two blocks from downtown Naperville

DIRECTIONS: From Chicago, take the Eisenhower Express-way, I-290, west to the East-West Tollway, I-88, west on I-88 to Naperville Road exit, south on Naperville Road to downtown Naperville, west on Aurora Avenue two blocks; Naper Settlement is between Aurora, Webster and Porter Avenues

23. OAK BROOK:

FULLERSBURG WOODS FOREST PRESERVE AND NATURE CENTER and OLD GRAUE MILL AND MUSEUM

Fullersburg Woods, 206 wooded acres along Salt Creek, are tucked in between the beautiful, old wealthy suburb of Hinsdale and the new wealthy sub-urb of Oak Brook. Part of the Forest Preserve District of DuPage County since 1920, they form a natural oasis in a recently developed area. A nature center, nature trails, and an operating 1850s grist mill are only a short ride away for west suburban families who crave a walk in the woods.

Graue Mill, a national historical landmark, is in Fullersburg Woods just northwest of the junction of Spring and York roads. Salt Creek provided the water power for the mill built by Frederick Graue, a German immigrant, in 1852. The massive three-and-one-half-story building is constructed of handmade red brick with a limestone foundation and trim, handhewn white oak posts and beams, and wooden pegs. Frederick Graue and his family operated the grist mill for 60 years, providing corn, wheat, oats and flour. Abraham Lincoln is said to have stopped at Graue's mill. The mill was a station on the Underground Railroad.

Eventually modern milling methods made the mill obsolete. After being closed for decades, it was partially restored by the Civilian Conservation Corps who had a camp in Fullersburg. The mill reopened in 1950, and is the only operating grist mill in Illinois. Millers demonstrate corn grinding using the restored wooden gearwheels and buhrstones powered by the huge wooden waterwheel. Corn meal and wheat flour can be purchased.

The mill's upper floors house a pioneer museum. The second floor replicates an old-fashioned barn complete with farm implements and vehicles, along with a sleigh. On the third floor, rooms are furnished as they would have been in the nineteenth century. There is a child's room, a Victorian drawing-room, a kitchen with a cast-iron stove, and a sitting room. The Old Country Store is the gift shop.

Fullersburg Woods' many decades of heavy use resulted in the death of trees and the pollution of Salt Creek. In an effort to restore the natural environment, the DuPage Forest Preserve District made a number of changes. In 1969, boating on Salt Creek was banned, and picnicking was restricted to a designated area. Fullersburg Woods is now a nature preserve, and the creek and forest have improved tremendously.

A 1 and ⅓-mile hiking trail winds past oak, cottonwood, sycamore and maple trees. Headphones can be rented to interpret the sights along this trail. Spring brings a variety of wildflowers, and most of them are identified along the wildflower trail. There is always wildlife and over 100 species of birds. Children cluster on the bank of Salt Creek, feeding the many ducks and geese.

An audio-visual show on the environment of Fullersburg Woods is shown in the Environmental Theater.

ADDRESS: Fullersburg Woods: 3609 Spring Road, Oak Brook, IL 60521; Graue Mill: P.O. Box 4533, Oak Brook, IL 60522-4533

TELEPHONE: Fullersburg Woods: 708-790-4900 and 708-790-4912; Graue Mill: 708-655-2090

HOURS: Fullersburg Woods: daily, from one hour after sunrise until one hour after sunset; Environmental Center: daily, 9 a.m. to 5 p.m., March-October; Graue Mill and Museum: daily, mid-April to mid-November, 10 a.m. to 5 p.m.

ADMISSION: Fullersburg Woods: free; Graue Mill: Adults, $2.00, Children 3-15, $0.50

FACILITIES: Fullersburg Woods: nature center, nature trails; Graue Mill: operating waterwheel grist mill; stoneground corn meal and whole wheat flour; gift shop; pioneer museum; special events on the third Sunday of each month, from April-November; NHL

LOCATION: Oak Brook is a western suburb in DuPage County, 18 miles from downtown Chicago; Graue Mill is located on York Road, two blocks north of Ogden Avenue (IL 34); Fullersburg Woods is located on Spring Road, about one-half mile north of Ogden

DIRECTIONS: Take the Tri-State Tollway, I-294, to Ogden Avenue west exit, west on Ogden about one-half mile to York Road, north on York Road about two blocks, Graue Mill parking lot on east side of York Road; or after turning on to York Road, stay left and enter Spring Road, follow Spring

Road north about one-third mile to Fullersburg Woods
parking lot

24. OAK PARK:
FRANK LLOYD WRIGHT HOME
AND STUDIO

People all over the world know and admire the
work of architect Frank Lloyd Wright and travel great
distances to see his buildings. Wright devotees make
pilgrimages to Oak Park to see where the architect
began his career, lived for 20 years in a house he built
for himself, developed his famous Prairie Houses and
practiced his profession. More than 20 Frank Lloyd
Wright homes can be seen in Oak Park, and there are
another half a dozen in adjacent River Forest. How
lucky we are in Chicago to have this great architectural
heritage nearby.

Wright's professional career spanned 70 years and
included over 430 buildings and designs. He is credited with creating a truly American style of architecture. By 1910, Wright's Prairie school of architecture
had gained world-wide recognition. Wright believed
that a building must be an inseparable part of its setting, that architecture should be organic, a blending of
nature and man-made forms, an integration of buildings and landscape.

Frank Lloyd Wright built his home in Oak Park for
himself and his new bride, Catherine Tobin, in 1889. At
that time, 22-year-old Wright worked for the architecture firm of Adler and Sullivan. Louis Sullivan lent his
young draftsman $5,000 to buy the lot and pay the
builder. As the second house ever designed by the
budding architect, its interest lies partly in its early

place in the historical evolution of Wright's architectural style. It was named a National Historic Landmark in 1976.

Sullivan and Adler fired Wright in 1893 for violating his contract by taking commissions to build houses on his own. Wright referred to these secret projects as "bootlegged" houses. After losing his job, Wright added an architecture studio to the home that he shared with Catherine and their six children so that he could pursue his practice. The years Wright operated his business from his Oak Park home represent an active, creative period in which he developed his Prairie House.

As he experimented with space, light, form, materials, furnishings and decorative arts, Wright often used his own home as a laboratory in which to test his ideas. The house in Oak Park was an informal, Queen Anne, shingle-style cottage which the young architect remodeled as his family grew. A children's playroom, a dining room and a kitchen were added in 1895, while the studio was added in 1898.

Wright left his wife, family and home in Oak Park in 1909 to pursue a love affair in Europe with Mamah Cheney, a neighbor whose husband had been his client. On his return from Europe, Wright built a home and studio called Taliesin in Spring Green, Wisconsin, for Mamah and himself. In 1911, he remodeled the Oak Park house to be used as a rental property, and the studio for Catherine and their children to live in. In 1925, Wright sold his Oak Park home and studio. It went through a succession of owners and alterations, and at one point the property was subdivided into seven apartments. It suffered a great deal of deterioration during those years.

Restoration of the Frank Lloyd Wright Home and Studio took 12 years and cost over $2,000,000. The property is now owned by the National Trust for Historic Preservation and has been restored and administered by the Frank Lloyd Wright Home and Studio Foundation, a non-profit foundation established in 1974 to acquire, restore and operate the property as a historic house museum and a center for public education on Wright. The building has been restored to its condition in 1909, the last year Wright lived and worked there. This date was a controversial choice because it implied removal of Wright's 1911 remodeling. Despite substantial deterioration of the foundations, masonry, sheathing, shingles, trim, art glass, skylights, and roofing, restoration work has been meticulous.

When you enter the Wright home on your guided tour, the living room is to your left and there is a light oak stairway in front of you. Couches are built into the living room's bays. The bays' diamond-paned windows provide plenty of light and a sweeping view. There are classical touches in the ceiling's dentil molding, the ceiling freize, and the statue on the steps. The color scheme is composed of two tones of green on the walls, and green velvet upholstery on sofas and doorway draperies. Wright wanted the walls to reflect nature's colors.

Off the living room in a small inglenook is a red brick fireplace with straight-backed, built-in settles on either side. On a wooden panel over the fireplace is engraved, "Truth is life. Good friend, around these hearth stones speak no evil word of any creature." Even in this early home, the hearth as a symbol of the heart of the home, the center of family warmth, was extremely important to Wright. Between the home and the studio, there are a total of six fireplaces.

The dining room is part of the 1895 addition and is consummate Wright. The red tile of the fireplace is also used on the floor. The only free-standing furniture, a large oak table, six high-backed chairs and a high chair, were designed by Wright. The most striking feature of this outstanding room is the large, rectangular ceiling grille which was a recessed lighting fixture, the first use of recessed, indirect lighting. The light illuminated only the table area, something Wright referred to as a room within a room.

Upstairs are girls' and boys' bedrooms separated by a wall that does not extend to the high ceiling. Wright did not value attics so the upper-story rooms have vaulted ceilings. The master bedroom has two murals of American plains Indians painted by Orlando Giannini in the arches of the ceiling vaults. A rather plain wooden bed designed by Wright and a simple chest furnish the room. Modern features are the built-in closets and the bathroom.

The children's upstairs playroom is the most stunning room in the house. It is a large, sunny room with a high arched ceiling with skylights, brick fireplace and walls, a large mural by Giannini over the fireplace, two enormous window seats with bands of art glass windows on two sides of the room, built-in bookshelves and drawers for toy storage, a built-in grand piano and an indoor balcony. What a playroom!

The studio complex consists of a foyer, a drafting room with balcony, an office and an octagonal library. The foyer has a long table on which architectural plans could be unrolled, skylights of green and orange glass, copper-colored walls and an unusual floor made of concrete and wood chips.

The drafting room, the main area of the studio, has 25-foot ceilings and a balcony work area that is supported by an intricate chain system. There are several drafting tables and stools at which Wright and his associates worked, a large brick fireplace, a domed atrium ceiling, and a huge safe in which architectural plans were placed each night to protect them from fire.

Wright met with clients in the octagonal library. The room contains a table and chairs designed by Wright, built-in cabinets with glass doors in which he kept samples of building materials, a skylight, copper-colored walls and a fireplace.

An architectural guide map of Oak Park and River Forest may be purchased at the Ginkgo Tree Bookstore at the Wright home or at the Oak Park Visitors Center, 158 Forest Avenue. This map indicates not only all of the Wright houses in those suburbs but also late-nineteenth- and early-twentieth-century buildings of other prominent architects. These buildings are all privately owned and may only be viewed from the outside.

Once a year, on the third weekend in May, the Frank Lloyd Wright Foundation sponsors a Wright Plus Housewalk which features guided tours of eight privately owned homes and two public buildings designed by Wright and his contemporaries. Tickets for this popular tour go on sale March 1.

The Frank Lloyd Wright Home and Studio Foundation formerly gave tours of Wright's Unity Temple, located at 875 Lake Street, in Oak Park. Due to recent questions about the structural soundness of the building, the Foundation has suspended tours. However, Unity Temple gives its own cassette-guided tours Monday-Friday from 2-4 p.m., and guided tours on Saturday and Sunday at 2 p.m. For information, call 708-848-6225.

ADDRESS: 951 Chicago Avenue, Oak Park, IL 60302
TELEPHONE: 708-848-1500
HOURS: Tours of Wright home and studio: Monday-Friday, 11
    a.m., 1 and 3 p.m.; Saturday and Sunday, continuously

from 11 a.m. to 4 p.m.; closed Thanksgiving, Christmas and
New Year's days
ADMISSION: Adults $5.00, youths 10-18 and seniors $3.00
FACILITIES: Guided tours; bookshop; annual housewalk on
the third weekend in May; NHL
LOCATION: Oak Park is adjacent to Chicago's west side, 10
miles west of downtown Chicago
DIRECTIONS: From Chicago, take the Eisenhower Express-
way, I-290, west to the Harlem Avenue exit, north on Har-
lem to Chicago Avenue, east on Chicago to Forest Avenue;
Public transportation: CTA rapid transit, the Lake
Street/Dan Ryan el to the Harlem/Marion stop; the Chi-
cago Northwestern-West line commuter train also serves
Oak Park.

25. SOUTH HOLLAND:
SAND RIDGE NATURE CENTER

Remnants of the Chicago area's geological past are
the focus of exhibits at Sand Ridge Nature Center, a
235-acre site in the Thorn Creek Division of the Cook
County Forest Preserves. In addition to the exhibition
building which emphasizes the natural history of the
Calumet region, the center has three nature trails,
naturalist directed hikes, and wildlife talks.

Sand Ridge Nature Center is located on the shore of
Lake Chicago, the glacial lake that was Lake Michigan's predecessor. Lake Chicago was formed 12,000
years ago as the glacier that covered most of Illinois
and Indiana melted, and meltwater was trapped by
rocks and boulders left by the retreating glacier. Lake
Chicago was 60 feet higher than Lake Michigan is
today.

Over a long period of time, water from Lake Chicago drained into the Chicago Outlet. Rivers formed

and carved out the valleys where the Des Plaines River and the Calumet Sag Channel flow today. As the lake's level fell, sandy beaches and ridges were formed. Since the level fell in stages, there are three former beach areas in the southern suburbs. Glenwood Beach formed 12,000 years ago, Calumet Beach formed 10,000 years ago, and the Toleston Beach formed 8,000 years ago. Lake Michigan's current shoreline dates back 6,000 years. Sandy Ridge is on Toleston Beach.

Don't bother bringing a beach umbrella and sunscreen. After the lake receded, the beach areas developed into prairies, forests and marshland. Towns now occupy this land. Come to Sand Ridge Nature Center to enjoy unspoiled nature by walking the three trails. Trail guides will help identify the trees, wildflowers, birds and wildlife along the way.

Lost Beach Trail extends two miles and loops along a forested beach ridge and sand dune. Dogwood Trail is a one-mile walk past a prairie restoration area, forests and marshes. Redwing Trail, one-half mile long, passes through oak forest and shrub to Red Wing Pond. All trails begin and end at the exhibition center. Picnicking is available at adjacent Shabbona Woods picnic area.

ADDRESS: Route 1, Box 72, South Holland, IL 60473
TELEPHONE: 708-868-0606
HOURS: Grounds: daily, 8 a.m. to 5:30 p.m. in summer, 8 a.m. to 4:30 p.m. in winter; exhibit building: March-October, 8 a.m. to 4:30 p.m. from Monday through Thursday, 8 a.m. to 5 p.m. on Saturday and Sunday; November-February, 8 a.m. to 4:00 p.m. from Saturday through Thursday; closed Thanksgiving, Christmas and New Year's days
ADMISSION: Free
FACILITIES: Nature center with exhibit building; 235 acres; 3

½ miles of nature trails; special programs for children and adults

LOCATION: South Holland is a southern suburb about 20 miles south of downtown Chicago, 4 ½ miles west of the Illinois-Indiana border

DIRECTIONS: From Chicago, take the Dan Ryan Expressway, I-90/94, south and continue on the Calumet Expressway, I-94, exit at U.S. 6/159th Street, east on 159th to Paxton Avenue, then north two blocks

26. WHEATON:
CANTIGNY

A well-kept secret in Chicago's western suburbs is the outstanding natural and historical recreational facility known as Cantigny. When Colonel Robert Mc-Cormick, editor and publisher of the Chicago Tribune since 1925, died in 1955, his will stipulated that his 500-acre estate be maintained as a public park and museum for the recreation, instruction and welfare of the people of the state of Illinois. His wishes have been carried out magnificently.

Cantigny is the site of one of the finest gardens in the Midwest, the restored 35-room McCormick Mansion, the First Division Museum, weekly outdoor summer concerts, large picnic areas, Freedom hiking trails and a tank park. This oasis in the suburbs offers something for everyone in the family.

The garden area, designed by landscape architect Franz Lipp, consists of eighteen self-contained groupings. Two-hundred thousand plants are planted each year. Bulbs bloom in the spring, while a riot of color predominates in the lush summer garden of perennials and annuals. Mums star in the fall.

The Fountain Garden's pool of water with a central

fountain is surrounded by large beds of impatiens in all hues, and light blue ageratum. Other floral displays are composed of snapdragons, celosia, tuberous begonias, nicotiana, and coreopsis. The Vegetable Garden displays combinations of ornamental vegetation with vegetables and a herb garden. In the Rose Garden, hybrid roses including tea roses, miniatures and standards can be seen.

The North and South Scalloped Gardens emphasize shade-loving flowering shrubs and evergreens. Plants requiring little moisture like birch, larch, redbud and creeping junipers are found in the Dryland and Rock Gardens. The Green Garden has yews, euonymus, winterberry, dwarf cotoneaster and Korean boxwood. Sedum and astilbe are found in the Douglas Fir Garden. Other gardens include the Octagon Garden, Flowering and Silver Foliage Shrubs Collection, Alder-Birch Collection, Ornamental Specimen Tree Collection, Ash-Dogwood Collection, Maple-Viburnum Collection, Columnar Tree Collection, Linden and Euonymus Collection and Bur Oak Flower Garden.

Guided tours of the McCormick Mansion begin in the Gold Theatre where an audio-visual show is presented. The original house built for Joseph Medill, Col. Robert McCormick's grandfather, in 1896 at a cost of $15,000, was a three-story, white-frame New England-style house designed by C. A. Coolidge. Joseph Medill was a lawyer and politician, the mayor of Chicago, and the principal owner of the *Chicago Tribune*. His grandson, Robert McCormick, was a lawyer, publisher and editor of the *Chicago Tribune*, and a member of the American Expeditionary Forces in France during World War I.

McCormick expanded the house in the 1930s, covering the frame house with Georgian pink brick and adding matching wings on either side. He then changed the name of the country estate from Red Oaks to Cantigny, the village in France near which the first American offensive in Europe was launched in 1918. The spacious 35-room house is furnished with many European antiques collected by the first Mrs. McCormick, and oriental artwork collected by the second Mrs. McCormick. Both the first and second floors are open to the public.

The library in the east wing of the house has 25-foot-high walls paneled with Brazilian pine, built-in bookcases, a hidden Art Deco bar, a large fireplace and portraits of members of the McCormick and Medill families. During the winter, concerts are held in the library. Colonel McCormick's office contains mementos of his life, including the marble desk he used in his Tribune Tower office.

Colonel McCormick's military career was the inspiration for the First Division Museum located in the former stables. During World War I, McCormick served in the First Division. This division, organized in June 1917, fought in France with the Allied armies. They captured the village of Cantigny from the Germans in the first American victory of World War I.

The museum tells the story of the First Division from its formation in 1917 through its participation in Viet Nam. It features dioramas of the battle of Cantigny and the landing at Omaha Beach on D-Day during World War II with accompanying audio commentaries. The museum also has a recreation of a World War I trench and a German pill box. Photographs and displays of weapons and uniforms portray the history of the First Division. A research library is also located in the museum. Having outgrown its space, a new First Division Museum is scheduled to open in 1992.

Many visitors to Cantigny return to enjoy a summer

picnic in the well-landscaped grounds and listen to the Sunday afternoon concerts which begin at 3 p.m. Concerts vary from classical, Dixieland, big band, pop, bluegrass, and country to ragtime. During the winter, chamber music concerts are held in the library monthly.

The tank park is a unique feature at Cantigny. Kids can climb on the six huge military tanks from World War II, Korea and Viet Nam. Although children are permitted to climb on the tanks, and the ground below is covered with chopped-up rubber tires to cushion falls, parental supervision is required. This playground may not appeal to those parents who oppose giving toy weapons to children, but kids, including our own, find the tanks great places to climb.

In 1989, a 27-hole golf course, tennis courts, and a club house with a restaurant were opened on Cantigny's grounds. Access to this area is by a separate entrance reached by traveling south on Winfield Road past the Cantigny entrance to Mack Road, east on Mack to golf course entrance.

ADDRESS: 1S151 Winfield Road, Wheaton, IL 60187

TELEPHONE: 708-668-5161

HOURS: Park: daily, 7 a.m. to dusk; Robert R. McCormick Mansion and First Division Museum: March-December, Tuesday-Sunday, 10 a.m. to 4 p.m., until 5 p.m. from Memorial Day to Labor Day, open weekends only in February, 10 a.m. to 4 p.m., closed January

ADMISSION: Free

FACILITIES: 500 acre estate; 10 acres of gardens; tours of restored McCormick Mansion; First Division Museum; outdoor summer concerts; indoor winter concerts; picnic area; trails; tank park; a golf course and tennis courts with clubhouse restaurant at a separate entrance; no food service at main park

LOCATION: In the western suburb of Wheaton, 30 miles west
of downtown Chicago

DIRECTIONS: From Chicago, west on the Eisenhower Expressway, I-290, to the East-West Tollway, I-88, west on I-88 to
Naperville Road exit, north on Naperville Road one-half
mile to Warrenville Road, west on Warrenville for three
miles to Winfield Road, north on Winfield Road for two
miles to Cantigny entrance; or take Roosevelt Road, IL 38,
from I-290, or I-294, or I-355, west to Winfield Road, south
on Winfield to entrance

27. WHEATON:

ILLINOIS PRAIRIE PATH

Chicago nature lovers who like to get out and hike
or bike will appreciate the 55-mile Illinois Prairie Path,
which runs along an abandoned railroad right-of-way
through the city's western suburbs. They can combine
exercise and family fun with bird watching, wildlife
observation, spring wildflowers and fall foliage along
this urban greenbelt without driving hours to get
there.

The Illinois Prairie Path exemplifies a national trend
to provide natural recreational areas within urban settings. Gratitude should be heaped on those naturalists
who have generously provided these facilities for us
city dwellers.

Following the route of the old Chicago, Aurora &
Elgin Railway, the Illinois Prairie Path passes through
Cook, DuPage and Kane counties. The Chicago,
Aurora & Elgin, an electric commuter line fondly
called the Third Rail, operated for almost a half century before going out of business in 1961. The idea for
converting the abandoned railroad right-of-way into a

nature trail came from May Theilgaard Watts, a naturalist at the Morton Arboretum.

In 1966, the Illinois Prairie Path, a not-for-profit group, was established by people who believed in May Watts' vision. Once the recreational potential of the railroad's right-of-way was recognized, there was work to be done to make it useable. Rails and ties had to be removed, as well as the trash that had been dumped along the roadbed. Next, paths had to be paved with hard-packed limestone grit so that they were suitable for bike riding. Volunteers did much of the work. In 1971, the Illinois Prairie Path was the first in Illinois to be designated a Recreational Trail of the National Trails System.

The Illinois Prairie Path is a Y-shaped trail with its three sections joined at Wheaton. Starting at Wheaton, one spur goes east for 15 miles through Glen Ellyn, Lombard, Villa Park, Elmhurst, Berkeley, Bellwood and Maywood, ending at First Avenue. Another spur from Wheaton travels northwest for 15 miles through Winfield, West Chicago, Wayne and Elgin. An 8-mile side spur to Geneva has not been completed. The third leg of the Y moves southwesterly from Wheaton, traveling through Warrenville into Aurora, with a 7-mile side spur going to Batavia.

Trail access is available in Bellwood, Berkeley, Elmhurst, Villa Park, Lombard, Glen Ellyn, Wheaton, Warrenville, Aurora, Winfield, Wayne, South Elgin and Elgin. The eastern section of the Prairie Path, from Wheaton to Maywood, is north of Roosevelt Road and south of St. Charles Road, running roughly parallel with both. Parking is available along many of the north-south streets which intersect with the path. All of the trails join in Wheaton at Carlton Avenue and Liberty Street. Parking is also available at the Roy C. Blackwell Preserve at Butterfield Road, (IL 56) and

Winfield Road in Warrenville, Pratt's Wayne Woods on Army Trail Road and Powis Road in Wayne, and Walnut Glen Park near downtown Glen Ellyn.

The entire path provides an opportunity for outdoor recreation but nature lovers will especially enjoy the trails west of Wheaton which are less residential than the eastern leg of the path. The western trails wind through farmlands, marsh, prairie and woods. Trees and wildflowers have been planted along the path.

The Illinois Prairie Path connects with the Fox River Trail, a 32-mile bicycle trail along the Fox River from Aurora to Algonquin. This scenic trail, which travels through the historic river towns of Aurora, St. Charles, Batavia, Geneva, and Elgin, is another superb recreational facility within easy reach of city dwellers. Connection points between the Illinois Prairie Path and the Fox River Trail are in Elgin, Batavia, Geneva and Aurora. For information, contact the Kane County Forest Preserve District, 719 Batavia Avenue, Geneva, IL 60134, 708-332-1242.

ADDRESS: P.O. Box 1086, Wheaton, IL 60189
TELEPHONE: DuPage County Division of Transportation: 708-682-7318; Illinois Prairie Path: 708-665-5310
HOURS: Daily, year-round
ADMISSION: Free
FACILITIES: 55-mile trail through Cook, DuPage and Kane counties; hiking; bicycling; horseback riding; cross-country skiing; Visitor Center in the Villa Park Historical Museum, Villa Avenue, Villa Park
LOCATION: Trail runs through western suburbs of Chicago, from near the Des Plaines River at First Avenue in Maywood west to Wheaton, then north to Elgin and south to Aurora
DIRECTIONS: The Eisenhower Expressway, I-290, leads to the western suburbs; also the East-West Tollway, I-88, which can be reached via the Tri-State Tollway, I-294

28. WILLOW SPRINGS:
LITTLE RED SCHOOLHOUSE NATURE CENTER

The Little Red Schoolhouse Nature Center features natural science and animal exhibits geared particularly to the curiosity and interests of children. Located in the Palos Hills Forest Preserve, it is one of four nature centers in the Cook County Forest Preserve. Long John Slough, just behind the schoolhouse, has a waterfowl viewing area. There are nature trails for hiking, a garden and an orchard.

The one-room schoolhouse which now serves as the nature center was built in Palos in 1886. At that time, its students came from nearby farms. The white-frame building was originally located on 99th Street. Flooding and other problems necessitated moving the school two-thirds of a mile to a new site on 104th Avenue during the summer of 1934. When many of the farms in Palos were acquired by the Cook County Forest Preserve District, school attendance dropped. In 1948, with only one student left, the school was closed. The school and its site were purchased by the Forest Preserve District in 1952. Once again it was moved—across 104th Avenue—where it was painted red and turned into a nature center.

The schoolhouse again serves an educational function as children come to see the animal and nature exhibits. Geared to the younger child, animal cages are placed very low so that children can see the snakes, rabbits, turtles, turtle doves, crows, toads, crickets, tropical fish or whoever else happens to be in residence. Nature science exhibits, which are changed seasonally, focus on native prairie grass, winter twigs, moths, a rattlesnake skeleton, and stuffed animals. An exhibit particularly enjoyed by kids is a tall cylinder with several curtained openings into which they stick their hands. After touching a natural object like bark or rabbit fur, they try to identify it.

Trails at the Little Red Schoolhouse Nature Center include the Black Oak Trail, a two-mile loop; White Oak, a one-mile loop and Farm Pond Trail, less than half a mile. Beginning at the nature center, the trails pass through woods, meadows, swamps, marshes, and ponds.

ADDRESS: 9800 S. Willow Springs Road, Willow Springs, IL 60480

TELEPHONE: 708-839-6897

HOURS: Parking lot and trails: March-October, Monday-Friday, 8 a.m. to 5 p.m., Saturday-Sunday, 8 a.m. to 5:30 p.m.; November-February, daily, 8 a.m. to 4:30 p.m.; Exhibit building: March-October, Monday-Thursday, 9 a.m. to 4:30 p.m., Saturday-Sunday, 9 a.m. to 5 p.m.; November-February, Saturday-Thursday, 9 a.m. to 4 p.m.; exhibit building closed on Friday; entire nature center closed on Thanksgiving, Christmas, and New Year's days

ADMISSION: Free

FACILITIES: Nature Center; nature trails for hiking; garden; orchard; waterfowl viewing area; arts and crafts fair on first Sunday in October

LOCATION: In Willow Springs, a southwestern suburb, in Palos Forest Preserve District

DIRECTIONS: From Chicago, take the Stevenson Expressway, I-55, south to La Grange Road/U.S. 12, 20, 45 south exit; south on La Grange Road to 95th St., west on 95th St. to 104th Avenue/Willow Springs Road, one-half mile south on 104th Avenue to nature center

PART 2:

Illinois

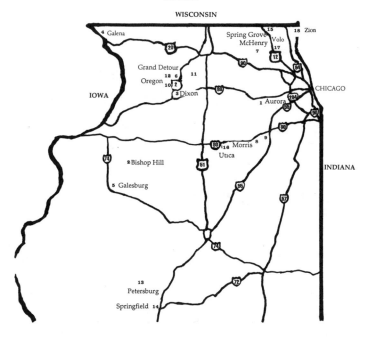

ILLINOIS

WISCONSIN

4 Galena

20

Grand Detour

Oregon
12 6
10 2
11

3 Dixon

IOWA

Spring Grove 15
McHenry Volo
7 17
12

90

80

18 Zion

94

CHICAGO
294
1 Aurora 55

80
90

80

80 16 Morris 8
Utica 9

74

2 Bishop Hill

51

55

INDIANA

5 Galesburg

57

74

72

13
Petersburg

Springfield 14

1. AURORA:
BLACKBERRY HISTORICAL FARM-VILLAGE

Take the kids to Blackberry Historical Farm-Village. It offers 60 well-landscaped acres, a manageable size, with live animals, a train and a carousel for young children, a horse-drawn carriage museum, and a re-creation of early Aurora's main street. On a sunny Sunday afternoon, not one of the many children at Blackberry was crying, a testimony to the site as a relaxing outing for Mom and Dad.

Blackberry's entrance fee includes admission to all rides and exhibits. The pony rides and carousel are favorites of the little ones. Another area they especially like is the Discovery Barn, which has pigs, goats, lambs, baby chicks, ducklings, roosters and rabbits. Animal feed can be ground by the children in the barn and fed to the animals in the barnyard.

Demonstrations are given in both the blacksmith

Illinois

shop and the weaving shop. Children can visit the 1880 one-room schoolhouse, Ingham School from Sugar Grove Township. The red brick building has hanging kerosene lamps, a cast iron stove with a coal bucket, wooden floors, long wooden benches, school desks made by Sears Roebuck, and a display of school-books.

A miniature train leaves from Big Rock Railway Station and circles little Lake Gregory, where kids and their parents can fish. The train stops at the 1840 Pioneer Farm which consists of a re-created two-room log cabin with a loft and not much more. After visiting the cabin, passengers can board the next train, climb on a horse and wagon, or walk back to the main area.

Blackberry has a fine collection of horse-drawn carriages and sleighs including hearses, a gypsy wagon, an 1880s popcorn wagon and a peddler's wagon, in the Carriage Museum. Farm Museum exhibits explain the seasons' relationship to farming. Farm instruments are displayed. The Early Streets Museum is an indoor museum that features the lighted shop windows of Aurora's Main Street as it was in 1900. Antique items related to each business are in the windows. Businesses include a toy store, grocery, barber shop, dress shop, hardware, furniture store, photography studio, tavern, and music store.

The Hunton House is on Patch Work Square. On its first floor are rooms furnished to reflect a Victorian home of the late 1890s. Upstairs is an exhibit of turn-of-the-century inventions related to housekeeping like the sewing machine, the washing machine and vacuum cleaners.

Gardeners will appreciate the extensive flower gardens located behind the entrance building. Blackberry's perennial exhibition garden displays a wide variety of flowers that are hardy for zone 5, which includes northern Illinois. All of the flowers are labeled. A guide to the perennial gardens, obtainable from the ticket sellers, provides information about proper growing conditions.

Picnic areas are scattered throughout the grounds in addition to a gazebo-style concession stand. Beautiful flowers, an outdoor setting, interesting historical exhibits, and animals to pet and ride, make Blackberry a good destination for a summer family outing.

ADDRESS: Galena Boulevard and Barnes Road, Aurora, IL 60506
TELEPHONE: 708-892-1550
HOURS: Daily, from last week in April through Labor Day, 10 a.m. to 4:30 p.m.; Friday-Sunday, Labor Day to mid-October, 10 a.m. to 4:30 p.m.
ADMISSION: Adults $5.50, children $4.25, seniors $3.50
FACILITIES: 60 acres; perennial gardens; pony rides; train ride; carousel; horse-drawn wagon ride; farm animals; museum of horse-drawn carriages and sleighs; log cabin; picnic areas; concession stand; gift shop; Early Streets Museum; Farm Museum; blacksmith shop; weaver's cabin
LOCATION: In Aurora, 35 miles west of Chicago
DIRECTIONS: From Chicago, take the Eisenhower Expressway, I-290, or the Tri-State Tollway, I-294, to the East-West Tollway, I-88, west on I-88 to Orchard Road exit, follow brown signs

2. BISHOP HILL
BISOP HILL

A gem of a town, Bishop Hill is a restored Swedish religious communal site as well as a living community of less than 200 people. Travelers to Bishop Hill will find the town to be a bit of nineteenth-century Sweden transplanted to western Illinois' prairies. Within driving distance from Chicago, it is virtually unknown to most city dwellers.

Bishop Hill was founded in 1846 by the Janssonists, a pietistical sect of Swedish immigrants who came to the United States to find the religious freedom denied to them in their native country. The Janssonists also came to Illinois to improve their economic condition. At the time of their departure, Sweden was in an economic depression caused by declining agricultural productivity and a rapidly growing rural population.

The Janssonists were named for their founder, Erik Jansson, a charismatic religious leader who preached a simple religion of the heart rather than a complicated theology. Originally members of the Swedish Reader or Lasare movement, the Janssonists believed that the Bible should be the sole guide to religious practice and conduct. They were fundamentalists who were dissatisfied with the state Lutheran church. Jansson experienced visions in which it was revealed to him that he and his followers were God's chosen people.

Because of the challenge that his unorthodox beliefs presented to the Lutheran church, Sweden's official religion, Jansson and his followers were persecuted. When Jansson was arrested in 1845 for burning Lutheran literature, he dispatched Olof Olsson to America to scout out a place to become the sect's New Jerusalem. On the recommendation of Jonas Hedstrom, a Swedish Methodist from Victoria, Illinois, Olsson choose a site in Henry County, Illinois, which had fertile land, good water and timber.

After a three-month ocean voyage, a trip across the Great Lakes, and a 150-mile trek on foot from Chicago, Erik Jansson and 400 Swedish immigrants arrived at Bishop Hill, named after the parish of Biskopskulla, Sweden, where Jansson was born. Since many of his followers could not afford to pay their passage to the United States, Jansson decided that the group's property should be held in common trust. While communal ownership was economically motivated, Jansson, who held total power in the community, also justified it on Biblical grounds.

Arriving at Bishop Hill in late fall, the colonists had to delay planting crops until spring. Their first winter on the Illinois prairie was a struggle to survive. They lived in dug-out shelters in the side of a ravine, or in tents. Ninety-six people died. One of the first buildings erected was the large church, a white-frame building that also contained living quarters. More than 20 major buildings were constructed of handmade brick at Bishop Hill in the following years, including a bakery, brewery, flour mill, and a 96-room apartment building called Big Brick.

Since Bishop Hill was a communal society, property was owned by the group and people lived and ate together in large units rather than in small family homes. There were two large dining rooms where several hundred people ate at one sitting. Under Jansson's watchful eye, religious regulations were strictly enforced.

Within five years the town, with a population of 800, had become quite prosperous. Farming was the major occupation but the community also ran a hotel for stagecoach travelers and sold handwoven linen cloth. The Janssonist settlement also had a school, hospital, dairy, tannery, brick kiln, hundreds of head of livestock and 12,000 acres of fertile farmland.

Jansson, who claimed to govern with divine authority, was the personal force that held the community together. His untimely death, only four years after founding the Illinois settlement, dealt a heavy blow to his followers. Erik Jansson was murdered in 1850 by

John Root, the husband of Jansson's cousin Lotta. Root
had decided to leave the colony and wanted to take his
wife and son with him. Lotta, however, refused to
accompany him. Root, whose attempts to take his family were thwarted by the colonists, attributed his problems to Jansson's hypnotic influence on his wife, and
in his anger murdered the colony's leader.

After Jansson's death, the Bishop Hill colonists
sought unsuccessfully to keep their community true to
their leader's teachings. Jonas Olsson, Jansson's suc-
cessor, permitted a more open way of life but could not
hold the group together as a communal society. In
1861, the colony was dissolved as a corporation, and
land and property were divided among the men. Men
35 or older received a full share and those under 35, a
half share.

After the colony's dissolution, Bishop Hill's settlers
went their own ways. Many joined other churches,
such as the Methodists. A few, including Jansson's
widow, joined the Shakers at Pleasant Hill in Kentucky. Still others remained at Bishop Hill, where their
descendants still reside, engaged in farming or in business.

The town of Bishop Hill experienced little growth or
change in the century which followed. Buildings
gradually fell into disrepair. A movement to restore
the Swedish settlement began in the 1940s. Of the 20
major colony buildings erected in the 1840s and 1850s,
15 remain, some of which surround the city park. Restoration by the state of Illinois and the Bishop Hill
Heritage Association has returned several buildings to
their 1861 appearance. Other buildings are used as
shops which sell antiques, crafts and Scandinavian
imports.

It is the large classical buildings that make this mid-
nineteenth-century Swedish town appear like a mi-

rage in western Illinois farm country. The 1848 Colony Church, a state historic site, was the community's first permanent building. The unheated sanctuary on the second floor of the three-story, white, gambrel-roofed church could seat 1,000 people. Services were held twice each weekday, three times on Sunday, and often lasted two hours. Twenty one-room apartments housed families on the other floors. Clothes, furniture and utensils belonging to the settlers are displayed.

Over 100 portraits of early settlers and village scenes painted by Olof Krans, who immigrated to Bishop Hill in 1850 when he was 11, vividly portray the lifestyle of the townspeople. Certainly one of Bishop Hill's treasures, Krans has been called one of America's finest folk artists. Krans' paintings are displayed in the Colony Church and the Steeple Building.

The 1854 Steeple Building is a three-story, Greek Revival, stucco-covered brick structure that was built as a hotel but used as a school. A two-story octagonal wooden cupola houses a clock with four faces, each of which has one hand that marks the hours only. Steeple Building exhibits focus on the history of Bishop Hill and its Swedish immigrants. A film is shown and there is a bookstore.

The Bjorklund Hotel, a State Historic Site, was a two-story building built in 1852. In 1861, a third story with hotel rooms, ballroom and a tower were added. The two-story Colony Store sells items made by village craftsmen.

Special celebrations at Bishop Hill include Valpurgis in April, Midsummer Festival in June, Sommarmarknad in August, Old Settlers' Day and Jordbruksdagarna in September, Julmarknad (Christmas Market) on Thanksgiving weekend, Lucia Nights in December and Julotta on Christmas morning.

Some original buildings are privately owned and

are now well-stocked craft and antique shops. Several restaurants are open, for lunch only, and serve Swedish-American food.

ADDRESS: P.O. Box D, Bishop Hill, IL 61419
TELEPHONE: 309-927-3345; 309-927-3899
HOURS: Daily, 9 a.m. to 5 p.m.; closed Thanksgiving, Christmas and New Year's days
ADMISSION: Free
FACILITIES: Restored Swedish communal society; state historic site; 15 original buildings which house museums and shops; antique and craft shops; restaurants
LOCATION: In Henry County in western Illinois, 157 miles west of Chicago
HOTELS/MOTELS: Jumer's Continental Inn, E. Main St, Galesburg 61401, 309-343-7151, 800-446-4690; Galesburg Inn, 565 W. Main St., Galesburg 61401, 309-343-3191; Oakwood Motel, U.S. 6 at jct. IL 82, Geneseo 61254, 309-944-3696
CAMPING: Shadow Lake Campground, Hwy. 92, Geneseo 61254, 309-944-4020; The Timber, Rt. 2, Cambridge 61238, 309-937-2314
DIRECTIONS: From Chicago, take the Stevenson Expressway, I-55, south to I-80 near Joliet, I-80 west to Geneseo exit, south on IL 82 about 20 miles to Co. 4, east on 4 about 4 miles to Co. 39, south on 39 about 2 miles

3. DIXON:

RONALD REAGAN BOYHOOD HOME

Praising the fine restoration of his boyhood home on a 1984 visit to Dixon, Ronald Reagan said that if the house on Hennepin had looked that good when he lived there, he might never have left. He did leave, however, when he was 21 and became a famous movie actor, governor of California from 1967-75 and president of the United States from 1981-89.

Although born in Tampico, Illinois, Ronald Reagan considered Dixon his home town. "Everyone has a place to come back to, and for me that place is Dixon, a place on the Rock River." Reagan spoke this line in a 1950 movie, *The Hasty Heart*, filmed in England. The line in the script was, "Everyone has a place to go back to, and for me it's Boston." Homesick after four months of filming abroad, Reagan got the director's permission to change the line. Dixon is justifiably proud of its former resident.

Ronald Reagan's parents, John Edward and Nelle Wilson Reagan, and their sons, Neil, 12, and Ronald, 9, moved to Dixon, Illinois (population 10,000), in 1920. They rented a house on Hennepin Avenue. The family had lived in Tampico, Chicago, Galesburg, and Monmouth before settling in Dixon. The future president would spend the rest of his childhood there.

Known as Jack, Ronald Reagan's father, an Irish Catholic, had been raised in Iowa. He supported his family by working in the retail shoe business. His wife, a Scottish Protestant, was a religious woman who taught Sunday School at the First Christian Church, as did her son Ronald. Ronald and Neil attended South Side School and Dixon High School. In high school, Ronald was president of the student body, a member of the drama club, the football team, the track team, and the newspaper staff. After learning to swim at the YMCA, he worked as a lifeguard at Lowell Park for six summers. He is credited with saving 77 lives.

The Reagan family home on Hennepin was built in 1891 by William C. Thompson and sold to Edward Donovan. The Donovan family still owned the house when it was rented to the Reagans from 1920 until 1923. Although the Reagan family remained in Dixon, they later lived in several other houses in town.

In 1980, the house on Hennepin Avenue was purchased by local citizens, and is now owned by the Ronald Reagan Home Preservation Foundation. The house had been divided into a multi-family dwelling and had undergone substantial change. After much research, it has been restored to its appearance in the early 1920s when the Reagans lived there.

Tours of the Reagan home begin in the house next door, which serves as a visitor center. An orientation film which focuses on President Reagan's 1984 visit to Dixon is shown there. Portraits of Ronald Reagan and his family hang on the walls, and commemorative gifts are for sale.

After viewing the film, you can visit the Reagan home which is staffed by knowledgeable docents. The two-story, white-frame, Queen Anne-style house has a front porch and a wood shingle roof. On the first floor is a parlor, family sitting room, dining room and kitchen. Three bedrooms and a bathroom are upstairs. When the Reagans moved there, it was considered a modern house, complete with indoor plumbing and central heat. Rooms are simply furnished with 1920-era antiques. None of the furnishings are original, but President Reagan and his brother were given pre-1920 Sears catalogues and asked to indicate the type of furniture that they remembered from their childhood.

The formal parlor is the only room with curtains. Other rooms had window shades. The children were not allowed in the parlor but did their homework and played board games in the sitting room. Oak dining room furniture includes an exact replica of Nelle Reagan's buffet. The dining room table is set with dishes that were bonuses from Jewel Tea food stores, just like Nelle Reagan's own. When Ronald, Nancy and Neil Reagan had lunch in the house during their 1984 visit, they used those dishes. The 1920s modern kitchen has a Detroit Jewel gas stove, a wooden ice box with a metal top, a metal sink, a free-standing kitchen cupboard with a built-in flour bin, and a linoleum floor.

On the second floor, the parents' bedroom has a brass bed covered with a quilt. A second brass bed is in the guest bedroom which was also used as a sewing room. The Reagan brothers shared a bedroom and an iron bed. Banners from Dixon High School and Eureka College decorate the wall. The bathroom has a very small sink, which is how the Reagans remembered it.

The barn that stood behind the house has been reconstructed on its original site. It had been used by Jack Reagan as a garage and now it houses a Model T Ford like the one Mr. Reagan owned. Next to the Reagan home is a small park with a statue of Ronald Reagan.

ADDRESS: 816 S. Hennepin Avenue, Dixon, IL 61021

TELEPHONE: 815-288-3404

HOURS: March-November: Monday and Wednesday-Saturday, 10 a.m. to 4 p.m., Sunday and holidays, 1-4 p.m., closed Tuesday; December-February: Monday and Saturday, 10 a.m. to 4 p.m. and Sunday 1-4 p.m., closed Tuesday-Friday

ADMISSION: Free

FACILITIES: Restored boyhood home of President Ronald Reagan; visitors' center with film and gift shop is handicapped accessible; adjoining small park with Reagan statue; NR

LOCATION: 100 miles west of Chicago

HOTELS/MOTELS: Best Western Brandywine Lodge, Sterling-Dixon Frwy., Dixon 61021, 815-284-1890; Super 8 Motel, 1800 S. Galena Avenue, Dixon 61021, 815-284-1800; The Presidential Inn, 1231 N. Galena Avenue, Dixon 61021, 815-284-3351

LODGES: White Pines Lodge, White Pines State Park, 6712 West Pine Road, Mt. Morris 61054, 815-946-3817

BED & BREAKFASTS: Colonial Inn, 8230 South Green Street,

Grand Detour, Dixon 61021, 815-652-4422; The Barber
House Inn, 410 West Mason Street, Polo 61064, 815-946-
2607; Riverview Guest House, 507 E. Everett, Dixon 61021,
815-288-5974; The Whitney B&B, 1620 Whitney Road,
Franklin Grove, 815-456-2526

CAMPING: White Pines Forest State Park, RR 1, Mt. Morris
61054, 815-946-3717; Lowden State Park, RR 2, P.O. Box 403,
Oregon 61061, 815-732-6828; Moore Park Campground, IL
5, Dixon 61021, 815-284-3725

DIRECTIONS: From Chicago, take the Eisenhower Expressway, I-290, or the Tri-State Tollway, I-294, west to the East-
West Tollway, I-88, west on I-88 to Dixon exit, U.S. 26, north
on U.S. 26 into Dixon

4. GALENA:

GALENA HISTORIC DISTRICT; U. S. GRANT HOME STATE HISTORIC SITE; OLD MARKET HOUSE STATE HISTORIC SITE

As a weekend respite for travelers who want to step
back in time, Galena offers a remarkably unchanged
nineteenth-century town built on hills (yes, hills)
along the Galena River, museums, restored house museums, good antique shops, and historic hotels and
B&Bs. Galena's historic district has steep streets lined
with hundreds of architecturally diverse mansions
constructed before 1900; 85 per cent of the town is
listed in the National Register of Historic Places. For
many Midwesterners, Galena represents the epitome
of a historical village. And, the town is only 160 miles
from Chicago.

Mid-nineteenth-century architecture creates the historic atmosphere in this town of under 4,000. Galena,
named after the Latin word for lead sulphide, was a

lead mining town and river trading port that boomed in the 1820s, was the richest town in Illinois in the 1840s, and went bust in the 1860s.

Settlers were attracted to what was known as the Fever River by its rich lead deposits. First mined by Indians, the lead caught the interest of a party of 30 French explorers in 1700. In 1807, the U.S. Congress took over the mines. Government leases were now necessary to occupy or work the mineral lands. Steam transportation, which began on the Mississippi in 1816 and reached the Upper Mississippi in 1823, facilitated shipping the ore and Galena became a busy river port and trading center.

The "lead rush" in Galena in the late 1820s drew many settlers from Kentucky, Virginia and other southern states. Lead mining created much prosperity. In 1845, Galena produced 27,000 tons of lead, 83 per cent of the country's supply. However, the boom did not last. After the surface veins were exhausted, the cost of mining lead made it unprofitable. Both the advent of the railroad in 1854, and the silting in of the Galena River contributed to the demise of river traffic. The town began to languish. Farming replaced mining as the economic base.

The town had been laid out in 1826 by a government lease agent, Lieutenant Martin Thomas. On hilly terrain, the town is built on terraces, ancient river beds cut out by the Galena River. The local architecture ranges from Greek Revival, Federal, Italianate, Queen Anne and Second Empire mansions to Cape Cod cottages and New England churches. Because of periodic fires in the business district, by the 1850s commercial buildings were required to be built of brick. These have survived with little alteration.

Ulysses S. Grant, Galena's most famous citizen, came to Galena from St. Louis in 1860 to work in the

leather goods store owned by his father and operated
by his brothers. When the Civil War broke out, Grant,
who was a veteran of the Mexican War, rose to the rank
of brigadier general and, in 1864, general-in-chief of
Union armies. In 1865 Grant returned to Galena after
the Union triumph over the Confederates and was
given a hero's welcome. Some grateful citizens of Galena presented Grant and his family with a home. Built
in 1859, it is an Italianate, bracketed, red brick two-
story house. From 1865 to 1867, Grant divided his time
between New York, Washington and Galena. In 1867,
he became secretary of war. After serving as president
of the United States from 1869 to 1877, and then taking
a world tour, Grant made occasional visits to his Galena home until 1881 when he moved to New York
City. Grant died in Mount McGregor, New York, in
1885.

In 1904, Grant's children gave the home to the city
of Galena. Now owned by the Illinois Historic Preservation Agency, the beautifully restored U. S. Grant
Home is a state historic site. Most of the furnishings
and artifacts in the home belonged to the Grant family.

Another state historic site in Galena is the Old Market House which was built in 1845 as Galena's public
market for produce. It was also the seat of city government and housed two city jail cells. The Greek Revival,
two-story, brick central block building has symmetri-
cal one-story wings. Inside the restored market house
is an exhibit on Galena's historical and architectural
heritage.

Just outside of Galena is the Vinegar Hill Historic
Lead Mine & Museum, an underground lead mine
opened in 1822. The museum features lead and ore
samples and mining tools: 8885 N. Three Pines Road,
Galena, 815-777-0588, open 9 a.m. to 5 p.m., daily May

through August, and on weekends during September and October; admission: adults $3.50, children $1.50.

In addition to the Grant home, there are other restored mansions to tour in Galena. The Belvedere Mansion and Gardens is a 22-room Italianate house, built in 1857 and now furnished in a formal Victorian style: 1008 Park Avenue, 815-777-0747; open daily, 11 a.m. to 5 p.m., Memorial Day through October; admission: $2.50.

Built of native limestone in 1826, the Dowling House may be the oldest house in Galena: 220 Diagonal Street, 815-777-1250; open daily, 10 a.m. to 5 p.m., Memorial Day to Christmas and weekends from January through May; admission: $2.50. A combination ticket for the Dowling and Belvedere houses costs $4.50.

The Old General Store Museum is a replica of a nineteenth-century general store which is operated by the Galena/Jo Daviess County Historical Society. Much of the store merchandise, now owned by the Illinois Historic Preservation Agency, was collected by Marie Duerrstein of Galena: 223 S. Main Street, 815-777-9129, open daily, 10 a.m. to 4 p.m., June through October and weekends during November and December.

Galena is an antique lover's paradise as many of the town's commercial buildings are now occupied by antique stores. Fifty to sixty antique shops operate in Galena and the surrounding area. There are also many galleries featuring pottery, watercolors, prints, paintings, leaded glass, and jewelry.

Galena is especially picturesque in fall. Downhill and cross-country skiing is popular in the area in winter.

ADDRESS: Grant home: 500 Bouthillier, Galena, IL 61036; Old

Market House: Market Square, Galena, IL 61036; Galena Convention & Visitors Bureau, 101 Bouthillier Street, Galena 61036

TELEPHONE: Grant home: 815-777-3310; Galena Convention & Visitors Bureau: 800-747-9377

HOURS: Grant home: Daily, 9 a.m. to 5 p.m.; closed Thanksgiving, Christmas, and New Year's days

ADMISSION: Grant home and Old Market House: free

FACILITIES: Historic town; historic district; Grant's home; Old Market House; Dowling and Belvedere mansions; antique stores; NR

LOCATION: Galena is in the extreme northwest corner of Illinois, a few miles east of the Mississippi River, just south of the Illinois-Wisconsin border, 160 miles from Chicago

MOTELS/HOTELS: Chestnut Mountain Resort, 8700 W. Chestnut Road, Galena 61036, 815-777-1320 and 800-397-1320; Eagle Ridge Inn & Resort, Box 777, the Galena Territory, U.S. 20 East, Galena 61036, 815-777-2444; Best Western Quiet House Suites, U.S. 20 East, Galena 61036, 815-777-2577; Grant Hills Motel, U.S. 20, Galena 61036, 815-777-2116

HISTORIC HOTELS: DeSoto House, 230 South Main Street, Galena 61036, 800-343-6562, 815-777-0090; Farmers' Home Hotel, 334 Spring Street, Galena 61036, 815-777-3456

BED & BREAKFASTS: Galena has over 40 B&Bs; lodging guide and list of vacancies available from the Galena Convention and Visitors Bureau, 101 Bouthillier Street, Galena 61036, 800-747-9377.

CAMPING: Palace Campground, U.S. 20 West, Galena 61036, 815-777-2466; Rustic Barn Campground, 3854 Dry Hollow Road, Kieler, WI 53812, 608-568-7797.

DIRECTIONS: From Chicago, take the North-West Tollway, I-90, which can be reached from the Kennedy Expressway, I-90/94, or the Tri-State Tollway, I-294, west toward Rockford, exit at U.S. 20 and continue west into Galena

5. GALESBURG:
CARL SANDBURG BIRTHPLACE

Poet, biographer, historian, two-time Pulitzer Prize winner, Carl Sandburg was an Illinois native. The son of Swedish immigrants, Sandburg was born and raised in the small community of Galesburg. His birthplace has been preserved by the state, which is justifiably proud of its native son.

Carl Sandburg was born 6 January 1878 to Clara and August Sandburg, the second of their seven children. August was a blacksmith for the Chicago, Burlington & Quincy Railroad.

Galesburg is named for the Reverend George Washington Gale, a Presbyterian minister from the "burned-over district" of western New York. In 1837, Gale came west to found Knox College for the training of frontier ministers. The town grew around the school. Knox's Old Main was the site of the fifth Lincoln-Douglas debate, and President Lincoln received his first honorary degree from Knox. Sandburg would receive a Pulitzer Prize for his biography of Lincoln.

The Carl Sandburg Birthplace State Historic Site is a white-frame cottage surrounded by a white picket fence. August Sandburg purchased the house in 1873 for $365.00. The family sold it in 1879 and bought a succession of larger houses in Galesburg. Carl's birthplace was saved from demolition by townspeople and children who collected Lincoln pennies to buy and restore the house.

Furnished with many Sandburg family belongings, the three-room house, parlor, kitchen and bedroom, reflects the lifestyle of a nineteenth-century working class family. A room was added to the house in 1949 and serves as a Sandburg museum. There are photo-

graphs of Sandburg's parents, a family Bible, first editions of Sandburg's poetry and history books, his type-
writer, and material relating to his Lincoln
biographies, the two-volume *Abraham Lincoln: The
Prairie Years* published in 1926, and the four-volume
Abraham Lincoln: The War Years published in 1939.

Behind the birthplace is Carl Sandburg Park. The
ashes of both Sandburg and his wife Lilian are buried
beneath Remembrance Rock in the park.

Galesburg is proud of its varied architectural heritage. Brochures for walking tours which pass by the
many Victorian houses can be obtained from the
Galesburg Visitors' Bureau at 140 East Main Street.

Each June, the city hosts Railroad Days with tours of
the Burlington Northern Railroad facilities. Galesburg's railroad heritage dates to 1854 and the town is
the junction point for the Burlington and Santa Fe
railroads.

ADDRESS: 313 E. Third, Galesburg, IL 61401
TELEPHONE: 309-342-2361
HOURS: Daily, 9 a.m. to 5 p.m.; closed Thanksgiving, Christ-
mas and New Year's days
ADMISSION: Free
FACILITIES: Restored birthplace of Carl Sandburg; Sandburg's
burial site
LOCATION: Galesburg is in western Illinois, about 180 miles
southwest of Chicago
MOTELS/HOTELS: Jumer's Continental Inn, E. Main St. at I-74,
Galesburg, 309-343-7151; Regal 8 Inn, 1475 Henderson St.,
Galesburg, 309-344-2401; Galesburg Inn, 565 W. Main St.,
Galesburg, 309-343-3191
CAMPING: Allison Lake Storey Campground, Lake Storey
Road, one mile north of U.S. 150, Galesburg, 309-344-1534;
KOA Galesburg East, RR. 1, Box 123, Knoxville, 61448,
309-289-4728
DIRECTIONS: From Chicago, take the Stevenson Expressway,

I-55, south to I-80, I-80 west to I-74, then I-74 south to Galesburg

6. GRAND DETOUR:

JOHN DEERE HISTORIC SITE

John Deere and agriculture are almost synonymous today. John Deere's invention of the steel plow launched the business that bears his name. Deere's first blacksmith shop in Grand Detour, Illinois, the site of his invention, has been reconstructed and can be visited at the John Deere Historic Site located in the scenic Rock River Valley of western Illinois.

In the 1830s, John Deere, a native of Vermont, was a struggling blacksmith whose forge had burned down twice. He was having difficulty supporting his wife and children. Other Vermonters told Deere about opportunities for blacksmiths in the new west, mentioning the Illinois settlement called Grand Detour. The town had been named by French explorers for the oxbow bend in the Rock River. According to an Indian legend, the river found the land so beautiful that it turned around for a second look.

In 1836, John Deere migrated to Grand Detour where he built a forge and started a much-needed business. He also built a small frame house and sent for his family, whom he had left in Vermont.

Most of Deere's customers were farmers who were discouraged by the difficulty they were having plowing the rich midwestern soil. Cast-iron plows that had worked well on the sandy eastern soil were constantly getting stuck in the heavy local clay even when pulled by teams of horses. Farmers had to stop every few feet to scrape the soil off the plow, making for slow progress.

In an effort to alleviate the farmers' problems, Deere designed a simplified plow with a steel blade made from a broken saw blade. From this, he developed a light-weight plow with a self-polishing steel blade that could be pulled by a single horse. Deere's plow zipped through the dense soil without the clay adhering to it. Interest in the young blacksmith's plow grew rapidly as farmers sang its praises.

Demand for Deere's invention quickly outgrew production. Deere needed steel for his plows. In 1847, after 11 years at Grand Detour, he moved to Moline, Illinois, located on the Mississippi River, where he could more easily receive shipments of materials. Deere began manufacturing in quantity; business mushroomed, eventually growing into today's large agricultural implements corporation.

John Deere's original blacksmith shop burned down in 1844. In 1962, a team of archaeologists from the University of Illinois excavated the site. They uncovered the outlines of the forge, the horse-drawn wheel that supplied the power, and many artifacts used in Deere's business.

The John Deere Foundation has carefully restored the site to its appearance in the mid-1830s. An audiovisual orientation shows the background of Deere and his plow, and there are knowledgeable guides stationed in each building. The well-landscaped grounds featuring flower beds and brick sidewalks are surrounded by a white picket fence. Adjacent to the restored area are nearly two acres of natural prairie which has been preserved by the Deere Foundation.

A museum focusing on the story of John Deere, blacksmithing, and farming on the Illinois frontier has been built over, but does not cover, the excavated shop floor. This exhibit hall tells the fascinating story of the archeological dig that uncovered Deere's blacksmith shop. A multi-media audio-visual program features "conversations" between John and his wife, Demarius, in addition to an explanation of the blacksmithing process. On the wall behind the original dirt floor is a mural illustrating Deere's blacksmithing career. Other exhibits in the museum tell the story of John Deere through photographs, tools found during the dig, and excerpts from books.

The John Deere home in Grand Detour had gone out of the Deere family but was repurchased by Mrs. Butterworth, a Deere granddaughter. The modest, white-frame Federal-style house was heated by a wood-burning stove. Although most of the furnishings now in the house did not belong to the Deere family, the sewing table in the parlor was Demarius Deere's. The 1830s kitchen has an iron stove, a dry sink and a pantry with a large pie safe. The parents' bedroom was on the first floor while the children slept upstairs. John Deere made two additions to the home to accommodate his growing family of nine children. Outside, there is a well on the porch and an attached open carriage house.

Mrs. Butterworth, the Deere granddaughter who re-acquired the site, lived for a time in a more elaborate neighboring house. Built by Mr. Dana, it is a two-story house with a parlor, a dining room with a fireplace and a sitting room on the first floor. Old photographs of Deere and his company are hung on the walls. This house has also been restored and serves as the Visitors' Center with a gift shop in the former kitchen.

A replica of the Deere blacksmith shop, in which the original self-polishing steel plow was invented, has been built. A working blacksmith demonstrates his craft using traditional tools and methods. Outside the shop is a display of plows and other agricultural implements.

After touring the Deere site, take a stroll around the tiny town whose population numbers in the hundreds. Grand Detour has the feel of a New England village with many stately old homes and broad lawns. It's hard to believe that this picturesque village is roughly 100 miles from Chicago.

ADDRESS: 8393 South Main, Grand Detour, Dixon IL 61021
TELEPHONE: 815-652-4551
HOURS: Daily, 9 a.m. to 5 p.m., April-November
ADMISSION: Adults and children 16 and over $2.00
FACILITIES: Restored home of John Deere; museum; blacksmith's shop with demonstrations; Visitors' Center; gift shop; NHL
LOCATION: 110 miles west of Chicago in the Rock River Valley
HOTELS/MOTELS: Best Western Brandywine Lodge, Sterling-Dixon Frwy., three miles west of Dixon on IL 2, Dixon 61021, 815-284-1890; V.I.P. Motel, 1326 IL 2 North, Oregon 61061, 815-732-6195; Super 8 Motel—Dixon, 1800 S. Galena Avenue, Dixon 61021, 815-284-1800
BED & BREAKFASTS: Colonial Inn, Rock Street, Grand Detour 61021, 815-652-4422; Barber House B&B, 410 W. Mason St., Polo 61064, 815-946-2607
LODGES: White Pines Lodge, White Pines State Park, 6712 West Pine Road, Mt. Morris 61054, 815-946-3817
CAMPING: White Pines State Park, RR 1, Mt. Morris 61054, 815-946-3717; Lake LaDonna Family Campground, Harmony Road, Oregon 61061, 815-732-6804; Lowden State Park, RR 2, P.O. Box 403, Oregon 61061, 815-732-6828; Lake Louise Camping Resort, IL 2, Byron, 815-234-8483
DIRECTIONS: From Chicago, take the Tri-State Tollway, I-294, or the Eisenhower Expressway, I-290, to the East-West Tollway, I-88, west on I-88 to the Dixon exit, then IL 26 north to IL 2; Grand Detour is six miles northeast of Dixon on IL 2, the John Deere Historic Site is located at the south edge of Grand Detour

7. MC HENRY:
MORAINE HILLS STATE PARK

Taking its name from the effects of the Wisconsinite stage glacier on its land, Moraine Hills State Park is a 1,690-acre state park where nature provides the recreational facilities. The park combines scenic beauty, plenty of hiking and biking trails, a variety of picnic and playground areas and pleasant fishing conditions in a region of northern Illinois that is sprouting more and more housing developments and strip malls. Indian tribes, including Sauk, Fox and Potawatomi, lived in the area from the seventeenth to nineteenth centuries. It is believed that the first white settler was Horace Long, who built a cabin in the southeast corner of the park in 1833.

Moraine Hills attracts lots of visitors when the weather is good. Most people head for the McHenry Dam area, a fine place for families because it has fishing, boating, concession stands, playground equipment and picnic tables. The McHenry Dam, built in 1907, originally had a hand-operated lock. A modern dam was constructed in 1937. Despite the dam's amenities, don't overlook the fact that Moraine Hills is a large park, and its other areas are scenic, uncrowded, and more relaxing, yet have plenty of facilities.

Over ten miles of bicycle/hiking trails, surfaced with crushed limestone, wander through diverse, unspoiled landscapes including wooded hills, ridges, forests, prairie, and bog, passing rivers, lakes and marshes. Bird watchers have found over 100 species of birds in the park which is also home to wildlife such as red fox, mink, opossum, raccoon, and white-tail deer.

Two less-than-a-mile boardwalk nature trails high-light the diverse geological character of the land cre-ated by the Wisconsinite glacier which came from the north and pushed over the Chicago area 14,000 years ago. The Pike Marsh Nature Trail, which is in a dedi-cated nature preserve, has a floating boardwalk ex-tending into the marsh so you can see the unique vegetation and the red-wing blackbirds that nest there. Marshes and bogs in Moraine Hills resulted from small glacial ice blocks that left depressions and kettle-holes in the earth.

The Lake Defiance Nature Trail provides a glimpse at one of the few glacial lakes in Illinois which remains relatively undeveloped. Lake Defiance was formed when a massive block of ice detached from the glacier and melted. Leatherleaf Bog, a dedicated nature pre-serve, is a glacially-formed area that exemplifies ket-tle-moraine topography. Its 120 acres consist of a large floating mat of sphagnum moss and leatherleaf sur-rounded by an open moat of water.

With a valid fishing license, which can be purchased at the concession stands, you can fish from the banks of Wilderness and Tomahawk lakes for largemouth bass, bluegills, green sunfish, bullheads, northern pike, and channel catfish. Bank fishing is prohibited at Lake Defiance but boat fishing in park rental boats is permitted. Fishing in the Fox River is permitted in the McHenry Dam area. A fishing pier accessible to handi-capped visitors is located at the north end of the McHenry Dam area.

Private boats may only be brought into the park by car top for use in the Fox River and lakes other than Lake Defiance. No trailers are allowed in the park and there are no launching facilities. Rental boats are avail-able at the McHenry Dam and Lake Defiance conces-sion stands. Swimming is not allowed in the park.

Picnic areas are located throughout the park. Playground equipment can be found at McHenry Dam and natural playground equipment is located at the Whitetail Prairie and Pike Marsh Day Use Areas. Trail booklets for the nature trails may be obtained at the Park Office.

During northern Illinois' long, cold winters, you can cross-country ski on more than ten miles of trails; cross-country skis can be rented at the Lake Defiance concession area. Sledding and tobogganing at the Whitetail Prairie Day Use Area or ice fishing on the lakes and the Fox River are other winter activities.

ADDRESS: 914 S. River Road, McHenry, IL 60050
TELEPHONE: 815-385-1624
HOURS: Daily, summer: 6 a.m. to 8 p.m.; spring and fall: 7 a.m. to 7 p.m.; winter: 8 a.m. to 5 p.m.; closed Christmas Day
ADMISSION: Free
FACILITIES: 1,690 acres; interpretive center; three small lakes; bicycle/hiking trails; nature trails; picnic areas; concession stands; fishing; cross-country skiing; boating; dedicated nature preserves; playgrounds
LOCATION: About 30 miles northwest of Chicago, on the Fox River, three miles south of McHenry
CAMPING: Chain O' Lakes State Park, 39947 N. State Park Road, Spring Grove 60081, 708-587-5512
DIRECTIONS: From Chicago, take the Eisenhower Expressway, I-290, west until it ends at IL 53, continue north on IL 53, exit at U.S. 12/Rand Road, follow Rand west for about 11 miles to IL 176 (Liberty St.), west for 3 ½ miles to River Road, north on River Road to park entrance

8. MORRIS:
GOOSE LAKE PRAIRIE STATE NATURAL AREA

Illinois was called the Prairie State because its landscape was open, grass-covered and treeless when white settlers first saw it. Prairie comes from the French word for meadow; three-fourths of Illinois was an expansive grassy meadow. Now, because Illinois' fertile soil is used for raising crops, prairie is so rare in the Prairie State that it has had to be given state protection in order to preserve it.

The largest prairie in Illinois, and one of the largest in the United States, is at Goose Lake Prairie. The state natural area began with the state's purchase of 240 acres in Grundy County in 1969; later additions brought the acreage to 2,600.

A visit to this prairie gives you some sense of the Illinois landscape which frontier settlers used to see— windswept grasslands without trees, not the most attractive scenery. Although Goose Lake Prairie would be more accurately described as interesting instead of beautiful, it has many rewards for the naturalist. Walking the seven miles of trails reveals a plethora of unusual birds, so bring your binoculars. We saw meadowlarks, red-winged blackbirds, upland sandpiper, and magnolia warbler. There's wildlife here too. We spotted fresh deer tracks, but we didn't spot the deer.

A trail guide, which can be picked up at the Visitor Center, will inform you of the variety of grasses which grow in the prairie, including big bluestem, Indian grass, switchgrass, prairie dropseed and little bluestem. Wildflowers are part of the prairie environment. Spring flowers include violet shooting star and blue-eyed grass, while in summer false indigo and blazing star can be enjoyed. Fall brings sunflowers, asters and goldenrod.

Despite its name, there is no longer a Goose Lake at Goose Lake Prairie. The lake after which the area is named was drained almost 100 years ago, so that the land could be farmed. Adjacent to Goose Lake Prairie is Heidecke Lake, a Commonwealth Edison cooling lake which has been leased to the Department of Conservation for fishing and hunting. It is a popular place to fish both from its rock-lined shore and from gasoline-powered motor boats. There are no beaches and swimming is not permitted.

A multi-media presentation is given in the Visitor Center's auditorium. Dioramas and exhibits depict life on the prairie when it was occupied by Indian tribes and later by white frontiersmen. There are also exhibits on prairie formation, prairie plants, flowers, and animals.

Goose Lake is an interesting site for naturalists but its charms are subtle and would not particularly appeal to younger children.

ADDRESS: 5010 N. Jugtown, Morris, IL 60450
TELEPHONE: 815-942-2899
HOURS: Daily, 6 a.m. to sunset; Visitor Center: daily, 10 a.m. to 4 p.m.; closed Thanksgiving, Christmas and New Year's days
ADMISSION: Free
FACILITIES: 2,537 acres of Illinois prairie; seven miles of nature trails; Visitor Center; bird watching; picnic areas; cross-country skiing
LOCATION: 60 miles southwest of Chicago, in Grundy County east of Morris, in the Illinois and Michigan National Heritage Corridor
DIRECTIONS: From Chicago, take the Stevenson Expressway, I-55, south to I-80, west on I-80 to exit at Morris, IL 47, then

south on IL 47 about three miles, then east on Pine Bluff
Road about four miles to Jugtown Road; or I-55 South to
Lorenzo Road, exit 240, west on Lorenzo for 7 ½ miles to
Jugtown Road, Jugtown one mile to entrance

9. MORRIS:

ILLINOIS AND MICHIGAN CANAL STATE TRAIL; ILLINOIS AND MICHIGAN CANAL NATIONAL HERITAGE CORRIDOR

Have you discovered northern Illinois' natural recreational jewel, the Illinois and Michigan Canal State
Trail? If you haven't, you're in for a real surprise.
Imagine a tree-lined, easy walking path with a canal
on one side and a river on the other side. Walking or
biking on the 60 miles of trail is a relaxing way to
exercise in a natural setting. And it's not far from
Chicago. The state trail has access points at Channahon Access, which is only 50 miles from Chicago; Gebhard Woods Access, 61 miles; and Buffalo Rock Access,
83 miles.

Completed in 1848, the Illinois and Michigan Canal
was a 96-mile man-made waterway connecting the
Great Lakes to the Illinois River which flowed into the
Mississippi River, thus providing a commercial shipping link between the East Coast and the Midwest.
Today's trail was the towpath which mules walked
while pulling the boats along the canal.

The development of the Illinois and Michigan Canal
area as a linear park for recreational and historical
purposes has been a joint project of the state and the
federal government. The state of Illinois' Department
of Conservation manages the 61-mile trail, which is

considered the spine of the National Park Service's Illinois and Michigan Canal National Heritage Corridor.

The National Park Service viewed the I & M Canal's open space near the Chicago metropolis as a prime cultural and recreational resource. In 1984, the U.S. Congress enacted legislation that recognized the unique contribution of the Upper Illinois River Valley transportation system to nineteenth-century American commercial expansion and industrialization by designating it the Illinois and Michigan Canal National Heritage Corridor. Extending from Summit to LaSalle, the Corridor is over 100 miles long and encompasses 42 communities, though much of the land is privately owned. Congress specified that the cultural, historic, natural, recreational, and economic resources of the Corridor be retained, enhanced and interpreted.

The possibility of water travel from the Great Lakes down the Mississippi River into the Gulf of Mexico was first envisioned hundreds of years ago. As early as the seventeenth century the French explorer, Louis Jolliet, found the portage between Lake Michigan and the Des Plaines River, a branch of the Illinois River, over which Indians carried their canoes. Jolliet realized that a canal could be constructed to connect Lake Michigan and the Illinois River. The corridor that links the Great Lakes to the Mississippi River basin reaches from the upper Illinois River at LaSalle-Peru to the mouth of the Chicago River at Lake Michigan.

Although it was begun in 1836, financial problems delayed the canal's completion until 1848. The canal operated for 85 years. When originally constructed, the 96 mile canal contained 16 lift locks, 12 wood-frame locktender's houses, 5 aqueducts built of stone piers and timber trusses, 5 crib dams, several feeder canals and a pumping station at Bridgeport. Virtually nothing of the canal remains in Chicago.

In 1836, when plans for the canal were being made, Chicago's Fort Dearborn was a small fur trading settlement and military outpost. The construction of the canal turned Chicago into a major inland port and stimulated the growth of the city into an important manufacturing and trade center. Chicago's population increased more than 600 per cent in the decade after the canal opened. The towns of Lockport, Joliet, La Salle, Channahon, Morris, Seneca and Ottawa developed to serve the commercial needs of the canal. Despite its success, the eventual obsolescence of the canal was signalled by the coming of the railroads, which offered faster freight transportation. Its usage ceased in 1933.

The I & M Canal State Trail features 60 miles of hiking, bird watching, picnicking, fishing and camping. Whether to enjoy the first buds on the trees in spring, the full bloom of summer, or the colorful fall leaves, you'll return there again and again. A total of 55 miles between Channon and LaSalle is available for hiking and biking.

Canoeing is available on approximately 28 miles of the canal; launch facilities are at Channahon, AuxSable, Gebhard Woods and LaSalle. Primitive camping is available at Channahon Access, and Gebhard Woods Access. Snowmobiling is allowed after a snowfall of four inches.

Access is available at small accesses with parking lots located along the trail. Closest to Chicago is Channahon Access, in the town of Channahon in Will County. This 18-acre park has picnic areas, two locks, fishing, canoeing and camping, in addition to a restored locktender's house.

Buffalo Rock Access, located between Ottawa and

Utica, is a 243-acre park on a bluff on the north bank of the Illinois River. Adjacent to the park is Effigy Tumuli, large earth sculptures of a water strider, snake, turtle, catfish and frog erected on an abandoned, 150-acre surface mine. The sculptures, which represent aquatic animals native to the area, are reminiscent of the mounds built by native Americans.

Gebhard Woods has 30 acres of forested, slightly rolling terrain. Facilities include picnicking, fishing, primitive camping, a restored canal aqueduct and an Information Center that is open daily from 10 a.m. to 4 p.m. The largest tree in the state, an eastern cottonwood that stands 120 feet tall and has a circumference of 32 feet, is one mile west of Gebhard Woods on the south side of the canal.

In the historic canal town of Lockport is the Gaylord Building, built in 1838 as a construction material warehouse for the I & M Canal. Located along the Illinois and Michigan Canal, the warehouse was built of dolomite limestone that was quarried locally. The two-story west wing of the Gaylord Building was the first structure to border the canal. The three-story Italianate east wing was added around 1860. The Gaylord Building received its name from one of its owners, George Gaylord, who operated a dry goods store there from 1878 to 1883.

The impressive limestone building, which is a National Historic Landmark, was restored in 1987 by Gaylord Donnelley, a grandson of George Gaylord. It now houses the Illinois and Michigan Canal Visitor Center. Audio-visual programs are given in its theater, and exhibits and information on the State Trail, and the National Heritage Corridor are available. It is open Tuesday-Sunday, 10 a.m. to 5 p.m.: 200 W. Eighth Street, Lockport 60441, 815-838-4830.

The Gaylord Building also houses the Illinois State

Museum Lockport Art Gallery, open Tuesday-Sunday, 10 a.m. to 5 p.m., 815-838-7400. A very charming restaurant, The Public Landing, is located in the restored lower level of the building and its historic atmosphere is enhanced by antique quilts hanging on the walls. Open for lunch and dinner; closed Mondays; 815-838-6500.

Lockport's historic canal town flavor can best be appreciated from the Lockport Historical Trail, a two-mile path paralleling the I & M Canal. Beginning at the site of the old boatyard area, the trail passes through the downtown historic district, by the Gaylord Building, the I & M Canal Museum, Pioneer Settlement managed by Will County Historic Society, the 1862 railroad station, and Lock 1, ending at Dellwood Park.

ADDRESS: P.O. Box 272, Morris, IL 60450
TELEPHONE: 815-942-0796; 815-942-9501
HOURS: State trail open daily; Gebhard Woods Information Center 10 a.m. to 4 p.m., daily; Illinois & Michigan Canal Visitor Center in Lockport 10 a.m. to 5 p.m., Tuesday through Sunday
ADMISSION: Free
FACILITIES: 60-mile hiking trail; 55 miles of bicycle trails; canoeing; fishing; picnic areas; primitive camping; state parks; special events; Effigy Tumuli (earth sculptures); Gebhard Woods Information Center; Visitor Center in Lockport; NHL
LOCATION: The linear park is southwest of Chicago and parallels I-80 for 55 miles; from Chicago, Channahon is 50 miles off of I-55, Morris is 61 miles off of I-80, and Ottawa is 83 miles
TRAIL ACCESS AREAS: Gebhard Woods Access, Box 272, Morris 60450, 815-942-0796; Channahon Access, Box 636, Channahon 60410, 815-467-4271; Buffalo Rock Access, Box 39, Ottawa 61350, 815-433-2220;
HOTELS/MOTELS: see Starved Rock State Park, Utica (#16)

CAMPING: Gebhard Woods, Box 272, Morris 60450, 815-942-0796; Channahon Access, Box 636, Channahon 60410, 815-467-4271; McKinley Woods, Rt. 52 and Cherry Hill Rd., Joliet, IL 60433, 815-727-8700

DIRECTIONS: From Chicago to Channahon, take the Stevenson Expressway, I-55, south to U.S. 6 exit, west on U.S. 6 for five miles to Channahon, then watch for signs; from Chicago to Gebhard Woods, take the Stevenson Expressway, I-55, south to I-80, I-80 west to Morris exit, IL 47, south on IL 47 for two miles, 1 ½ miles west on Jefferson St.; from Chicago to Buffalo Rock Access, take the Stevenson Expressway, I-55, south to I-80, I-80 west to Ottawa exit, IL 23, south on IL 23 to IL 6, west on IL 6 to Boyce Memorial Drive, south to Dee Bennett Road; the Visitor Center in the Gaylord Building in Lockport is 35 miles southwest of Chicago, take the Stevenson Expressway, I-55, south to IL 53 exit, south on IL 53 to IL 7, east to Lockport

10. OREGON:
CASTLE ROCK STATE PARK

Newest of the three Rock River Valley state parks, Castle Rock State Park was established in 1978, although natural lands preservation groups had begun acquiring land as early as 1921. These groups wanted to preserve the natural beauty of the area for future generations to enjoy.

Located along the west bank of the Rock River, Castle Rock received its name from a spectacular butte of St. Peter sandstone overlooking the river. Sandstone rock formations, deep ravines, rolling hills, and a wide river with five islands, provide scenic variety in Castle Rock. Walking on the six hiking trails is the best way to appreciate it. There is also a two-mile nature trail with 28 markers identifying trees and wildflowers.

Fishermen and boaters are drawn to the river. They can fish along one and one-half miles of shoreline for catfish, bass, northern pike, walleye and crappie. Or they can launch a boat from the park's boat ramp. Canoeing is also popular and the park's only campground must be accessed by canoe.

710 acres, a third of the park, is a dedicated nature preserve reserved for scientific study. The Old Orchard and Aspen Ridge picnic areas are handicapped accessible.

ADDRESS: R.R. 2, Oregon, IL 61061
TELEPHONE: 815-732-7329
HOURS: Open year-round; closed Christmas and New Year's days
ADMISSION: Free
FACILITIES: 1,995 acres; hiking trails; nature trail; designated nature preserve; picnic areas; playgrounds; fishing; boating; boat ramp; canoe campground—boat access only
LOCATION: see White Pines Forest State Park (#12), three miles south of Oregon on IL 2
DIRECTIONS: see White Pines Forest State Park (#12)

11. OREGON:
LOWDEN STATE PARK

Lorado Taft's 50-foot statue of an Indian on a 250-foot bluff overlooking the Rock River is the most outstanding feature of Lowden State Park. The concrete statue depicts a blanket-wrapped man with folded arms, gazing across the river. Named "Eternal Indian" by Taft but informally dubbed "Blackhawk" by the public, the statue was sculpted in 1910 as a tribute to the Indians of the Rock River Valley. Eighty-year old Blackhawk has suffered some weather damage and is getting a facelift from the Illinois Department of Conservation.

Illinois tribes inhabited the scenic valley until 1730 when they were driven out by displaced Sac and Fox from the east. A century later, the remaining Indian tribes were forced into Iowa, as white settlers pushed the frontier steadily west. The Black Hawk War of 1832 marked the end of the Indian era in Illinois.

Lowden State Park was established by the state of Illinois in 1945. The property had been owned by Wallace Heckman, a Chicago attorney and a patron of the arts, who founded Eagle's Nest Art Colony on the site. From 1898 until 1942, artists, sculptors, and writers, including Lorado Taft, lived in cottages on the bluff and pursued their work, drawing inspiration from the natural beauty of the river valley. It was during his years at the summer colony that Taft was inspired to sculpt Blackhawk. Though originally part of the park, the Eagle's Nest area became Northern Illinois University's Lorado Taft Field Campus in 1951. It is used for classes in natural science and outdoor education.

Lowden has four miles of hiking trails, some of which follow the Rock River, the western boundary of the park. Boaters, water skiers and fishermen on the river can look up at Blackhawk perched majestically above them. A launching ramp and boat docks are located adjacent to the park. Spectacular fall color draws many visitors to the heavily-wooded park with its abundant maple, oak, hickory and cherry trees. 140 campsites are available for overnight stays.

ADDRESS: P.O. Box 403, Oregon, IL 61061
TELEPHONE: 815-732-6828
HOURS: Open year-round; closed Christmas and New Year's days
ADMISSION: Free

FACILITIES: 207 acres; 140 campsites; picnic areas; hiking
    trails; boating; launching ramp; fishing; 50-foot American
    Indian statue by Lorado Taft
LOCATION: see White Pines Forest State Park (#12), one and
    one-half miles north of Oregon on River Road
CAMPING: Lowden State Park, P.O. Box 403, Oregon 61061,
    815-732-6828
DIRECTIONS: see White Pines Forest State Park (#12), then
    follow IL 2 north from Dixon, Lowden is one and one-half
    miles north of IL 64 on River Road

12. OREGON:
WHITE PINES FOREST STATE PARK

One hundred miles west of our heavily populated,
overbuilt metropolitan area is a peaceful, scenic, rural
region called the Rock River Valley. Yes, I am talking
about Illinois, and it's less than two hours from Chicago. If you haven't discovered this area yet, maybe
it's time you did. But let's not all go at the same time
so we don't destroy its uncommercialized natural
beauty. Right now, chain restaurants and motels are at
a minimum as are shopping centers and cutesy country craft shops.

Instead, rolling, pastoral countryside with picturesque barns, natural beauty, historic sites, country inns
and an old-fashioned atmosphere are its attractions.
When you're hungry, have a great sandwich at Arthur's Deli in Dixon, dinner at the rustic White Pines
Inn in White Pines State Park, or at Maxson Manor in
Oregon, a supper-club on the river. For families with
children, nature lovers, history buffs, boaters, and
stressed-out city folks, the Rock River Valley is a good
choice for a low-key weekend.

White Pines Forest State Park is a favorite Rock

River Valley destination because it combines outstanding natural scenery with comfortable cabins and a pleasant restaurant. A completely self-contained destination, you can have an enjoyable week without leaving the park.

Hiking the seven trails is the best way to appreciate the heavily-forested rolling terrain and the variety of wildflowers. Moss-covered limestone bluffs loom over meandering Pine Creek. Fisherman try their luck in the stocked stream while little children try to catch elusive tadpoles. The virgin white pines, after which the park was named, constitute the southern-most stand of its kind in the Midwest.

Another special feature of the park is that, in several spots, the creek is crossed by fords rather than bridges. Water covers the roads shallowly and cars have to ford the stream. Pedestrians get to do a balancing act on boulders.

The 25 log cabins and the restaurant were built by the Civilian Conservation Corps in the 1930s. As part of the Build Illinois project, the cabins have recently been renovated. The one-room cabins accommodate four people, are air conditioned and heated, have private baths, telephone and television. The restaurant has also been renovated and can serve 225 people in several rooms.

The 150-mile Rock River is reserved exclusively for boaters and fishermen. It has never been improved for commercial navigation. The wide, swift river is a good place for canoeing.

ADDRESS: 6712 W. Pines Road, Mt. Morris, IL 61054
TELEPHONE: 815-946-3717
HOURS: Park: open year-round, closed Christmas and New Year's days; White Pines Inn cabins and restaurant: open March 1 through mid-December

ADMISSION: Free

FACILITIES: 385 acres; picnic areas; five miles of hiking trails; 25 cabins; White Pines Inn restaurant; 107 campsites; gift shop; dinner theater; fishing; playgrounds; cross-country skiing

LOCATION: In northwestern Illinois' Rock River Valley, ten miles north of Dixon, eight miles west of Oregon

CABINS: White Pines Forest State Park, 6712 White Pines Road, Mt. Morris 61054, 815-946-3817

CAMPING: White Pines Forest State Park, 6712 White Pines Road, Mt. Morris 61054, 815-946-3717

DIRECTIONS: From Chicago, take the Eisenhower Expressway, I-290, or the Tri-State Tollway, I-294, to the East-West Tollway, I-88, west on I-88 to IL 26, Dixon, exit 70, IL 26 north through Dixon to Lowell Park Road, then east to Pines Road, right on Pines Road for one and one-fourth miles to park

13. PETERSBURG:

LINCOLN'S NEW SALEM STATE HISTORIC SITE

The village of New Salem, on the Sangamon River, is indelibly linked in the nation's memory to the Illinois years of Abraham Lincoln, America's sixteenth president. It was in this crude frontier village that Lincoln worked as a young man, first sought political office, and decided to become a lawyer. His life would take him from New Salem to nearby Springfield as a lawyer and state legislator, to Washington as a congressman, back to Springfield, and then on to the nation's presidency.

New Salem, where Lincoln lived from 1831 to 1837, was founded in 1829 by James Rutledge and his nephew John Camron, a millwright and Cumberland

Presbyterian preacher. Recognizing the commercial potential of the place, Rutledge and Camron erected a dam and built a water-powered saw mill and grist mill. Like other frontier mill sites, New Salem's attracted nearby farmers and those who wanted to do business with them.

On 23 October 1829 a surveyor, Reuben Harrison, officially plotted the land that became the village of New Salem. Soon, the first business establishments opened. Samuel Hill and his partner, John McNeil, began a store above the mill. William Clary opened a saloon. Henry Onstot established a cooperage. James and Rowan Herndon opened a store. On 25 December 1829 New Salem's post office was established. In 1831, Dr. John Allen, a physician, began a medical practice.

Like others who came to the village, twenty-two year old Abraham Lincoln was drawn to New Salem by the Sangamon River. In April 1831, Lincoln was a member of a crew whom Denton Offutt had hired to pole a flatboat loaded with produce from Springfield down the Sangamon River and on to New Orleans. On April 19, Offutt's heavily-laden flatboat became marooned on the dam at New Salem. Directed by Lincoln, the crew off-loaded some of the cargo to lighten the load and successfully eased the boat over the dam. Impressed by Lincoln's quick action, Offutt offered him a job in a store that he planned to open at New Salem. Lincoln accepted. Although the store only operated for a short time, Lincoln made New Salem his home.

Lincoln was politically ambitious and in March 1832 became a candidate for the Illinois legislature. During the campaign, the Black Hawk War broke out when the famous Indian chief led his tribe, the Saux and Fox Indians, back into Illinois from across the Mississippi. Enlisting in the 4th Regiment of Mounted Volunteers,

Lincoln was elected captain of his company. He served until 10 July 1832, when he left the Volunteers to resume his election campaign.

Defeated on 6 August 1832 in his first bid for public office, Lincoln purchased Rowan Herndon's share in the Herndon-Berry Store which was renamed the Berry-Lincoln Store. In January 1833, the business was moved to the Warburton building, now known as the Second Berry-Lincoln Store. On May 7, Lincoln was appointed New Salem's postmaster, a position he held until 1836 when the office was relocated to Petersburg.

Lincoln was successful in his second campaign for the state legislature in 1834 and was re-elected in 1836. On 9 September 1836, he was licensed to practice law and he was admitted to the Illinois bar on 1 March 1837. He then left New Salem for Springfield to practice law in the state capital.

Like many other frontier settlements, New Salem enjoyed a quick start but never developed, and its fortunes began to decline. No efforts were spent to make the river more navigable, and trade drifted from New Salem to other towns. After the post office's relocation to Petersburg, many citizens left the town. When the legislature made nearby Petersburg county seat of newly created Menard County in 1839, New Salem's few remaining citizens gave up and left. New Salem became a frontier ghost town.

As Lincoln's historical stature grew, sites related to the life of the martyred Civil War president gained a deeper significance for Americans. In 1906, William Randolph Hearst, the newspaper magnate, purchased New Salem and conveyed it in trust to the Old Salem Chautauqua Association, an organization that promoted the site's historic reconstruction. In 1919, the Chautauqua Association conveyed the town to the state of Illinois, and in 1931 the state began reconstructing its buildings. In the 1930s, the Civilian Conservation Corps also aided the effort by reconstructing buildings.

Today, New Salem Village, in New Salem Historic Site, is a reconstructed living history museum of log cabins, shops, stores, a school and a tavern that appear as they did when Lincoln lived there. All of the structures, which are on their original foundations, are accurate reproductions based on historical maps, deeds, and documents. The only original building is the Onstot Cooper Shop which had been moved to Petersburg and has been moved back to its former foundation.

Interior furnishing and artifacts include items used by New Salem's residents, and other early-nineteenth-century period pieces such as wheat cradles, flax shuttles, chests, candle molds, rope beds, and pewter utensils. Flower, herb, and vegetable gardens authentically recreate the village milieu at the time of Lincoln.

Buildings line both sides of the village road. The Onstot Cabin and Cooper Shop, built in 1835, has barrels and the cooper's tools on display. Behind the cooper's shop is the Trent Brothers' Cabin, built in 1832 by Alexander Trent, a corporal who served with Lincoln in the Black Hawk War.

The Mentor Graham School House is named for Mentor Graham, a self-educated schoolmaster, who ran the subscription school. Prior to the establishment of tax-supported common or public schools, pupils paid a tuition rate, or subscription, which ranged from 30 to 85 cents a month. The school's simple interior contains four half-log benches, a table, and fireplace. Near the school are the cabins of Isaac Gulihur, another veteran of the Black Hawk War; Robert Johnson, a wheelwright and cabinet-maker; and Isaac Burner, a short-time resident.

The First Lincoln-Berry Store, located south of the main street, was built by James and Rowan Herndon in 1831. It was operated by Rowan Herndon and William Berry until 1832, when Herndon sold his interest in the store to Lincoln.

The Lukins and Ferguson Cabin, built in 1831 by Peter Lukins, consists of two rooms, one of which was used as a cobbler's shop by Alexander Ferguson. Cobbler's tools are on display.

Dr. John Allen's Cabin is the residence of one of New Salem's prominent citizens. A Dartmouth College graduate, physician, and businessman, Dr. Allen was a Yankee living on the Illinois frontier. Following the New England tendency to social reform, Allen organized a temperance society and a Sunday School.

The Rutledge Tavern, built in 1828 as the home of James Rutledge, the town's founder, was converted into a tavern and inn in 1831. A native of South Carolina, Rutledge was a quiet and studious man who had a personal library of 30 books. He founded a local debating society in which Lincoln practiced the oratory that would make him a powerful stump speaker in his debates with Stephen A. Douglas in the campaign for the United States Senate. Although Lincoln lost that election, he would defeat Douglas, again his rival, for president in 1860. Rutledge was the father of Ann Rutledge who was linked romantically with the young Lincoln by his early biographer, William Herndon. The truth of the love between Lincoln and Ann Rutledge is unknown, however.

The museum, a modern stone building, contains exhibits of Lincoln's surveyor's instruments, as well as furniture, and early nineteenth century tools and implements. When we visited New Salem, a quilting demonstration and an exhibition of antique quilts was in progress.

The Rutledge Saw and Grist Mill reproduces the 1829 water-driven combination sawmill and gristmill that sparked New Salem's rise as a community. The original mill was sold to Jacob Bale in 1832 and operated until 1853. William Clary's Grocery Store, a simple log building, opened in 1829, and was a favorite gathering place of those waiting to have their grain ground.

Located on a bluff overlooking the River is Denton Offutt's General Store, which opened in 1831, with Lincoln as clerk. Like other frontier general stores, it sold a wide variety of goods, ranging from food to fire arms.

The Second Lincoln-Berry Store, a frame structure, was built by George Warburton in 1831. It passed through several owners and was rented by Abraham Lincoln and William Berry.

During the summer and fall, a number of special events are held at New Salem, ranging from quilt shows, summer festivals, prairie story-telling days, traditional music performances, and candlelight tours.

The *Talisman*, a replica of the steamboat that plied the Sangamon River, provides boat trips. The original 95-foot-long *Talisman* had difficulty in navigating the narrow, and often shallow, Sangamon River. On one of its voyages, Rowan Herndon and Abraham Lincoln assisted the captain in negotiating the Sangamon's narrow channel. The steamboat was destroyed by fire in 1832. Now, the new and somewhat smaller *Talisman* again navigates the Sangamon. Except for Mondays and holidays, it makes 2 and ½-mile narrated excursions upstream from New Salem hourly, beginning at 10 a.m., May through August. In September and October, it operates on weekends only: Adults $1.50, children 4-12 $1.00; 217-632-2219 or 217-632-7681; Talisman River Boat, Box 337, Petersburg, 62675.

Your Obedient Servant, A. Lincoln, an outdoor drama presented by the Great America People Show Company chronicles Lincoln's life. It is presented at 8 p.m. nightly, except Mondays, from mid-June through late August in the outdoor amphitheater: The Great American People Show, Box 401, Petersburg 62675; 217-632-7754.

ADDRESS: R.R. 1, Box 244A, Petersburg, IL 62675
TELEPHONE: 217-632-7953; 217-632-7611
HOURS: Daily, 9 a.m. to 5 p.m., late April through late October; 8 a.m. to 4 p.m. rest of year
ADMISSION: Free
FACILITIES: Reconstructed early nineteenth-century frontier settlement; state historic site; museum; crafts and souvenir shop; Hilltop concession stand; picnic areas; steamboat rides; outdoor drama; Visitor Center; River Ridge Restaurant; NR; partially handicapped accessible
LOCATION: In central Illinois on IL 97; two miles south of Petersburg, 20 miles northwest of Springfield, 200 miles southwest of Chicago
BED & BREAKFAST: Carmody's Clare Inn, 207 South 12th St., Petersburg 62675, 217-632-2350
HOTELS/MOTELS: see Springfield (#14)
CAMPING: Lincoln's New Salem State Park, RR 1, Box 244A, Petersburg 62675, 217-632-7953; NSPOA Campground, PO Box 102, Petersburg 62675, 217-632-2977
DIRECTIONS: From Chicago, take the Stevenson Expressway, I-55, south to Williamsville, exit 109, then 20 miles west to New Salem

14. SPRINGFIELD:
LINCOLN SITES

Illinois is called the land of Lincoln and Springfield, its state capital, is the heart of the historic places that were significant in the sixteenth president's life.

Begin your visit at the Lincoln Home Visitor Center, 426 South Seventh Street, for an orientation to the Lincoln sites in the area. Open daily from 8:30 a.m. to 5 p.m; 217-492-4150.

The Lincoln Home National Historic Site is the most popular Lincoln site. In 1844, Lincoln purchased the house, located at Eighth and Jackson Streets, from the owner, Reverend Charles Dresser, the minister who officiated at Lincoln's wedding to Mary Todd.

The frame home, originally one-story, was built in 1839 at a cost of $1,500. Lincoln added the second story to accommodate his wife and four sons, Robert, Edward, William, and Thomas. The family lived in the house, the only one Lincoln ever owned, for seventeen years, until they moved to the White House in 1861.

The house has been painstakingly restored to its appearance in 1860. The interior consists of a kitchen and dining room, the double formal parlors, the informal sitting room, and four bedrooms. The rooms are furnished with items owned by the Lincolns or with period pieces. In 1887, Robert Todd Lincoln donated the home to the state. It has been administered by the National Park Service since 1972. Open daily from 8:30 a.m. to 5 p.m.; free; 426 South Seventh Street, Springfield 62701, 217-492-4150.

The Great Western Depot, at Monroe Street between Ninth and Tenth Streets, where Lincoln delivered his farewell address before departing for Washington, is open to visitors. On 11 February 1861, Lincoln told the crowd that had assembled to see him off, "To this place, and the kindness of these people, I owe everything." The Depot's restored waiting rooms feature a multi-media presentation and an exhibit on Lincoln. Open daily, 9 a.m. to 5 p.m., from April 1 through November 1; admission.

The Old State Capitol State Historic Site, at Fifth and Adams streets in downtown Springfield, was the center of Illinois' government from 1839 to 1876. Restored to its original appearance, the site is maintained and operated by the Illinois Historical Preservation Agency. Designed by the architect John Rague, the Capitol is a distinguished example of the Greek Revival architectural style that was popular for early nineteenth-century public buildings. It features a domed cupola and Doric porticos.

The first floor contains the restored offices of the state auditor, secretary of state, supreme court and treasurer. On the second floor are the governor's office and reception room, and the chambers of the senate and the house of representatives. Lincoln served as a state representative from 1834 to 1841. Here, as the Republican nominee for U.S. senator, he delivered his famous speech in 1858, saying, "A house divided against itself cannot stand. I believe this government cannot endure, permanently, half slave and half free." It was also here that his body lay in state on 3 May 1865, returned to Springfield after his assassination. An original handwritten copy of Lincoln's "Gettysburg Address" is permanently displayed. On most Fridays and Saturdays, living history tours are conducted by guides costumed in 1850s styles. The Illinois State Historical Library is housed on a level beneath the Old State Capitol. The Old State Capitol is open daily, 9 a.m. to 5 p.m.; closed Thanksgiving, Christmas and New Year's days; free. 217-785-7961.

One-half block east of the Old State Capitol is the Lincoln-Herndon Law Offices State Historic Site, located at 209 South Sixth Street at the corner of Adams Street. Built in 1840, it is the only surviving structure in which Lincoln maintained a law office. The Court, located one floor below Lincoln's office, is restored to its appearance when it was the only federal court in Illinois. Open daily from 9 a.m. to 5 p.m.; closed on Thanksgiving, Christmas and New Year's days; 217-785-7289.

Lincoln's Tomb State Historic Site, located in Oak Ridge Cemetery, on Springfield's north side, is the final resting place of Abraham Lincoln. He was buried in the cemetery on 4 May 1865. Construction of the tomb began in 1869. Lincoln's coffin was transferred to the present tomb when it was dedicated in 1874. After thieves attempted to steal the body and hold it for ransom in 1876, his remains were buried beneath the floor of the burial chamber in 1901. The bodies of Mary Todd, his wife, and three of his sons, Edward, William, and Thomas, are also interred in the monument. The tomb contains a bust of Lincoln by Gutzon Borglum, a model of Chester French's statue of the president, and bronze tablets of the "Gettysburg Address," the "Farewell Address" to Springfield, and the "Second Inaugural Address." Open daily from 9 a.m. to 5 p.m.; closed Thanksgiving, Christmas and New Year's days; free; 217-782-2717.

In addition to the Lincoln sites, Springfield has several other interesting historical sites. The Illinois State Museum on Spring and Edwards streets, has exhibitions on the state's history and natural history. The museum is open daily from 8:30 a.m. to 5 p.m. and on Sundays and holidays from 1:30-5 p.m; closed Thanksgiving, Christmas, New Year's, and Easter days; 217-782-7386.

The Dana-Thomas House State Historic Site, 301 East Lawrence Avenue, built between 1902 and 1904, is an excellent example of Frank Lloyd Wright's early Prairie style of architecture. The interior is furnished with furniture, lighting fixtures, and art glass windows designed by Wright. Open daily, from 9 a.m. to 4 p.m., with the last tour beginning at 4 p.m.; closed Thanksgiving, Christmas, and New Year's days; free; 217-782-6776.

In addition to the historic sites, visitors to Springfield may also tour the modern state government buildings. The Illinois State Capitol is open from 8 a.m. to 4 p.m; guided tours are available from 8 a.m. to 3:30 p.m. on weekdays; free. Information about attractions in Springfield is available from the Springfield Convention and Tourism Commission, 219 South Fifth St., Springfield 62701, 217-789-2360.

LOCATION: Springfield is in central Illinois, almost 200 miles southwest of Chicago

HOTELS/MOTELS: Hampton Inn, 3185 S. Dirksen Parkway, Springfield 62703, 217-529-1100; Mansion View Lodge, 529 S. 4th St., Springfield 62701, 217-544-7411, 800-252-1083; Ramada Renaissance, 701 E. Adams St., Springfield 62701, 217-544-8800

CAMPING: Lincoln's New Salem State Park, RR 1, Box 244A, Petersburg 62675, 217-632-7953

DIRECTIONS: From Chicago, take the Stevenson Expressway, I-55, south to Springfield; most sites are in downtown Springfield

15. SPRING GROVE:
CHAIN O'LAKES STATE PARK

Because of its proximity to Chicago and its facilities for outdoor sports, Chain O'Lakes State Park is usually crowded on summer weekends. The park has grown from an initial 840 acres acquired by the state in 1945, to over 6,000 acres today. Ninety-five acres have been set aside as a nature preserve.

The name refers to ten of the Fox chain of lakes that were formed by glaciers. These lakes represent the largest concentration of natural lakes in the state. The state park borders three of them, and the Fox River runs through the park.

All this water makes fishing and boating the most popular activities. Bluegill, walleye, crappie, bass, northern pike, catfish and bullheads can be caught along the banks of the river and lakes as well as from the docks and fishing piers. There are two launching ramps for boats, and boat rentals are available.

While boaters crave action, nature lovers enjoy walking the two mile nature trail from which they can peacefully observe the woods, wildflowers, birds and animals. The area is composed mainly of fresh-water bog over deep peat deposits. Trees in the park include Scotch pine, oak, cherry, hickory, elm, birch, sumac and spruce. Wildlife residents include chipmunks, ground squirrels, gophers, deer, rabbits, mink, opossum, skunk, raccoons and fox.

Chain O'Lakes has an especially nice feature, a short circular nature trail that is handicapped accessible. There are eight miles of trails for horseback riders, six picnic areas and three campgrounds.

During northern Illinois' long winters, sporting enthusiasts use the park for ice skating, ice fishing, sledding, cross-country skiing, and access is provided for snowmobiling in frozen areas. Pheasants may be hunted, by permit only, during hunting season, when the park is closed for all other activities.

ADDRESS: 39947 North State Park Road, Spring Grove, IL 60081

TELEPHONE: 708-587-5512

HOURS: Daily, during daylight hours; closed Christmas day; closed to other activities during hunting season

ADMISSION: Free

FACILITIES: 6,063 acres; lakes; Fox River; fishing; fishing piers; boating; boat launches; boat rentals; hiking trails; handicapped accessible trail; horse riding trail; nature preserve; picnic areas; campgrounds

LOCATION: In northeastern Illinois, McHenry and Lake counties, 20 miles west of Lake Michigan and four miles south of the Illinois-Wisconsin border, about 45 miles northwest of Chicago

CAMPING: Chain O'Lakes State Park, 39947 N. State Park Road, Spring Grove 60081, 708-587-5512

DIRECTIONS: From Chicago, go north on the Kennedy Expressway, I-90/94, or the Tri-State Tollway, I-294, continuing north on the Tri-State Tollway, I-94, to IL 173, west to park

16. UTICA:

STARVED ROCK STATE PARK

In an area surrounded by flat Illinois farmland and corn fields there are deep canyons, flowing waterfalls, soaring cliffs, spectacular geological rock formations, and a wide river, all of which were produced by continental glaciation. Less than two hours from Chicago, Starved Rock State Park is a 2,630-acre site on the Illinois River with 18 canyons carved from sandstone by running water. Heavily forested trails climb to high cliffs to give breathtaking views of the Illinois River Valley. A state park since 1911, Starved Rock is an exceptional outdoor recreational site that has been popular with generations of Chicagoans and downstate residents. A recent multi-million-dollar renovation of its lodging facilities has made it even more attractive.

The Illinois River Valley was formed by a series of floods as glacial meltwaters broke through moraines, sending torrents of water surging across the land, eroding sandstone and other sedimentary rocks. Canyons were formed by streams feeding into the Illinois River which wore away the sandstone during the period of glacial melt, 20,000 years ago. Starved Rock, for which the park is named, is a section of the Illinois River bluff which rises 125 feet straight up from the water.

The Indian legend which gave the rock its name relates to the murder of an Ottawa chief, Pontiac, by a member of the Illinois tribe which lived along the river. To avenge Pontiac's death, battles were fought between the Illinois and the Ottawas and their allies, the Potawatomi. Eventually, the Illinois took refuge on top of a high sandstone butte where they were surrounded by Ottawa and Potawatomi. Although the Illinois were able to defend this position, their food ran out. Many warriors died of starvation and the butte became known as Starved Rock.

Although this incident was said to have occurred in the 1760s, archaeologists say that there was Indian habitation on the site as early as 8000 b.c. Archaic Indians were hunters who camped on or below the bluffs, which were used as lookout spots. Evidence of tool-making left by these hunters include hammerstones, scrapers, drills, grinding tools, and spear-

points. Later, Woodland, Hopewellian and Mississippi
Indian farming communities occupied the area, living
in both shelter caves and structures built in open areas.
Cooking pots as well as burial mounds containing
their dead have been found.

A French exploring party led by Louis Jolliet and
Father Jacques Marquette in 1673, brought the first
Europeans into the area. In 1675, Father Marquette
returned and founded the Mission of the Immaculate
Conception for the Kaskaskia Indians, a sub-tribe of
the Illinois. In 1682, French explorers, Robert Cavalier
Sieur De La Salle and Henri Tonti claimed the entire
Mississippi Valley for France. To protect that claim, a
chain of forts was built by La Salle including, in 1682,
Fort St. Louis in the vicinity of Starved Rock. In 1702,
the French ordered Fort St. Louis to be abandoned. It
had disappeared by 1720 and no traces of it remain
today.

Starved Rock's magnificent canyon scenery can best
be appreciated by hiking its 15 miles of trails which
lead to all of the canyons, many of which have waterfalls. Since St. Louis waterfall is spring-fed, it can be
seen year round while others may only appear during
the rainy season. Usually, Ottawa, LaSalle and French
canyons have waterfalls. Since steep cliffs can be dan-
gerous for young children, families with small children should stay on the flatter areas along the river,
picnic groves and playgrounds.

The park abounds with wildflowers, plants, trees,
wildlife and birds. Vegetation varies with the terrain.
In the rock walls of the canyons grow lichens, mosses,
liverworts, ferns, Canada yews and blue harebells.
Cottonwood, black willow and ash trees grow on the
wet, level Illinois River flood plain. Red oak, basswood, and sugar maples thrive in the sandy soil of
north-facing slopes, while on the sandy bluffs grow

black and white oaks, red and white cedars, and white pines. Spring plants include marsh marigolds, skunk cabbage and wild iris. Wildflowers add to the natural beauty; they include trillium, may apple, dutchman's breeches, flowering spurge, shooting star, orange columbine, yellow partridge pea, black-eyed susans, jack-in-the-pulpits, hepatica and spiderworts. You're also likely to see witch hazel, wild hydrangea, serviceberry and northern honeysuckle. Watch out for the poison ivy which grows throughout the park.

Animal life includes squirrels, rabbits, chipmunks, deer, raccoon, opossum and beaver. Bird watchers should keep an eye out for red-tailed hawks, owls, swallows, vireos, catbirds, yellow-bellied sapsuckers, scarlet tanagers, cedar waxwings, nuthatches, chickadees, indigo buntings and rock doves, all of whom inhabit the park. Eagles can be seen in winter.

In addition to great scenery, the Starved Rock State Park lodge, a rustic stone and log building built in the 1930s by the Civilian Conservation Corps, provides lodging and food in the park. A successful get-away trip involves total immersion in the setting. Leaving the natural site you came to see in order to find lodging and dinner on a highway strip of look-alike motels and fast-food restaurants destroys the illusion. For non-campers, finding a natural site with lodging can be difficult. Starved Rock Lodge, which now has a new hotel wing with a lobby, has a total of 93 rooms. Other recent additions are an indoor swimming pool, hot tub, children's pool, and saunas.

ADDRESS: P.O. Box 116, Utica IL 61373
TELEPHONE: 815-667-4726
HOURS: Open daily; closed Christmas and New Year's days
ADMISSION: Free
FACILITIES: 2,630-acre park; lodge with 71 rooms; dining

room; 22 cabin rooms; Visitor's Center; 133-site campground; hiking trails; guided hikes; horseback riding trails; equestrian campground; boat ramps; canoe rentals; fishing; picnic areas; special events

LOCATION: Approximately 100 miles southwest of Chicago, one mile south of Utica, midway between Ottawa and La Salle-Peru, four miles south of I-80

LODGE: Starved Rock State Park, P.O. Box 471, Utica 61373, 815-667-4211

HOTELS/MOTELS: Ottawa Inn-Starved Rock, 3000 Columbus St., at jct. IL 23 and I-80, Ottawa 61350, 815-434-3400; Howard Johnson, I-80 and IL 251, Peru 61354, 815-224-2500; Super 8, 1851 May Road, Peru 61354, 815-223-1848; Motel 6, 1900 May Road, Peru 61354, 815-224-2785; Super 8, I-80 and IL 23, Ottawa 61350, 815-434-2888

CAMPGROUNDS: Starved Rock State Park, Box 116, Utica 61373, 815-667-4726; LaSalle/Peru KOA, RR 1, Box 477, Utica 61373, 815-667-4988; White Oak Camping Resort, P.O. Box 156, Utica 61373, 815-667-4758

DIRECTIONS: From Chicago, take the Stevenson Expressway, I-55, south to I-80, follow I-80 west to IL 178 exit, south on IL 178 to IL 71, east on IL 71 to park entrance

17. VOLO:

VOLO BOG STATE NATURAL AREA

A unique natural phenomenon can be observed at Volo Bog, a dedicated Illinois Nature Preserve as well as a National Natural Landmark. Volo Bog is the only quaking bog in the state, exhibiting all the stages of natural succession of a bog. It was formed when the Wisconsinite glacier retreated from northeastern Illinois approximately 12,000 years ago, leaving large blocks of glacier ice behind. The melting ice left depressions in the earth called kettle-holes. When filled with water, these kettle-holes became lakes and ponds.

Bogs and marshes formed when ponds and lakes were gradually filled in by concentric rings of plants, starting at the banks of the lakes and spreading toward the center.

Volo Bog was once a kettle-hole lake which covered 50 acres and was 50 feet deep. Now it consists of an open pool of water in the center of a bog in which waterlilies, spatterdock and duckweeds grow. Surrounding the pool is a floating mat composed of sphagnum moss, cattails, ferns and sedges. Beyond that is a ring of shrubs including sumac, willow, adler, and leatherleaf. The next ring is composed of a tamarack forest, conifers that lose their needles in winter, then a secondary shrub zone of poison sumac, winterberry holly, quaking aspen and buckthorn. Beyond the shrubs is a marsh/sedge meadow with blue-joint grass and reed canary grass. Next grow black willow, and then the deciduous trees, including red maple, yellow birch and serviceberry. As each ring slowly moves toward the center, the bog will eventually be filled in and become low, wet woods. Bogs are a middle stage in the progression from lake to woods.

The Volo Bog has been designated a preserve because wetlands, which are vanishing at an alarming rate, are vital to the survival of all life forms. They replenish ground water that supplies wells, collect silt from upland erosion that would choke streams, provide food and water for many animal species, and prevent flooding by soaking up water from melting snow, thawing ground and heavy storms. Wetlands collect, store and purify rain water which is gradually returned to the water cycle through evaporation and plant transpiration.

In 1958, the Illinois Chapter of the Nature Conservancy recognized the significance of the bog and raised money to rescue it from the threat of land devel-

opers. Forty-seven acres of bog land were purchased
and in 1970, ownership was transferred to the Illinois
Department of Conservation, which bought additional
acreage to protect and enlarge the area. Now totaling
869 acres, the natural area includes two other bogs,
prairie restoration areas, hardwood forest, and succes-
sional fields.

Because of the unstable ground and the delicacy of
the bog, visitors must stay on the designated half-mile
trail at all times. The trail is a floating boardwalk
which crosses the wet areas of the bog and marsh. Out
on the boardwalk, surrounded by the thick vegetation
and the signs warning of hazardous soils and poisonous plants, we had an eerie feeling that we were in a
nature horror film where killer tomatoes or triffids
were going to get us. However, the feeling passed, we
survived, and we actually enjoyed the unique bog environment.

Each season has its own special look at Volo Bog,
which is home to 25 species of endangered plants. In
spring, the wetland is flooded with several feet of
water from melting snow and spring rains. Spring
flowers including marsh marigold, white violet, blue
flag, and the blueberry and cranberry can be enjoyed.
Bird watchers may glimpse some rare species as flocks
of migratory waterfowl and song birds use the bog for
resting, feeding and nesting.

In summer, when the bog is no longer flooded, it
becomes a breeding ground for large numbers of in-
sects, especially the mosquito, deer fly and dragonfly.
Other residents of the bog include turtles, frogs,
snakes, muskrat, deer, mink, shrew, foxes and weasels.
Birds commonly sighted are red winged blackbirds,
catbirds, cedar waxwings and common yellowthroats.
Larger birds include the sparrow hawk, turkey vul-
ture, great blue heron, Canadian geese, ducks, red-

tailed hawks, and owls. Marsh wildflowers and bog plants are in full bloom. Look for New England aster, swamp milkweed, broad-leaved arrowhead, ragged fringed orchid, starflower, grass pink and marsh bell-flower.

Fall presents changing colors—gold of the tamarack needles, red of the poison sumac and green of the sphagnum moss. In winter, the only colors are the red berries of the winterberry holly and red leaves of the leatherleaf.

The Tamarack View Trail is an easy two-and-three-quarters-mile hiking trail through meadows and woods. The Visitor Center has exhibits on all aspects of the bog including native plants and animals, Illinois' valuable wetlands, geological history of Volo Bog and birds' nests that incorporate bog materials.

A wide variety of educational programs for adults and children is offered including topics such as Pond Life, Bog Communities, Birds, Animal Tracking, Family Insect Safari, Wetland Seminars, Nature Photography, Guided Bird Walks and Astronomy Sessions. Guided bog tours leave from the Visitor Center at 11 a.m. and 1 p.m. on Saturday and Sunday.

ADDRESS: 28478 W. Brandenburg Road, Ingleside, IL 60041
TELEPHONE: 815-344-1294
HOURS: Daily, 8 a.m. to 4 p.m.; closed Christmas and New Year's days; interpretive trail: 8 a.m. to 8 p.m. June-August, 8 a.m. to 4 p.m. September-May; guided bog tours: Saturday and Sunday, 11 a.m. and 1 p.m.; Visitor Center: 9 a.m. to 3 p.m., Thursday-Sunday June-August, Saturday and Sunday September-May
ADMISSION: Free
FACILITIES: 869 acres; Visitor Center; interpretive bog trail; two and three-fourth-mile Tamarack View hiking trail; guided bog tours on weekends; educational programs for children and adults; picnic area; gift shop

LOCATION: Northeastern Illinois in Lake County, 45 miles northwest of Chicago

DIRECTIONS: From Chicago, take the Tri-State Tollway, I-294, north, continuing on I-94 to exit at Belvidere Road, IL 120, west on IL 120 for 12 miles to town of Volo, then north on U.S. 12 to Sullivan Lake Road, west on Sullivan Lake Road to Volo Bog; or, take the Northwest Tollway, I-90, to IL 53 exit, IL 53 north to U.S. 12/Rand Road, then northwest on IL 12 about 19 miles to Sullivan Lake Road, just north of town of Volo, then west on Sullivan Lake Road

18. ZION:

ILLINOIS BEACH STATE PARK

The Chicago area's finest natural and recreational feature is Lake Michigan. Much of the valuable lakefront property has been developed for private homes. Fortunately, some Lake Michigan frontage has been preserved for public use. Over 4,000 acres of lakefront and almost seven miles of beach at Illinois Beach make this state park one of Illinois' best. For weekenders, a comfortable lodge adds the final touch for a great getaway.

The park actually has two units, both of which are on the lake. The Northern Unit has beach access, five miles of trails that can be used for hiking, biking and cross-country skiing, fishing in the beach area and in Sand Lake which has a handicapped fishing pier, and picnic areas with picnic shelters. The larger Southern Unit has swimming beaches, bath houses, campgrounds, hiking trails, fishing, picnic areas, a nature preserve with an Interpretive Center, and a 96-room lodge.

Although its water doesn't warm up until late August, swimming in Lake Michigan is the primary attraction for most visitors to the park. Wide sandy beaches make a good playground for both adults and kids. Fishing, picnicking and beach walking are popular pursuits along the shores of this vast lake.

The attractive lodge provides all the comforts of a resort, including a good restaurant, cocktail lounge, olympic-size indoor swimming pool, whirlpool, tennis courts, health club and video game room. Even in winter, when outdoor activities may be limited to cross-country skiing, facilities at the lodge can keep family members busy. The view is great, year round.

The park is endowed with natural features such as dunes, forests, prairie, marsh, the Dead River and the residues of glacial lakeshores. The long process by which prehistoric Lake Chicago, formed by glacial meltwaters, lowered to the level of present-day Lake Michigan involved a series of new shorelines. The corrugated ridges visible in Illinois Beach State Park's dune area are remnants of those shorelines.

Illinois Beach State Park is the site of Illinois' first nature preserve. Selected because it contains 16 different natural plant communities and displays plant succession from shore to forest, the nature preserve contains 900 acres. Protection of its 60 endangered types of plants and animals is a goal of the preserve. The bald eagle and the peregrine falcon have been spotted there. Almost four miles of hiking trails run through the nature preserve. The Interpretive Center has exhibits and audiovisual programs on the park.

Hiking trails in the park are good places to observe the park's 600 species of plants, oak and pine forests, marshes, and its birds, mammals, reptiles and amphibians.

The nearby town of Zion, originally a religious commune, was founded in 1900 by John Alexander Dowie, a Scotsman. Dowie advocated divine healing and established a religion called the Christian Catholic Church. He then started a separate community, which he called City for God, for himself and the followers of his church. The 10,000 residents of this church-owned, autocratic theocracy pledged to avoid alchohol, tobacco, opium, drugs, medicines, pork, gambling, theaters, opera houses, dance halls, circuses, pharmacies, physicians and houses of ill-fame. Economic difficulties led to the deposition of Dowie in 1906. The theocracy collapsed. Eventually property was transferred from the church to individuals, and Zion became a secular community.

Shiloh House, a 25-room Swiss-style mansion built for Dowie and his family, is now the home of the Zion Historical Society. Original furnishings, antiques, religious artifacts and manuscripts are displayed: 1300 Shiloh Boulevard, Zion 60099, 708-746-2427; open 2-5 p.m., weekends from May through August.

ADDRESS: Lakefront, Zion, IL 60099
TELEPHONE: 708-662-4811
HOURS: Daily, dawn to 8 p.m.
ADMISSION: Free
FACILITIES: 4,160 acres on Lake Michigan; beaches; swimming; beach houses; concession stands; playground; picnic areas; fishing; boating; boat launch; hiking trails; nature preserve; Interpretive Center; cross-country skiing; 244 campsites; 96-room lodge with restaurant, conference facilities, indoor pool; tennis courts
LOCATION: In extreme northeast corner of Illinois, on Lake Michigan, north of Waukegan and south of Illinois-Wisconsin state line, about 28 miles north of Chicago's northern border
LODGE: Illinois Beach Resort, Sheridan Road and Wadsworth, Zion 60099, 800-424-6065 (IL), 800-424-6060 (outside IL)

CAMPING: Illinois Beach State Park, Lakefront, Zion 60099, 708-662-4811

DIRECTIONS: From Chicago, take the Edens Expressway, I-94, north, continuing north on I-94, the Tri-State Tollway, to exit at IL 173, east to Sheridan Road, turn north for Northern Unit or south for Southern Unit

Clarke House, Chicago, Il.

Jane Addams' Hull-House Museum, Chicago, Il.

Lincoln Park Conservatory, Chicago, Il.

Garfield Park Conservatory, Chicago, Il.

Historic Pullman, Hotel Florence, Chicago, Il.

Robie House, Living Room, Chicago, Il.

Foxes at Willowbrook Forest Preserve and Wildlife Haven, Glen Ellyn, Il.

Edward L. Ryerson Conservation Area, Deerfield, Il.

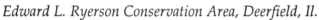

Cantigny, Robert R. McCormick Museum, Wheaton, Il.

Frank Lloyd Wright Home and Studio, Oak Park, Il.

Little Red Schoolhouse Nature Center, Willow Springs, Il.

The train at Blackberry Historical Farm-Village, Aurora, Il.

Steeple Building, Bishop Hill, Il.

Ronald Reagan Boyhood Home, Dixon, Il.

A view of the town of Galena, Il. (Photo courtesy of Galena/Jo
Daviess County Convention & Visitors Bureau)

Old Market House State Historic Site, Galena, Il. (Photo
courtesy of Galena/Jo Daviess County Convention &
Visitors Bureau)

John Deere Historic Site, Statue of John Deere, Grand Detour, Il.

Moraine Hills State Park, McHenry, Il.

Goose Lake Prairie, Morris, Il.

Lowden State Park, Blackhawk Statue, Oregon, Il.

Lincoln Law Office, Springfield, Il.

New Salem State Historic Site, Onstot Cooper Shop, Petersburg, Il.

Illinois Beach State Park, Zion, Il.

Conner Priarie, Mrs. Curtis in the kitchen, Noblesville, In.
(Photo courtesy Conner Prairie)

President Benjamin Harrison Memorial Home, Indianapolis, In.
(Photo courtesy President Benjamin Harrison Foundation)

The Gerald Ford Museum, Grand Rapids, Mi.

Yankee Springs Recreational Area, Middleville, Mi.

A circus wagon at Circus World Museum, Baraboo, Wi.

Old World Wisconsin, Koepsell House in German Area, Eagle, Wi.

Mid-Continent Railway, North Freedom, Wi.

Pendarvis House, Mineral Point, Wi.

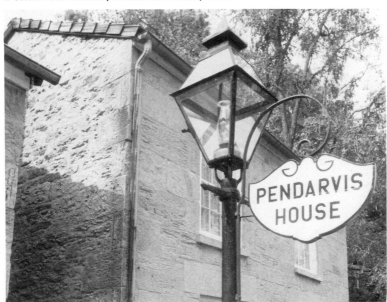

Old Wade House, Greenbush, Wi.

Taliesin, Spring Green, Wi.

PART 3:

Indiana

INDIANA

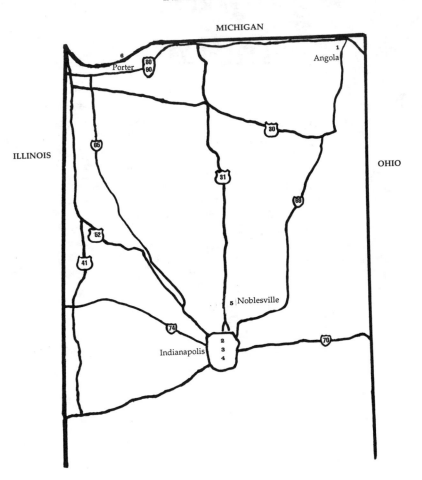

1. ANGOLA:
POKAGON STATE PARK

Pokagon State Park has been a favorite weekend destination of our family for years. We've found all seasons enjoyable. Winter evenings spent careening down the quarter-mile toboggan slide leave happy memories, despite the long walk back up for just one more time, with Dad hauling the toboggan. Walks in the woods during crisp fall days were often rewarded by sighting a silent deer or two. Summer meant swimming in Lake James. Pokagon is one of Indiana's finest state parks, providing a natural refuge and plenty of entertainment for families.

Named after Potawatomi Indian Chief Simon Pokagon, the park lies on 1,200 acres of rolling, heavily wooded land bordering on Lake James and Snow Lake. The Potawatomi Indians inhabited the site until the early 1800s when they sold more than 1,000,000 acres, including what is now Chicago, to the U.S. government for three cents an acre.

The park was established in 1925 and much of the construction work was completed by the Civilian Conservation Corps from 1934 to 1942. The CCC built roads, nature trails, the toboggan slide, the saddle barn, camping areas, and a bathhouse, in addition to planting trees.

The Potawatomi Inn, built in 1927, is a cozy lodge

that retains the charm of an earlier era despite its modern addition with pool, sauna, and whirlpool.

The best way to enjoy the variety of trees, wildflowers, birds and wildlife is to hike any of the six trails which cover a total of eight miles. The park also has a nature center and a naturalist who often presents programs in the inn.

Summer activities revolve around the beaches on Lake James and include swimming, sunbathing, fishing and boating. Rowboats and paddleboats may be rented. Camping is another warm-weather activity, with over 400 campsites available.

Pokagon offers a good antidote to the winter blahs. Its refrigerated, quarter-mile toboggan slide produces shouts of delight from both big and little kids as they speed along at 35 miles per hour. Depending on the weather, the toboggan operates weekends, from Thanksgiving through February. A somewhat more peaceful but still vigorous outdoor activity is cross-country skiing on the park trails. Both cross-country ski equipment and toboggans can be rented at the park.

The nearby town of Angola has restaurants and antique shops. Many of the local Amish people come into town by horse and buggy.

ADDRESS: Rt. 2, Box 129, Angola, IN 46703
TELEPHONE: Park: 219-833-2012; inn: 219-833-1077
HOURS: Daily, year round
ADMISSION: $2.00 daily fee for non-commercial vehicles
FACILITIES: 1,200 acres; Lake James; swimming; boating; fishing; hiking trails; nature center; 430 campsites; lodge with indoor pool, sauna and whirlpool; cross-country ski trails; quarter-mile toboggan slide; playground; picnic areas
LOCATION: In extreme northeast corner of Indiana, 153 miles

east of Chicago, about ten miles west of Ohio border, three
miles south of Michigan border, six miles north of Angola

INNS: Potawatomi Inn, Pokagon State Park, 6 Lane 100A Lake
James, Angola 46703, 219-833-1077

CAMPING: Pokagon State Park, 1080 West St. Rd. 727, Angola
46703, 219-833-2012

DIRECTIONS: From Chicago, take the Tri-State Tollway, I-294,
south to I-80/94 eastbound, or take the Dan Ryan Expressway, I-90/94, south to I-94 to I-80/94 eastbound; continue
east on the Indiana Tollway, I-80/90, across Indiana to I-69,
exit 144, south on I-69 to IN 727 West, exit 154, west to park

2. INDIANAPOLIS:
THE CHILDREN'S MUSEUM
OF INDIANAPOLIS

Called a "jewel of an institution" by the *Chicago
Tribune*, the Children's Museum of Indianapolis aims
to delight children of all ages, and it succeeds admira-
bly. Founded in 1925, it was one of the first children's
museums in the United States and now lays claim to
being the largest in the world.

The museum, which attracts nearly 1.5 million visitors each year, has a collection of 140,000 items ranging
from the historical to the futuristic. Housed in a modern building, the functionally and attractively designed interior consists of a central atrium surrounded
by spiral ramps that lead to five floors of galleries,
exhibits, and hands-on activities.

Among the galleries is Playscape, an exhibit for preschoolers and their parents in which play stimulates
children to use building bricks, make toy trains, meas-
ure sand and water, and make crayon rubbings of
mummies and dinosaurs. The Pastimes exhibit, located in the Clowes Gallery, features radios, movies,

jukeboxes and television, to explore how Americans use their leisure time.

The Science Spectrum gallery, with its Indiana Bell Think Tank and the You've Got to Have Heart exhibit, has 40 hands-on science experiments through which children can explore the space program, energy use, astronomy, electricity, computers, and chemistry. The museum even has a simulated limestone cave with stalactites and stalagmites that children can enter.

One of the museum's largest and most popular artifacts is the turn-of-the-century carousel located in the Toys and Dolls Gallery. Rides can be taken on the fully operational carousel equipped with its original 1919 Wurlitzer organ and 41 Dentzel animals.

The Mysteries in History gallery challenges youngsters to become historians and archaeologists by discovering clues about the past using archaeology, documents, oral history, and photographs. The gallery, which hosts a simulated archaeological dig, also has exhibits of an 1830s Indiana frontier farm cabin, and an early 1900s small town street.

The Passport to the World gallery, which includes 50,000 folk art objects and toys, transports visitors from Indiana to the world. Here, youngsters learn about other peoples and cultures by taking a simulated ride on an elephant in India, wearing children's costumes from other countries, and participating in the festivals of other cultures.

The new, 130-seat, domed SpaceQuest Planetarium features high-tech space voyages like Time Trek, a 35-minute jaunt through the galaxy on a time machine giving visitors a chance to explore how the universe has changed over billions of years.

In the Eli Lilly Center for Exploration, an innovative 15,000-square-foot gallery, children ten and over use museum resources like synthesizers, a darkroom, carpentry shop, state-of-the-art audio equipment, and computers to explore and develop special projects of their own design.

Performances of puppetry, mime, opera, dance, and clowns are presented in the museum's 350-seat Ruth Allison Lilly Theater.

ADDRESS: 3000 North Meridian Street, Indianapolis, IN 46206
TELEPHONE: 317-924-5431, 317-921-4002
HOURS: Memorial Day to Labor Day, Monday-Wednesday and Friday-Saturday, 10 a.m. to 5 p.m., Thursday 10 a.m. to 8 p.m., and Sunday, noon to 5 p.m.; rest of year, Tuesday, Wednesday, Friday and Saturday, 10 a.m. to 5 p.m., Thursday, 10 a.m. to 8 p.m., and Sunday, noon to 5 p.m.; closed Thanksgiving, Christmas, and New Year's days
ADMISSION: Adults $4.00, seniors $3.00, annual pass for children 2-17 $3.00; SpaceQuest Planetarium $1.00, carousel ride $0.50
FACILITIES: Children's museum; changing exhibits; planetarium; gift shop; restaurants; wheelchair accessible
LOCATION: In Indianapolis on Meridian Street (U.S. 31) bordered by 30th and Illinois Streets, about 175 miles southeast of Chicago
HOTELS/MOTELS: Canterbury Hotel, 123 S. Illinois St., 46225, 317-634-3000; Embassy Suites, 110 W. Washington St., 46204, 317-236-1800; Hilton at the Circle, 31 W. Ohio St., 46204, 317-635-2000; Hyatt Regency Indianapolis, 1 S. Capitol Ave., 46204, 317-632-1234; Holiday Inn, Union Station, 123 W. Louisiana St., 46225, 317-631-2221; Ramada Inn, 501 W. Washington St., 46204, 317-635-4443; Westin Hotel, 50 S. Capitol Ave., 46204, 317-262-8100
CAMPING: Indianapolis KOA NE, 5896 West 200 North, Greenfield 46140, 317-894-1397; Kamper Korner, 1951 W. Edgewood Ave., Indianapolis 46217, 317-788-1488; Mohawk Campground, 756 W 375N, Greenfield 46140, 317-326-3393; Mounds State Park, Anderson 46013, 317-642-6627
DIRECTIONS: From Chicago, take the Dan Ryan Expressway,

I-90/94, south or Tri-State Tollway, I-294 south to I-80/94, east, follow I-94/80 east in Indiana to I-65 exit, south on I-65 to Indianapolis, take the Dr. Martin Luther King Jr. exit to 29th Street, follow 29th Street to Illinois Street. Parking is accessible from Illinois St.

3. INDIANAPOLIS:
PRESIDENT BENJAMIN HARRISON MEMORIAL HOME

The President Benjamin Harrison Memorial Home was the home of the twenty-third president of the United States. Benjamin Harrison (1833-1901) was born in North Bend, Ohio, the son of a distinguished American political family. His grandfather, General William Henry Harrison, who defeated the Indian chief Tecumseh at the battle of Tippecanoe, was the ninth president of the United States. His father, John Scott Harrison, served as a congressman from Ohio.

After graduating from Miami University, Benjamin Harrison practiced law in Cincinnati. He married Caroline Lavinia Scott in 1853, and the couple moved to Indianapolis in 1854, where he established a law practice. He served in the Civil War as an officer in the 70th Indiana Volunteer Regiment and was promoted to brigadier general for his distinguished service. He was elected to the U.S. Senate as a Republican, and served from 1881 to 1887.

Harrison was the Republican nominee for president in 1888. He defeated incumbent Grover Cleveland, the Democratic candidate, in a close election. President Harrison served one term and then was defeated by Cleveland, once again his opponent in the election of 1892. He returned to his home in Indiana in 1893.

Harrison's home on North Delaware was designed in the Italianate style by architect H. T. Brandt, and built at a cost of $24,818. Completed in 1875, the large brick house of 16 rooms was then home to the Harrisons and their two children, Mary and Russell.

When he returned to Indianapolis in 1893, Harrison modernized the house by adding central heating, plumbing, and electricity, and enlarged it by adding several rooms and a front porch. Caroline, Harrison's first wife, died while he was president. He married Mary Lord Dimmick in 1896 and their daughter Elizabeth was born in the house.

The Harrison home was purchased in 1937 and restored by the Arthur Jordan Foundation. It was completely refurbished a second time in 1974. Most of the furnishings are original to the Harrison family. The tour is guided by a trained docent who explains the history of the home and its furnishings.

Special celebrations take place on the Fourth of July, Harrison's birthday on August 20, and during the Christmas season.

ADDRESS: 1230 North Delaware Street, Indianapolis, IN 46202

TELEPHONE: 317-631-1898

HOURS: Monday-Saturday, 10 a.m. to 4 p.m.; Sundays, 12:30-4 p.m.; closed Easter, Thanksgiving, Christmas and New Year's days and the first two weeks of January

ADMISSION: Adults $2.00; 1st-12th grade students and college students with I.D. $1.00

FACILITIES: Restored home of 23rd U.S. president; special events; NHL

LOCATION: In Indianapolis, about 175 miles southeast of Chicago

HOTELS/MOTELS: see Children's Museum, Indianapolis (#2)

CAMPING: see Children's Museum, Indianapolis (#2)

DIRECTIONS: From Chicago, follow directions to Indianapolis

in Children's Museum (#2); from southbound I-65, use Meridian St. exit, proceed east (Meridian becomes 11th Street), cross 11th Street to Delaware, turn left, go north on Delaware to the Harrison Home, first house on left after interstate overpass

4. INDIANAPOLIS:

JAMES WHITCOMB RILEY HOME

Preserved by peers of the Indiana poet, the James Whitcomb Riley Home is the Victorian house in which Riley (1849-1916) lived the last 23 years of his life. The home was owned by Major and Mrs. Charles L. Holstein, Riley's friends, and had been built by John R. Nickum, Mrs. Holstein's father, in 1872. Shortly after Riley's death there, the Holstein house was purchased by a group of Riley's friends, including Booth Tarkington, who later formed the James Whitcomb Riley Memorial Association. The Association preserved the house as it was on Riley's death in July, 1916.

The house provides a glimpse at the lifestyle of well-to-do Victorians in small-town Indiana around the turn of the century. In addition to the Holsteins and Riley, there was a household staff of four.

The solidly constructed brick building sits on a stone foundation and is topped by a slate roof. The rooms on the first floor consist of a long entrance hall, drawing room, library, formal dining room, family dining room, and kitchen. The second floor has five bedrooms and a bathroom. Hand-carved hardwood woodwork, decorated ceilings, bordered wall-to-wall carpeting, marble fireplaces, and crystal chandeliers are found throughout the house, complementing the fine Victorian furniture.

Riley's room contains the poet's desk, a Wayman Adams painting of his poodle, a self-portrait, his clothing and a wicker invalid's chair. His easy chair and favorite books are in the library.

Owned and maintained by the James Whitcomb Riley Memorial Association, the house is a National Historic Landmark.

ADDRESS: 528 Lockerbie Street, Indianapolis, IN 46202
TELEPHONE: 317-631-5885
HOURS: Tuesday-Saturday, 10 a.m. to 4 p.m.; Sunday, noon to 4 p.m.; closed Monday
ADMISSION: Adults $1.00, students $0.25, children under 12 free when accompanied by an adult
FACILITIES: Museum home of James Whitcomb Riley; gift and book store; NHL
LOCATION: Near downtown Indianapolis, 175 miles southeast of Chicago
HOTELS/MOTELS: see Children's Museum, Indianapolis (#2)
CAMPING: see Children's Museum, Indianapolis (#2)
DIRECTIONS: From Chicago: see Children's Museum (#2); in Indianapolis: from Monument Circle, north on Meridian Street three blocks to Vermont Street, east on Vermont five blocks to East Street, south one-half block to Lockerbie Street, east to 528 Lockerbie

5. NOBLESVILLE:
CONNER PRAIRIE

American history can be learned in a variety of ways. One relaxing and interactive method is visiting outdoor museums, which combine history and recreation. These non-traditional museums provide a particularly painless way to introduce children to their country's heritage. An especially fine outdoor, or liv-

ing history, museum is Conner Prairie, founded in
1964 by Eli Lilly and owned by Earlham College.

At Conner Prairie's 250 acres, visitors find three
historic areas: a re-creation of an 1836 Indiana pioneer
village; the restored 1823 home of William Conner, an
early settler; and a hands-on pioneer craft area, along
with a modern visitor center.

Conner Prairie takes its name from William Conner,
a trader and scout whose mother was born in a Dela-
ware-Moravian settlement in Ohio. In 1802, Conner
established a trading post on the White River, near
present-day Noblesville. The area was inhabited by
Delaware Indians and, because Conner spoke their
language, he quickly gained their trust. His trading
post prospered. Conner married Mekinges, daughter
of Chief Anderson, a Delaware, and the couple had six
children.

A prominent man, Conner occasionally served as a
scout and an interpreter at Indian councils for William
Henry Harrison, who was serving as governor of the
Northwest Territory. When Indiana became a state in
1816, two-thirds of its land was owned by Indians.
Conner helped negotiate the Treaty of St. Mary, Ohio,
in 1818 whereby Indian tribes, including the Delaware,
relinquished their rights to a large piece of central
Indiana land referred to as the New Purchase. The
Indians agreed to move westward across the Mississippi River. Ironically, the large group of Delawares
who moved west in 1820 included Mekinges and the
six Conner children. William Conner remained in Indiana, where he was elected to the state legislature three
times.

In 1823, William Conner built a brick, Federal-style
mansion on a bluff overlooking a 200-acre prairie for
his second wife, Elizabeth Chapman, and their family,
which grew to ten children. The Conner house was the

core around which Conner Prairie developed. When Eli Lilly, a grandson of the founder of the pharmaceutical house by that name, purchased the house in 1934, it had fallen into disrepair. Lilly carefully restored and furnished the house with authentic period pieces.

Wishing to depict the lifestyle of an early Indiana settler, Lilly relocated several original log buildings including a barn, cabin, trading post, distillery and spring house from nearby Brown County to the Conner estate. Lilly then donated the property to Earlham College, who added the village area.

Prairietown is a re-creation of an 1830s Indiana community. In the village, costumed interpreters recreate life in 1836. They have names, ages, occupations, families, and pasts. Visitors are greeted as if they were neighbors who had just dropped in to chat. First-person interpretation, listening to people talk as if they were in the early nineteenth century, usually surprises visitors at first. However, children find it delightful and everyone adjusts quickly to conversing as if they had stepped back 150 years in time.

The village has 39 early nineteenth-century structures, businesses as well as simple homes. The Golden Eagle is an inn run by Martha Zimmerman with a ladies' parlor, bar room, dining room, kitchen and three sleeping rooms. Also in the village is a school house, Dr. Campbell's office, George Whitaker's and his son James' general store, Ben Curtis' blacksmith shop, Isaac and Lucinda Baker's pottery shed, and the McClure carpenter shop, along with homes and barns. All buildings contain furniture and artifacts appropriate to the period.

Participation is the byword of the Pioneer Adventure Area where guests are encouraged to try pioneer activities like weaving, cooking, spinning, quilting, log splitting, wood carving, candle dipping or soap making.

An orientation film is shown in the theater of the modern visitor center. The Weaver Gallery features permanent and changing exhibits related to Indiana history. Governor Noble's Eating Place, a restaurant featuring traditional Hoosier-style cooking, is also in the museum center as is the gift shop. During the Christmas season, candlelight tours of the village are given. Symphony concerts are presented in the museum's amphitheater during the summer.

ADDRESS: 13400 Allisonville Road, Noblesville, IN 46060
TELEPHONE: 317-776-6000, 24-hour information line: 317-776-6004
HOURS: May through October, 10 a.m. to 5 p.m., Tuesday-Saturday, noon to 5 p.m., Sunday; April and November, 10 a.m. to 5 p.m., Wednesday-Saturday, noon to 5 p.m., Sunday; candlelight tours in December; closed Easter and Thanksgiving
ADMISSION: Adults $8.00, seniors $7.25, children 6-12 $5.00
FACILITIES: Re-created 1836 Indiana pioneer village; restored William Conner home; Pioneer Adventure Area; 39 historic buildings on 288 acres; Visitor Center with Weaver Gallery, theater, restaurant, bakery and museum shop; handicapped-accessible nature trail
LOCATION: In central Indiana, six miles north of Indianapolis, four miles south of Noblesville, 170 miles southeast of Chicago
HOTELS/MOTELS: Waterfront Inn I & II, 409 W. Jackson St., Cicero 46034, 317-773-5115; Quality Inn Castleton Suites, 8275 Craig St., Castleton 46250, 317-841-9700
CAMPING: see Children's Museum, Indianapolis (#2)
DIRECTIONS: Follow directions to Indianapolis area in Children's Museum (#2); from I-65, take I-465 east to Allisonville Road, exit 35, north on Allisonville Road for six miles to Conner Prairie

6. PORTER:
INDIANA DUNES NATIONAL LAKESHORE and INDIANA DUNES STATE PARK

Mention the word dunes to Chicagoans and you'll unleash a torrent of memories. The dunes are connected with coming-of-age rituals like being old enough to get the car, being permitted to travel 50 miles away with your friends and without any parents, and going on dates. For generations, the dunes have traditionally been a favorite spot for the day after the prom. We felt a twinge of nostalgia when our daughters continued the tradition.

What Chicagoans might not be aware of is the naturalists' long struggle to preserve the dunes which finally proved successful in 1966 when the Indiana Dunes was declared a National Lakeshore, a part of the National Park System. Within, or at least surrounded by, the National Lakeshore is Indiana Dunes State Park, which has been in existence since 1927.

The battle to establish Indiana Dunes National Lakeshore lasted 50 years. Beginning in the late nineteenth century, the industrial revolution brought steel mills, meat-packing plants and oil refineries to Lake Michigan's southern shore. Only the sand dunes between Michigan City and Gary remained untouched. As early as 1913, conservationists, afraid that all of the lakeshore, its huge sand dunes and its unique ecology, would be lost to industrialization, tried to preserve that stretch of dunes by having it declared a national park. Their efforts were unsuccessful.

In 1916, the state of Indiana became interested in

founding state parks to commemorate its centennial year. After two parks were established, their popularity convinced state leaders to create more. Several years of efforts by conservationists persuaded the state legislature to authorize funds for Indiana Dunes State Park in 1923. Four years passed before the state completed the purchase of the 2,200 acres that now comprise the park.

Finally, after more of the southern lakeshore was lost to a power station, a steel finishing plant, and Burns Harbor, the U.S. Congress authorized the purchase of 6,539 acres for the Indiana Dunes National Lakeshore in 1966; the park was formally established in 1972. Congress voted to enlarge the National Lakeshore by 3,300 acres in 1976, 500 acres in 1980, and 853 acres in 1986.

Indiana Dunes National Lakeshore is considered an urban national park, which means that it is located near a large city and is relatively small compared to other national parks. Traditionally, federal policy called only for the establishment of vast parks in areas of natural grandeur far away from population centers. During the Kennedy administration, national park policy changed to include smaller, recreation-oriented parks, near large cities.

The national lakeshore is located along the southern edge of Lake Michigan between Gary on the west and Michigan City on the east. It is not one continuous piece of property, but is interrupted by the Port of Indiana. Its 13,000 acres include 13 and ½ miles of lakefront, beaches, and huge sand dunes. Many dunes are covered with dense forests, bogs, and marshes.

Swimming and sunbathing, the most popular activities at the dunes, are possible at West Beach, Kemil Road, Central Avenue and Mount Baldy. West Beach, the most developed beach, has 3 and ½ miles of sandy beaches, a beach house, visitors center, picnic area, concession stands and lifeguards, along with five miles of hiking trails.

The National Lakeshore Visitor Center, located at U.S. 12 and Kemil Road, offers exhibits and literature about the dunes, an orientation slide program, and ranger-led hikes and other programs for visitors. It is open daily, 8 a.m. to 5 p.m.

A historical attraction is the Bailly Homestead, the site of an 1830s homestead established by French Canadian fur trader Joseph Bailly. Restored buildings include the 1835 hewn-log house, the coachman's house, storehouse and a cemetery. Nearby is the Chellburg farm, which is a restored 1900 farm including a farmhouse, barn, and chicken house.

The state park has three miles of Lake Michigan shoreline for swimming, 1,800 wooded acres, a nature center, picnic areas, a modern campground, and a 9 and ⅕-mile hike/bike trail called the Calumet Trail, which leads to the National Lakeshore.

Conservationists were originally attracted to the dunes because of their fascinating ecology. Change is a constant factor in sand dune ecology. The dunes were created by northwesterly winds blowing across Lake Michigan, which picked up sand from the shore and redeposited it a short distance inland when they were slowed down by hills and dunes. Shoreline dunes, called active dunes, change the most. The newest dunes are at the shore and they increase in age as they are more distant from the lake. Older dunes develop plant life and forests which make them stable. Mount Baldy, a 120-foot-high dune, advances inland four or five feet each year, burying everything in its path.

Plant life in the dunes is extremely diverse because the climatic zones of north and south meet here. Plants range from southern dogwood to prickly pear cactus, tundra mosses to northern jack pine to eastern white pine. This environment supports 1,000 species of flowering plants and ferns, and 75 kinds of trees. Bird-watchers have documented almost 300 species of birds. Thirty types of mammals live in these dunes.

Henry Chadler Cowles, a botany professor at the University of Chicago, developed his theory of plant succession, or ecological succession, at the dunes around the turn of the century. Ecological succession refers to the orderly, progressive sequence of replacement of biotic communities over a given area. The rapidly changing environment of the dunes provided a natural laboratory in which to study the interactive relationship between plants and their environment. The changes that occurred there simulated the plant adaptation that took centuries elsewhere.

ADDRESS: Lakeshore: 1100 N. Mineral Springs Road, Porter, IN 46304; Park: 1600 North, 25 East, Chesterton, IN 46304

TELEPHONE: Lakeshore: 219-926-7561; Park: 219-926-1952

HOURS: Lakeshore: daily; Visitor Center: daily, 8 a.m. to 5 p.m., closed Thanksgiving, Christmas and New Year's days; Park: daily

ADMISSION: Lakeshore: $2.50 per vehicle; Park: $2.00 per vehicle

FACILITIES: Lakeshore: 13,000 acres, visitor center, beaches, swimming, fishing, picnic area, hiking trails, biking, horse trail, bathhouse, interpretive talks, Bailly Homestead and Chellberg Farm, food concession in summer, cross-country skiing; Park: 2,182 acres, beaches, swimming, beach house, campgrounds, picnic areas, snack bar, hiking trails, biking, Calumet Trail, cross-country skiing

LOCATION: On the southern shore of Lake Michigan, between Gary and Michigan City

BED & BREAKFAST: Creekwood Inn, U.S. 20, IN 35 at I-94, Michigan City 46360, 219-872-8357

HOTELS/MOTELS: Indian Oak Inn Resort & Spa, I-94 at Chesterton Exit, Chesterton 46304, 219-926-2200; Howard Johnson, 6161 Melton Rd., Portage 46368, 219-762-2136; Holiday Inn, 6200 Melton Rd., Portage, 46368, 219-762-5546; Knights Inn, 201 W. Kieffer Rd., Michigan City 46360, 219-874-9500; Red Roof Inn, 110 W. Kieffer Rd., Michigan City 46360, 219-874-5251

CAMPING: Indiana Dunes State Park, Chesterton 46304, 219-926-4520; Yogi Bear's Jellystone Park Camp Resort, PO Box 810, 5300 Old Porter Road, Portage 46368, 219-762-7757; Michigan City KOA, 1601 North U.S. 421, Michigan City 46360, 219-872-7600

DIRECTIONS: From Chicago, take the Dan Ryan, I-90/94, or the Tri-State Tollway, I-294, south, stay on I-94 into Indiana, exit at IN 49, north to state park; or exit at IN 249, north to U.S. 12, east on U.S. 12 to national lakeshore

PART 4.

Michigan

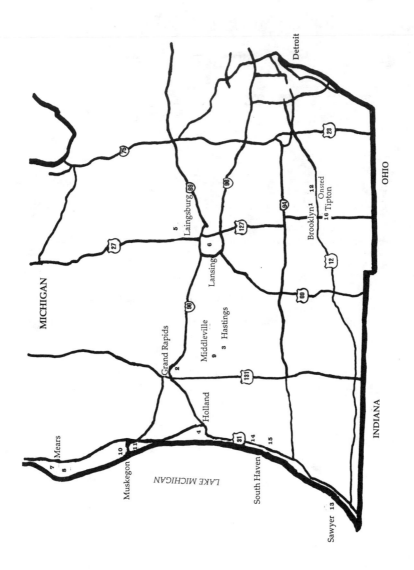

1. BROOKLYN:
WALKER TAVERN HISTORIC COMPLEX

The Walker Tavern Historic Complex is a restored 1840s stagecoach tavern that focuses on Michigan's frontier stagecoach period, from 1825 to 1853. In the days when Michigan was being settled, this frontier tavern was located at the junction of two early overland roads, the Detroit-Chicago Road and the La Plaisance Bay Turnpike which ran inland from Monroe on Lake Erie. The Chicago Road, which traced the route of the Old Sauk Trail, was the main artery of settlement in the southern part of the state.

In the 1830s, the U.S. Government sold land in Michigan for $1.25 an acre. Pioneers from the east caught "Michigan Fever" and bought the cheap, fertile land. Sylvester and Lucy Walker came from Cooperstown, New York, in 1837. When they arrived at Cambridge Junction, they found the two-story frame tavern and took over its operation in addition to farming. The Walkers bought the property in 1843.

Michigan

Lucy Walker was a good cook and her husband kept her supplied with food from the family farm, orchard, and dairy. The Walker Tavern was well located, at the junction of roads carrying stagecoach, wagon, horseback and pedestrian traffic. Traveling was extremely arduous because the roads were rough and often washed out. Travelers needed inns at frequent intervals where they could get rest, food and spirits. Walker Tavern had a reputation for providing fine food and lodging, and became a favorite gathering place for the local community. Business was so brisk that Walker constructed a larger three-story brick hotel across the road in 1852-53.

In the 1850s, transportation changed dramatically when railroads began to replace stagecoach travel. A relic of the stagecoach era, the original two-story, white-frame Walker Tavern has been restored to its appearance in the mid-1840s. Many nineteenth-century furnishings decorate the bar room, parlor, kitchen and dining room. A reconstructed nineteenth-century barn displays a blacksmith and wheelwright's shop. The Visitor Center has an audio-visual program and exhibits on the settlement of Michigan.

ADDRESS: 13220 M-50, Brooklyn, MI 49230
TELEPHONE: 517-467-4414
HOURS: Daily, 10 a.m. to 5 p.m., Memorial Day through Labor Day
ADMISSION: Free
FACILITIES: Visitor Center; restored frontier tavern and wheelwright barn; picnic area
LOCATION: Junction of U.S. 12 and MI 50, 25 miles southeast of Jackson, in Irish Hills area, 175 miles northeast of Chicago
HOTELS/MOTELS: Walter J. Hayes State Park, Onsted (#12)
CAMPING: Walter J. Hayes State Park, 1220 Wampler's Lake Road, Onsted 49265, 517-467-7401; Irish Hills Resort Kamp-

ground, 16230 U.S. 12, Cement City 49233, 517-592-6751;
Juniper Hills Campground, 13500 U.S. 12, P.O. Box 427,
Brooklyn 49230, 517-592-6803
DIRECTIONS: Same directions as Hayes State Park (#12) to
Jackson, exit I-94 at U.S. 127 south, south on U.S. 127 to MI
50, then south on MI 50 towards junction with U.S. 12, park
entrance is on MI 50, one-quarter mile north of the junction

2. GRAND RAPIDS:
GERALD R. FORD MUSEUM

Gerald Ford is an adopted son of Michigan. Born
Leslie Lynch King, Jr. in Omaha, Nebraska, in 1913,
Ford was raised in Grand Rapids, Michigan, by his
mother and stepfather, Gerald R. Ford, Sr., whose
name he took. Ford Sr. adopted his stepson in 1935.
Ford Jr. represented Michigan's Fifth Congressional
District in the U.S. House of Representatives from 1948
to 1973, becoming House minority leader in 1965.

President Gerald Ford, the thirty-eighth president
of the United States, served in that office from 9 August 1974 until 20 January 1977. Ford assumed the
presidency in unique circumstances. He was the first
vice-president who became president because of the
resignation of his predecessor, and the first man ever
to become president without having been elected to
national executive office.

The successful candidates in the presidential election of 1972 were Richard Nixon for president, and
Spiro Agnew for vice-president. Spiro Agnew resigned
in October 1973, and Gerald Ford was appointed as
vice-president on 6 December 1973. The Watergate
scandal resulted in the resignation of President Nixon
on 9 August 1974 and the appointed, not elected, vice-
president, Gerald Ford, was sworn in as president the
same day.

Ford had the unenviable task of restoring popular confidence in the nation's democratic process. The people's faith in the political system had been eroded by the Watergate scandal, which involved the highest levels of the Executive Branch of the government. In his inaugural address, Ford declared, "My fellow Americans, our long national nightmare is over....As we bind up the internal wounds of Watergate, more painful and more poisonous than those of foreign wars, let us restore the golden rule to our political process."

The Gerald R. Ford Presidential Museum is not a presidential library, although it is in the hands of the National Archives and Records Administration. The Ford Library is located in Ann Arbor. The museum in Grand Rapids was originated by a group of local people known as the Gerald R. Ford Commemorative Committee. They wanted it to be a commemoration of Ford's life, and a testimony to the esteem the people of Grand Rapids felt for Jerry Ford. The committee planned the museum and raised the funds, and it was later transferred to the federal government.

The Gerald R. Ford Museum, modern and impressive architecturally, is a triangular, two-story building with a mirrored east wall. It is situated on a six-acre site on the west bank of the Grand River. Ah-Nab-Awen Bicentennial Park, which is a memorial to the Indian tribes who used this site as a trading place, separates the museum from the river. On the other side of the Grand River is the imposing Amway Plaza Hotel and the Grand Center, a convention center.

Beautifully displayed exhibits in the museum focus on Ford's life, his congressional years, his presidency, his 1976 presidential campaign, and gifts from dignitaries and heads of state. There is a full-scale replica of the White House Oval Office as it looked during the

Ford years. It contains many of Ford's personal belongings which he donated to the museum. There is also a model of the White House indicating what each room was used for.

President Ford's administration coincided with America's Bicentennial, in 1976. An exhibit features a slide presentation of the Bicentennial celebrations, along with gifts marking the Bicentennial made by Americans from every state.

Ford's most controversial decision was the presidential pardon of former president Richard Nixon; an exhibit contains documents related to that issue.

Ford's unsuccessful campaign for the presidency in 1976, which many have attributed to the unpopular Nixon pardon, is the subject of another exhibit. His successful 1948 campaign for Congress, in which a quonset hut, also displayed, served as Ford's campaign headquarters, is in stark contrast to the elaborate presidential campaign.

Other exhibits include a history timeline in which Ford's career is placed in the context of 100 years of American history; a boyhood display, featuring photographs and artifacts that relate to Ford's family, scouting years, sports and education; Ford's romance and marriage to Betty Bloomer Warren; and Betty Ford as First Lady. There is a video on Gerald Ford's appointment as vice-president, and an exhibit on Nelson Rockefeller, also an appointed vice-president, who served under Ford.

A 28-minute film entitled *Gerald R. Ford: The Presidency Restored* is shown in the auditorium. There is a museum shop which sells books, campaign posters, puzzles, slides and Ford memorabilia.

While in Grand Rapids, visit the Public Museum of Grand Rapids, a favorite of children. There are exhibit rooms on fish and reptiles, birds and skeletons, and mammals. Most of the mammal exhibits include groupings of adults and their young.

Gaslight Village recreates an 1890s Grand Rapids evening street scene. As you walk on the wooden sidewalk or the cobblestone street with a trolley on its tracks, you can look in the windows of an authentically furnished fire station, police station, gunsmith shop, telegraph office, saddle shop, drug store and doctor's office. Another exhibit, called Heritage Hall, features artifacts, crafts and costumes from the nations whose descendants live in Grand Rapids. Featured are Mexico, South America, Latvia, Poland, Africa, Germany, Holland and France.

In the same building as the museum is the Chafee Planetarium which features weekend shows in its Sky Theatre. Plans are being made for a new Public Museum on the west bank of the Grand River with a projected opening in winter 1992. Open Monday-Friday, 10 a.m. to 5 p.m.; Saturday and Sunday, 1-5 p.m.; admission charged; 54 Jefferson SE, Grand Rapids 49503, 616-456-3977.

The Blandford Nature Center has 143 acres of woods, including maple trees which are tapped in March, fields, hiking trails, ponds, and wildlife. Children will enjoy the farm animals at the demonstration farm, as well as the one-room school house, log cabin, general store and blacksmith's shop. The interpretive building and animal hospital are open Monday-Friday, 9 a.m. to 5 p.m.; Saturday and Sunday, 2-5 p.m., 1715 Hillburn NW, Grand Rapids 49504, 616-453-6192.

ADDRESS: 303 Pearl Street, NW, Grand Rapids, MI 49504-5353
TELEPHONE: 616-456-2675
HOURS: Monday-Saturday, 9 a.m. to 4:45 p.m.; Sunday, noon to 4:45 p.m.; closed Thanksgiving, Christmas, and New Year's days

ADMISSION: Adults $1.50, children under 16 free

FACILITIES: Gerald R. Ford Presidential Museum; audio-visual presentation; accessible to handicapped; gift and book shop

LOCATION: Grand Rapids is in west central Michigan, about 25 miles east of Lake Michigan and 77 miles north of the Michigan-Indiana border, 184 miles from Chicago

BED & BREAKFAST: Bed & Breakfast of Grand Rapids, 455 College Ave. SE, Grand Rapids 49503, 616-451-4849

HOTELS/MOTELS: Amway Grand Plaza Hotel, Pearl at Monroe, Grand Rapids 49503, 616-774-2000; Days Inn-Downtown, 310 Pearl NW, Grand Rapids 49503, 616-235-7611; Hampton Inn, 4981 28th St. SE, Kentwood 49508, 616-956-9304

CAMPING: Duke Creek KOA Kampground, 15190 White Creek Avenue, Cedar Springs 49319, 616-696-9648; Grand Rogue Campgrounds, 6400 West River Drive, Belmont 49306, 616-361-1053

FOR MORE INFORMATION: Grand Rapids/Kent County Convention & Visitors Bureau, in the Grand Center, 245 Monroe NW, Grand Rapids 49503-2246, 616-459-8287

DIRECTIONS: From Chicago, take the Dan Ryan Expressway, I-90/94, or the Tri-State Tollway, I-294, south into Indiana, continue on I-94 into Michigan, take I-196 near Benton Harbor north to Grand Rapids area, then U.S. 131 South, exit at Pearl Street East, Gerald R. Ford Museum is in downtown Grand Rapids

3. HASTINGS:

CHARLTON PARK VILLAGE AND MUSEUM

Charlton Park Village and Museum provides a good combination of Michigan history and scenery. It is a restored 17 building turn-of-the-century village and recreation area on Thornapple River and lake. Now administered by the Barry County Parks and Recreation Commission, Charlton Park was the brainchild of Irving Delos Charlton, a Hastings native who was a college teacher of mechanics and agricultural engineering and a farmer. In 1936, he donated 210 acres to Barry County especially for this purpose.

Mr. Charlton was an avid collector of late-nineteenth-century and early twentieth-century artifacts, with a special interest in old coins and bills, and agricultural equipment. After Mr. Charlton's death, Barry County purchased historic buildings in which his artifacts could be displayed. A turn-of-the-century, mid-Michigan agricultural village has now been recreated at Charlton. Most of the buildings are original structures that were built in the late 1800s and were moved to the village from nearby towns.

The Irving D. Charlton Memorial Museum, a two-story stone house, contains the gift shop and exhibits on the development of the Great Lakes region, especially Michigan and Barry County. The bank, in the Hastings Mutual Building which was built in Hastings in 1908, is furnished with antique teller's cages and furniture. A lawyer's office and an insurance office are on the second floor. Other town businesses include the Thornapple Press, the General Store and the Hardware Store, all of which have original storefronts. The Lee School, a one-room schoolhouse, was built in 1869 and moved to the village from nearby Woodland Township. The Hastings Township Hall dates from 1886 while the Carlton Center Church was built in 1885. The oldest building is the Bristol Inn, built in 1852. It was a stagecoach stop and tavern in Bristol Lake. The Blacksmith Shop and the Carpenter Cooper Shop came from the Niethamer farm in Woodland.

Charlton Park, located on the Thornapple River and lake, is a recreational as well as historical site, making it a fine destination for a full-day's outing. After touring the village, children can swim at the beach, or play at the playground. There's a picnic area, boat launch and nature trails.

Special events are held at the village throughout the year. An ice-fishing festival is held in February, car show on Father's Day in June, Fourth of July Civil War Encampment, gas and steam engine show in July, antique auto and fire-fighting shows in August, folk life festival in September, and an old-fashioned Christmas in December.

ADDRESS: 2545 Charlton Park Road, Hastings, MI 49058
TELEPHONE: 616-945-3775
HOURS: Thursday-Sunday, noon to 5 p.m., Memorial Day-Labor Day; weekends only from Labor Day until third weekend in October
ADMISSION: Adults $3.00, senior citizens $2.00, children 5-15 $1.00; recreation area: $2.00 per car but free to purchasers of historic village tickets
FACILITIES: 17 buildings; craft demonstrations; guided tours; special events; gift shop; recreation area with swimming, boating, picnic areas, nature trails, playground
LOCATION: In south central Michigan between Hastings and Nashville, 25 miles north of Battle Creek, 175 miles from Chicago
HOTELS/MOTELS: Howard Johnson, 2590 Capital Ave. SW, Battle Creek 49015, 616-965-3201; Regal 8 Inn, 4775 Beckley Road, Battle Creek 49017, 616-979-1141; also see listings for Gerald R. Ford Museum, Grand Rapids (#2)
CAMPING: Yankee Springs Recreation Area, 2104 Gun Lake Road, Middleville 49333, 616-795-9081; Barry's Resort, 2875 S. Charlton Park Rd., Hastings 49058, 616-945-4762; Gunlake Parkside Park, 2430 Briggs Rd., Middleville 49333, 616-795-3140
DIRECTIONS: From Chicago, take the Dan Ryan Expressway, I-90/94, or the Tri-State Tollway, I-294, south to I-80/94,

then east to I-94 North into Michigan, at Battle Creek, take I-94 Business to MI 37, MI 37 north toward Hastings to MI 79, east on MI 79 to village

4. HOLLAND:
HOLLAND STATE PARK

The most heavily visited state park in Michigan, Holland State Park's greatest attraction is its wide beach which extends for 1,800 feet along the Lake Michigan shore. Visitors come for the day to enjoy the lake, sand dunes and beach, along with the 1907 Holland Harbor lighthouse, known as Big Red.

The 142-acre state park is divided into two separate areas; one fronts Lake Michigan, while the other fronts Lake Macatawa. Ottawa Beach Road, which has a parallel walkway/bike path, connects the two. The park has 368 modern campsites with 147 at the Lake Michigan unit and 221 at the Lake Macatawa unit. Because of the popularity of this park, campground reservations can be made after the first of the year for the following summer.

The town of Holland was settled in 1847 by immigrants from the Netherlands who had seceded from the established Dutch church and were looking for religious freedom. The town is still occupied primarily by people of Dutch heritage. Holland's annual Tulip Time Festival, featuring hundreds of thousands of tulips in bloom, is held in mid-May.

The Netherlands Museum, 8 E. 12th Street, features fine collections of Dutch furniture, Delft pottery and pewter, and exhibits relating to Dutch settlement in Michigan. Windmill Island Municipal Park, 7th and Lincoln Avenue has a five-story restored windmill from the Netherlands, called De Zwaan. The windmill can be toured and flour ground in the mill may be purchased. You can visit the Deklomp Wooden Shoe and Delftware Factory at 12755 Quincy Street, or the Wooden Shoe Factory, 447 U.S. 31 at 16th Street in Holland and watch the craftsmen at work. There are many Dutch restaurants in the town.

ADDRESS: 2215 Ottawa Beach Road, Holland, MI 49424

TELEPHONE: 616-399-9390

HOURS: Daily, 8 a.m. to 10 p.m. for day use; campgrounds open 24 hours a day

ADMISSION: Daily Michigan state park vehicle permit $3.00, annual vehicle permit $15.00; Michigan resident seniors' annual permit $3.75; camping $12.00 per night from April 15 to October 15, $10.00 rest of year

FACILITIES: Beach; swimming; picnic areas and picnic shelter; playground; beach house; concessions; boat launch; fishing; 368 modern campsites

LOCATION: In west central Michigan on Lake Michigan, seven miles west of Holland, approximately 140 miles from Chicago

BED & BREAKFASTS: Old Wing Inn, 5298 E. 147th Avenue, Holland 49423, 616-392-7362; Maplewood Hotel, 428 Butler Street, P.O. Box 1059, Saugatuck 49453, 616-857-2788; Twin Gables Country Inn, 900 Lake Street, Saugatuck 49453, 616-857-4346; Wickwood Inn, 510 Butler Street, Saugatuck 49453, 616-857-1097

HOTELS/MOTELS: Comfort Inn, 422 E. 32nd St., Holland 49423, 616-392-1000; Holiday Inn, 650 E. 24th St., Holland 49423, 616-394-0111; Point West Inn, Southshore Dr., Lake Macatawa, Holland 49434, 616-335-5894; Lake Shore, 2885 Lake Shore Dr., Saugatuck 49453, 616-399-9390

CAMPING: Holland State Park, 2215 Ottawa Beach Road, Holland 49424, 616-399-9390

DIRECTIONS: From Chicago, take the Dan Ryan Expressway, I-90/94, or the Tri-State Tollway, I-294, south into Indiana, continue on I-94 into Michigan, I-94 to I-196/U.S. 31 North to U.S. 31 North exit; U.S. 31 to Lakewood Boulevard, west to Douglas Ave. which becomes Ottawa Beach Road, to park entrance

5. LAINGSBURG:

SLEEPY HOLLOW STATE PARK

Only 15 miles northeast of Michigan's state capital is a state park with a modern campground, picnic areas, a large lake known for good fishing and boating, including rental paddle boats.

This area of Michigan originally had few lakes for recreational purposes and flood control was also a problem, so Little Maple River was dammed. The result was Lake Ovid, a 410-acre lake which has a one-half-mile beach area with a beach house, a picnic area, a playground and a concession building. There are three islands in the lake, the largest of which is connected to the shore by a foot bridge.

Fishermen try their luck in the well-stocked lake which has tiger muskellunge, pike, largemouth bass, smallmouth bass, bluegill, sunfish, crappie, rock bass, perch, catfish and bullheads. A fishing pier is on the west side of the lake, and there is even a fisherman's night entrance, open from 10 p.m. to 8 a.m., on the west side of the park, off Shepardsville Road. During those hours, the other park entrances are closed.

Boating is a popular activity at Lake Ovid. Electric motors are allowed, but not gasoline engines. A boat-rental concession at the south end of the lake rents canoes, rowboats, and paddle boats by the hour. Boat rentals are available late May through September.

Acquisition of land for Sleepy Hollow State Park was begun in the mid-1960s. One of the former land owners also contributed to naming the park. The landowner's name was I. B. Crane, reminiscent of Ichabod Crane from *The Legend of Sleepy Hollow*. The terrain in this central Michigan park consists mainly of farmlands that have reverted to meadows and grassy fields interspersed with stands of hardwoods. Sixteen miles of trails, including one that circles Lake Ovid, are good places to unwind and do some bird watching. You can pick berries, apples and nuts in season. Trailheads are located on the east side of the lake near the picnic area, and at the west end of the beach parking lot.

ADDRESS: 7835 E. Price Road, Laingsburg, MI 48848
TELEPHONE: 517-651-6217
HOURS: Daily, 8 a.m. to 10 p.m.
ADMISSION: Daily Michigan state park vehicle permit $3.00; annual state park vehicle permit $15.00
FACILITIES: 2,600 acres; lake; swimming; beach house; concession building; picnic areas; hiking trails; fishing; boating; boat launch; boat rental; 181 modern campsites; cross-country skiing; snowmobiling; ice fishing
LOCATION: In south central Michigan, 15 miles northeast of Lansing off U.S. 27, about 200 miles from Chicago
BED & BREAKFAST: Classic Bed & Breakfast, 505 E. Walker, St. Johns 48879, 517-224-6897
HOTELS/MOTELS: University Inn, 1100 Trowbridge Road, East Lansing 48823, 517-351-5500, 800-221-8466; Holiday Inn, 300 Mac Avenue, East Lansing 48823, 517-337-4440; Capri Motel, 1204 S U.S. 27, St. Johns 48879, 517-224-4239; Hub Motel, 2451 N. U.S. 27, St. Johns 48879, 517-224-2324
CAMPING: Sleepy Hollow State Park, 7835 Price Road, Laingsburg 48848, 517-651-6217
DIRECTIONS: From Chicago, take the Dan Ryan Expressway, I-94, or the Tri-State Expressway, I-294, south to I-80/94 in Indiana, continue north on I-94 to Michigan, then I-94 to exit I-69/U.S. 27 North near Battle Creek, stay on U.S. 27 when I-69 and U.S. 27 separate north of Lansing, U.S. 27 to Price Road, east on Price about seven miles to park

6. LANSING:

MICHIGAN HISTORICAL MUSEUM

The Michigan Historical Museum is in a strikingly modern, solid-looking, granite-and-glass five-level building with two atriums. The museum focuses on Michigan history from its geological beginnings through the nineteenth century using artifacts, audio-visual displays, and a variety of exhibits in 12,500 square feet of exhibit space.

The 312,000 square-foot building, officially called the Michigan Library and Historical Center, has the Library of Michigan on the west side and the State Historical Museum and State Archives on the east side. Books and artifacts that had previously been in at least five different locations in Lansing are now housed in the library and museum complex.

The building itself, designed by architect William Kessler and completed in 1989, is reason enough to visit. Native Michigan materials such as limestone and copper were used to integrate the interior with the outdoors, emphasizing the theme of Michigan as an outdoor state. Chair upholstery and carpeting are Great Lakes blue, and elevators are wood-paneled. The two glass atriums, 93 feet high in the west wing and 73 in the east wing, and the central courtyard and rotunda with its 47-foot white pine tree surrounded by a glass mosaic pool, bring plenty of sunlight inside.

Michigan, as a state of great natural resources, water, forests and minerals, dictated the theme of displays in the east atrium. A huge topographical map of Michigan depicting the Great Lakes, rivers and lakes dominates the space. Underneath the map are samples of local rock, including shale, gypsum, coal, iron ore, and sandstone, while three man-made white pine trees represent the forests of Michigan.

The Prehistoric Man gallery focuses on the Paleo-Indians who first inhabited the land now known as Michigan. These hunters wore caribou clothing and hunted caribou and mastodon. The subject of the Woodland exhibit is the arrival of European fur traders, explorers, missionaries, soldiers and settlers, beginning in the 1620s. The inevitable conflict between the Indians and Europeans is the topic of the exhibit called Two Cultures Struggle.

Early Michigan industries, including lumbering and copper and iron mining, are the subjects of other displays. The mining gallery features a replica copper mine with tunnels and drafts. Displays on the miners who settled the Upper Peninsula's communities include artifacts and family photos. In the lumbering exhibit is the facade of lumber baron Charles Hackley's Muskegon mansion with its intricately carved woodwork. A sawmill, complete with tools, machinery, photos and a ten-foot wheel used to drag logs out of the forest, is also part of this exhibit. Other exhibits include Rural Michigan, Growth of Manufacturing, Statehood and Settlement.

The State Archives contains about 80,000,000 documents, 330,000 photographs, and 500,000 maps and drawings. The Library of Michigan holds 5,200,000 books and manuscripts dating to 1805, which can be accessed by 80 computer terminals.

While in Lansing, take the children to Impression 5 Science Museum, a fascinating museum geared to interactive learning, with more than 240 hands-on exhibits. Open daily; admission fee; 200 Museum Drive, Lansing 48933, 517-485-8116.

Other attractions in the Lansing area are the Carl G.

Fenner Arboretum, a 120-acre nature park with hiking trails and picnic area, 2020 E. Mt. Hope Avenue, Lansing 48910, 517-483-4224; the Potter Park Zoo on the Red Cedar River which has 400 animals, pony rides, children's train, canoe rentals, playgrounds and picnic areas, 1301 S. Pennsylvania Avenue, Lansing 48910, 517-483-4222; and the Woldumar Nature Center, a 188-acre wildlife preserve, 5539 Lansing Road, Lansing, 517-322-0030. East Lansing is the home of Michigan State University, a Big Ten university with a large, attractive campus.

ADDRESS: 717 West Allegan Street, Lansing, MI 48918
TELEPHONE: 517-373-3559
HOURS: Monday-Friday, 9 a.m. to 4:30 p.m.; Saturday, 10 a.m. to 4 p.m.; Sunday, 1-5 p.m.
ADMISSION: Free
FACILITIES: State historical museum; handicapped accessible; educational programs; shares building with State Archives and Library of Michigan
LOCATION: In downtown Lansing, two blocks west of the state capitol; 195 miles from Chicago
HOTELS/MOTELS: Days Inn, 500 S. Capitol, Lansing 48933, 517-482-1000; Best Western Midway Motor Lodge, 7711 W. Saginaw Highway, Lansing 48917, 517-627-8471; Holiday Inn-South, 6501 S. Pennsylvania Avenue, Lansing 48911, 517-393-1650; Radisson, 111 N. Grand Avenue, Lansing 48933, 517-482-0188; most of the chain motels are represented in the Lansing area
CAMPING: Lansing Cottonwood Campground, 5339 Aurelius Road, Lansing 48911, 517-393-3200; Sleepy Hollow State Park, 7835 Price Road, Laingsburg 48848, 517-651-6217
DIRECTIONS: From Chicago, take the Dan Ryan Expressway, I-94, or the Tri-State Tollway, I-294, south to I-80/94 in Indiana, continue on I-94 North/East into Michigan; I-94 to I-69 exit, north on I-69 to Lansing, then take I-496 to downtown Lansing exits

7. MEARS:
HART-MONTAGUE BICYCLE TRAIL STATE PARK

Parallel eight-foot-wide paved bike, walking and equestrian trails along 22 miles of abandoned Chesapeake & Ohio Railroad right-of-way comprise the linear state park known as the Hart-Montague Bicycle Trail. This new trail is about seven miles inland from the Lake Michigan shoreline. Traveling primarily through peaceful countryside with cherry and apple orchards, forested areas, wetlands, fields planted with crops, and small rural towns, its terrain varies from flatlands to gently rolling hills.

The south trailhead is in Montague, at Stanton Boulevard, while the north trailhead is in Hart. The trail may also be accessed at Shelby, New Era, Rothbury and Mears. During winter months, the trail is used for cross-country skiing and snowmobiling. Equestrian use is permitted from Rothbury south to Fruitvale Road on the west side of the trail corridor. The trail is wheelchair accessible from many locations. Food, bicycle rentals, and trail passes are available in the villages that the trail runs through. Trail passes may also be purchased from the rangers patrolling the trail.

ADDRESS: Silver Lake State Park, Route 1, Box 254, Mears, MI 49436
TELEPHONE: 616-873-3083
ADMISSION: Trail passes: daily individual $2.00, daily family $5.00, annual individual $10.00, annual family $25.00
FACILITIES: 21-mile trail for walking, biking and horseback

riding; cross-country skiing; snowmobiling; wheelchair accessible from many locations

LOCATION: In western Michigan, near to and parallel with the Lake Michigan shore, 18 miles north of Muskegon, 175 miles from Chicago

BED & BREAKFAST: Wells 602 Bed & Breakfast, 602 State Street, Hart 49420, 616-873-3834; Rooms at The Inn, 515 State Street, Hart 49420, 616-873-2448; Duneland Inn, Mears 49436, 616-873-5128

HOTELS/MOTELS: Gateway Motel, Hart 49420, 616-873-2125; Hart Motel, 715 State, Hart 49420, 616-873-2151; Dune View Resort, Mears 49436, 616-873-3074; Flora-Dale Resort, Mears 49436, 616-873-3212; The Resorter, Mears 49436, 616-873-3069; Sandy Shores, Mears 49436, 616-873-3003; Silver Sands Resort, Box 318, Mears 49436, 616-873-3769; Windhaven Resort, Mears 49436, 616-873-3476; Double J Resort Ranch, Rothbury, 616-894-4444

CAMPING: Silver Lake State Park, Rt. 1, Box 254, Mears 49436, 616-873-3083; John Gurney Park, E. Main Street, Hart 49420, 616-873-4959; Hide-A-Way Campground, Mears 49436, 616-873-4428; Holiday Resort, Rt. 1, Box 97B, New Era 49446, 616-861-5220; Timberview Campground, Shelby 49455, 616-861-5286

DIRECTIONS: From Chicago, take either the Dan Ryan Expressway, I-90/94, or the Tri-State Tollway, I-294, south to I-80/94 East to Indiana, continue on I-94 North into Michigan to exit I-196/U.S. 31 North near Benton Harbor, stay on U.S. 31 N after I-196 and U.S. 31 separate around Holland, exit at Colby Road, east to Montague

8. MEARS:
SILVER LAKE STATE PARK

Silver Lake State Park is a popular, 2,860-acre park on the shore of Lake Michigan. Two thousand of those acres form a mile-wide strip of sandy beaches and high sand dunes between Lake Michigan on the west and Silver Lake on the east. The almost treeless, wind-swept sand hills provide a huge outdoor sandbox for adults and children to play in.

The combination of four miles of Lake Michigan shoreline and the sparkling blue water of Silver Lake, whose western edge is a huge dune, provides recreation and beautiful scenery. You can run down a steep sand dune right into the lake. Hiking to the top of a dune to get a panoramic view of vast Lake Michigan is also fun. Whether or not you feel like hiking, there is about a 300-yard walk from the lighthouse area parking lot to the Lake Michigan beach, so relax and enjoy it. The wide beach provides plenty of space for all.

Though most visitors come to swim, sunbathe, and climb the dunes, Silver Lake State Park also attracts a large number of people who drive off-road vehicles (ORVs). Four hundred and fifty acres at the north end of the park are reserved for drivers who ride up and down the dunes in their four-wheelers, dirt bikes and dune buggies. The pedestrian and ORV areas are separate and strictly regulated, so there is no danger to pedestrians. The state park requires ORV drivers to wear helmets and harness straps, and their vehicles must have a current ORV Michigan registration, and comply with other safety regulations. Contact the park directly about these regulations which differ from those found statewide.

If you want to ride the dunes but don't drive an ORV, you can take a Mac Wood's Dune Ride. Mac Wood's is a licensed concessionaire in the state park who provides eight-mile dune rides in large, open-air vehicles with a driver.

On the southeast side of Silver Lake there are 249 modern campsites. Other facilities include a beach house, picnic area, and playground. Sailing and fishing are available on Silver Lake which has a boat launch area. There is even an 1880s lighthouse, Little Point Sable Lighthouse, which you can visit at the south end of the park.

ADDRESS: Route 1, Box 254, Mears, MI 49436

TELEPHONE: 616-873-3083

HOURS: Daily, 8 a.m. to 10 p.m.

ADMISSION: Daily Michigan state park vehicle permit $3.00, annual vehicle permit $15.00

FACILITIES: 2,860 acres on Lake Michigan shore; sand dunes; swimming; fishing; boating; 249 modern campsites; picnic areas; playground; off-road vehicle area on sand dunes; dune rides; lighthouse

LOCATION: In western Michigan on the shore of Lake Michigan, about 40 miles north of Muskegon, 200 miles from Chicago

BED & BREAKFAST: The Pentwater Inn, 180 E. Lowell, P.O. Box 98, Pentwater 49449, 616-869-5909; Duneland Inn, Mears 49436, 616-873-5128

HOTELS/MOTELS: Dune View Resort, Mears 49436, 616-873-3074; The Resorter, Rt. 1, Silver Lake, Mears 49436, 616-873-3069; Windhaven Resort, Mears 49436, 616-873-3476; Flora-Dale Resort, Mears 49436, 616-873-3212

CAMPING: Silver Lake State Park, Rt. 1, Box 254, Mears 49436, 616-873-3083; Silver Hills Camp/Resort, Box 387, Hazel Road, Mears 49436, 616-873-3976; Silver Lake Campground, Rt. 1, Box 313, Mears 49436, 616-873-3912; Jellystone Park, Mears 49436, 616-873-4502

DIRECTIONS: From Chicago, take the Dan Ryan Expressway, I-94, south, or the Tri-State Tollway, I-294, south to I-80/94 East to Indiana, continue on I-94 North into Michigan to exit I-196/U.S. 31 N near Benton Harbor, stay on U.S. 31 N after I-196 and U.S. 31 separate around Holland, exit U.S. 31 at Shelby Rd., then west to Co. Rd. B15 (16th Avenue); north to the park

9. MIDDLEVILLE:
YANKEE SPRINGS RECREATION AREA

Yankee Springs' 5,000 scenic acres offer such a wide variety of recreational choices that they attract 750,000 visitors a year. Facilities include 17 miles of hiking trails, nine lakes for fishing, rustic and modern campgrounds, outdoor centers with cabin camping, swimming beaches, and panoramic overlooks.

This popular recreation area got its name from a nineteenth-century stagecoach inn formerly on the site. The Yankee Springs Inn, operated by Yankee Bill Lewis, was on the stage road between Kalamazoo and Grand Rapids.

Swimmers should head to Gun Lake, which offers a beach, picnic areas, concession stands, as well as a boat launch. Gun Lake is also the best fishing lake among the nine lakes, stocked with walleye, bass, and perch.

Hiking the 17 miles of trails is a good way to enjoy the scenic beauty of south central Michigan. Yankee Springs and the adjoining 15,000-acre Barry Game Area are moderately hilly and heavily wooded, with many lakes, streams, bogs and marshes.

Two-mile-long Hall Lake Trail begins across from the Long Lake Outdoor Center, winds through the pines and along the shore of Hall Lake to Graves Hill, a scenic overlook. Another panoramic overlook can be reached on the Chief Noonday Trail. This four-mile trail begins near Chief Noonday Road and travels to the McDonald Lake overlook. A second four-mile trail is the Deep Lake Trail, which winds through the bog area at the south end of Deep Lake leading to the Devil's Soupbowl, a kettle lake formation remaining from the glacial period. The longest trail is Long Lake

Trail. Its five miles travel through bog land to Graves Hill and the Devil's Soupbowl.

The thickly wooded park has oaks, maples, hickories, dogwoods, sumacs, white pines and white cedars. During the spring, hikers will see the delicate white dogwoods in bloom, while fall features the vivid colors of the hardwoods. Wildlife in Yankee Springs and the adjoining game preserve include deer, grouse, pheasants, Canadian geese, and red-tailed hawks.

ADDRESS: 2104 Gun Lake Road, Middleville, MI 49333
TELEPHONE: 616-795-9081
HOURS: Daily
ADMISSION: Daily Michigan state park vehicle permit $3.00, annual vehicle permit $15.00
FACILITIES: 5,014 acres; 340 campsites; picnic area; playground; beach; beach house; boat launch; swimming; fishing; hiking trails; horseback riding; snowmobiling; cross-country skiing
LOCATION: Halfway between Kalamazoo and Grand Rapids, about 65 miles north of Michigan-Indiana border, 30 miles east of Lake Michigan, 160 miles from Chicago
HOTELS/MOTELS: Gun Lake Motel, Patterson Road, Middleville 49333, 616-792-2028
CAMPING: Yankee Springs Recreation Area, 616-795-9081, has the following facilities: Gun Lake Campground, 220 modern sites; Deep Lake Campground, 120 rustic sites; Horsemen's Campground and Staging Area, 25 sites for equestrian use; Organization Campground, for organized youth groups; Chief Noonday Outdoor Center and Long Lake Outdoor Center have cabins and bunk houses for groups.
DIRECTIONS: From Chicago, take the Dan Ryan Expressway, I-90/94, or the Tri-State Tollway, I-294, south to I-80/94 East into Indiana, continue on I-94 into Michigan, exit I-94 at U.S. 131 N around Kalamazoo, U.S. 131 N to exit 61, follow Co. Road A42 east for seven miles to Briggs Road, turn right

10. MUSKEGON:
HACKLEY & HUME HISTORIC SITE

Muskegon's Hackley & Hume Historic Site is a fine restoration of two late-1880s Victorian houses that were built by lumber barons Charles H. Hackley and Thomas Hume.

In the 1880s, Michigan's forests provided vast amounts of lumber for railroad ties for the country's rapidly expanding railroads, and for the Midwest's growing cities and farms. Timber was cut in logging camps, shipped to lakeshore sawmills to be cut into lumber, then shipped to Chicago via Lake Michigan. The lumber boom made millionaires out of men like Hackley and Hume, but by 1900 Michigan's forests were virtually depleted and the boom turned to bust. Muskegon grew up on the boom and managed, with a good deal of help from Hackley, to survive the bust.

Hackley built a home for himself with Thomas Hume building a home next door, and shared the carriage barn between them. These elaborate Victorian renditions of Queen Anne architecture have been carefully restored and are known for their hand-carved woodwork, stenciled walls and ceilings, stained glass windows, ceramic tile fireplaces, and original and period furniture.

Also in the Muskegon area is the USS *Silversides* & Maritime Museum. The USS *Silversides* is a navy submarine that was commissioned a week after the attack on Pearl Harbor and served with the Pacific Fleet. It was decommissioned in 1969, having been used as a reserve training boat since 1947. The *Silversides* was saved from the scrapyard by the Combined Great

Lakes Navy Association which began its restoration and moved it to Muskegon in 1987. Tours are given daily from May 1 through September 30 and on weekends during April and October, 10 a.m. to 6 p.m.; admission: adults $2.50, children 5-11 and seniors $1.50; located on the channel, Pere Marquette Park; P.O. Box 1692, Muskegon 49443, 616-755-1230.

ADDRESS: West Webster Avenue at the corner of Sixth Street, Muskegon, MI 49440
TELEPHONE: 616-722-7578
HOURS: 1-4 p.m., Wednesdays, Saturdays and Sundays, mid-May through September
ADMISSION: Adults $2.00, students $1.00, children under 12 free
FACILITIES: Two Victorian homes and carriage barn; NR
LOCATION: In Muskegon, at the corner of West Webster Avenue (U.S. 31 Business South) and Sixth Street
HOTELS/MOTELS: see P. J. Hoffmaster State Park (#11)
CAMPING: see P. J. Hoffmaster State Park (#11)
DIRECTIONS: see P. J. Hoffmaster State Park (#11)

11. MUSKEGON:
P. J. HOFFMASTER STATE PARK and GILLETTE NATURE CENTER

The eastern shore of Lake Michigan is a long summer sandbox for adults and children alike. Sugar sand beaches, towering dunes, thick forests, miles of hiking trails and modern campgrounds are just some of the features that draw thousands and thousands of people to Michigan's lakeshore state parks. P. J. Hoffmaster State Park is one of those parks with an additional attraction, the Gillette Nature Center. Named for Michigan conservationist E. Genevieve Gillette, the center, which opened in 1976, is housed in a modern building near a huge sand dune that can be viewed from a glass wall in the lobby.

Gillette is an interpretive center which focuses on the natural history of the sand dunes of the Great Lakes. Michigan boasts the world's largest accumulation of sand dunes bordering a body of fresh water. Exhibits explain ecological plant succession, the principles of which were developed by University of Chicago botanist Professor Henry Cowles at the Indiana dunes in the late 1890s.

From a Grain of Sand is an exhibit which uses dioramas and graphics to explain the sand dune environment. The ecological zones from beach, including wet beach, storm beach, pioneer dune grass; to foredune with cottonwood and sand cherry; to trough, including conifer zone and interdunal pond; to backdune, including white pines, black oak; to barrier dune; to climax forest, are well illustrated. Nine-projector multi-media presentations on the dunes and seasonal nature subjects are shown in the auditorium. The center also has a gift shop, art gallery and seasonal exhibits. Hands-on exhibits as well as live pond animals such as snakes and frogs get a lot of attention from the children.

Near the Gillette Nature Center is the Dune Climb Stairway, 165 steps up one of the park's highest sand dunes. At the top is an observation deck from which there is a magnificent view of Lake Michigan and its towering dunes. Other trails from the nature center lead through the wooded dunes and down to the beaches.

The ten miles of hiking trails in Hoffmaster's 1,043 acres are ideal for bird watching and observing wild flowers in spring, and are used for cross-county skiing in winter. The day use area has 2 and ½ miles of sand beaches, picnic areas, a concession stand, and a beach house.

ADDRESS: 6585 Lake Harbor Road, Muskegon, MI 49441
TELEPHONE: 616-798-3711
HOURS: State park: daily, 8 a.m. to 10 p.m.; Gillette Nature Center: summer: 9 a.m. to 6 p.m., Tuesday-Sunday; winter: 1-5 p.m., Tuesday-Friday and 10 a.m. to 5 p.m., Saturday and Sunday; closed Monday
ADMISSION: Daily Michigan state park vehicle permit $3.00; annual vehicle permit $15.00
FACILITIES: 1,043 acres; Lake Michigan beach; forest-covered sand dunes; beach house; concession store; picnic areas; hiking trails; 333 modern campsites; cross-country skiing; Gillette Nature Center: a sand dune interpretive center with a theater, audio-visual program, lectures, guided hikes, ecological exhibits, hands-on exhibits, gift shop and art gallery
LOCATION: On eastern shore of Lake Michigan, south of Muskegon, 180 miles from Chicago
HOTELS/MOTELS: Days Inn, 150 Seaway Dr., Muskegon 49444, 616-739-9429; Holiday Inn, Seaway Dr. at Hoyt St., Muskegon 49444, 616-733-2601; Seaway, 631 Norton Ave., Muskegon 49441, 616-733-1220; Hilton Muskegon Harbor, 939 3rd St., Muskegon 49440, 616-722-0100
CAMPING: P. J. Hoffmaster State Park, 6585 Lake Harbor Road, Muskegon 49441, 616-798-3711; Muskegon State Park, 3560 Memorial Drive, North Muskegon 49445, 616-744-3480
DIRECTIONS: From Chicago: take the Dan Ryan Expressway, I-90/94, or the Tri-State Tollway, I-294, south to I-80/94 East into Indiana, continue on I-94 into Michigan, exit at I-196/U.S. 31 near St. Joseph/Benton Harbor, stay on U.S. 31 when I-196 and U.S. 31 separate near Holland into Muskegon, exit at Pontaluna Road, west on Pontaluna to park

12. ONSTED:

WALTER J. HAYES STATE PARK

Like the Wisconsin Dells, Michigan's Irish Hills is a naturally scenic area that has been overshadowed by commercial fun. Every type is represented: water slides, go-karts, miniature golf, Wild West amusement parks, etc. However, tucked into the Irish Hills are nature-oriented and historic sites which are not commercial, but are fun. The region took its name from Irish settlers who thought the rolling hill scenery looked like the hills of Ireland.

The Walter P. Hayes State Park, at 654 acres, is not one of Michigan's bigger parks but the combination of two lakes and green, rolling hills makes it a popular destination in summer.

The park is divided by MI 124 with Wampler's Lake and the day-use area on the west, and Round Lake and the campgrounds on the east. Wampler's Lake has a 1000-foot-long sand beach, a bathhouse, picnic area, concession stand, boat rental and boat launch. The Round Lake area has 210 modern campsites and its own boat launch. A two-mile hiking trail from the campground winds through the wooded hills. It is used for cross-country skiing in the winter.

The campgrounds are being redeveloped and may only be open on a limited basis until the new facilities are completed. Call for information.

ADDRESS: 1220 Wampler's Lake Road, Onsted, MI 49265
TELEPHONE: 517-467-7401
HOURS: Daily
ADMISSION: Daily Michigan state park vehicle permit $3.00, annual vehicle permit $15.00
FACILITIES: 654 acres; 210 modern campsites; picnic area; hiking trails; swimming; fishing; beach house; boat launch

LOCATION: In Irish Hills area of southeastern Michigan, 170 miles from Chicago

HOTELS/MOTELS: Holiday Inn East, 3750 Washtenaw Ave., Ann Arbor 48104, 313-971-2000; Knights Inn, 830 Royal Drive, Jackson 49202, 517-789-7186; Carlton Lodge, 1629 W. Maumee, Adrian 49221, 517-263-7000; Days Inn, 1575 W. Maumee, Adrian 49221, 517-273-5741

CAMPING: Walter J. Hayes State Park, 1220 Wampler's Lake Road, Onsted 49265, 517-467-7401

DIRECTIONS: From Chicago, take the Dan Ryan Expressway, I-90/94, or the Tri-State Tollway, I-294, south into Indiana, continue on I-94 into Michigan, exit at Jackson onto U.S. 127 South, U.S. 127 to U.S. 12 East, U.S. 12 East to junction with MI 124

13. SAWYER:

WARREN DUNES STATE PARK

"Let's go to the dunes!"

"OK, which ones?"

"Michigan is prettier and not so crowded."

This conversation takes place thousands of times each summer among Chicagoans, and has for generations. When Chicago gets hot, and Chicago does get very hot in summer, it means that it's time to go to the dunes.

Among dunes aficionados, there is a running debate about which is better—the Indiana dunes or Michigan's Warren Dunes. Arguments can and often are made on either side, but it usually comes down to personal taste. The reality is that the Indiana dunes and Warren Dunes are both outstandingly beautiful recreational sites and, because they are relatively close to a huge urban area, they are popular and crowded in summer. Warren Dunes is further from Chicago so it is less crowded, though it draws over 1,000,000 visitors each year. In the Michigan state park system, only Holland State Park attracts more tourists annually.

But don't let the crowds discourage you. Despite the large number of annual visitors, Warren Dunes' 4,705 acres and 2,100-car parking lots accommodate everyone comfortably. If you haven't been to Warren Dunes, you've missed one of the finest natural sites in the Midwest, and if you have, you don't need to be convinced. The dunes are a popular destination for teenagers as well. And as parents know, one of the best ways to amuse small children for hours is to take them to the lakeshore, where they can run in and out of the water and dig in the sand. Just bring a sand pail and some shovels.

Warren Dunes State Park is located on the east shore of Lake Michigan, with over three miles of wide sand beaches backed by spectacular sand dunes which rise as high as 240 feet. Swimming in always-bracing Lake Michigan, sunbathing on the white beaches, and viewing the beauty of the lake and dune scenery are the most common activities of visitors, but the park offers other possibilities.

Climbing wind-swept sand dunes is an enjoyable way to expend time and energy. Although these sand mountains don't compare to the Rockies, they present their own challenges as the sand keeps giving way under your feet. Some of the higher dunes have been named Pikes Peak, Mt. Fuller, Mt. Randal and Tower Hill. The last-mentioned dune is used by adventuresome hang gliders who appreciate the winds off the lake for carrying them aloft, and the sand for soft landings. Warren Dunes State Park is the only Michigan state park that permits hang gliding. Gliders must be certified and obtain a gliding permit from the park headquarters.

Warren Dunes is a year-round recreational site and hiking on over 6 miles of trails can be enjoyed in all seasons. Trails lead through the dunes, along Lake Michigan and into the forests; for in addition to the beaches and sand dunes, the park contains large sections of heavily wooded hilly terrain. These oak and hickory woods provide striking colors in autumn. There is a trail head near the northern parking lot of the beach area.

Camping is, of course, one of the preferred ways to spend time at the dunes. The 197 modern campsites operate at full capacity on summer weekends and it is a good idea to make reservations.

Two other nearby natural areas come under the auspices of Warren Dunes State Park, but are not contiguous with it. Warren Woods is a 311-acre natural area which has one of Michigan's only surviving stands of virgin hardwood forests. This forested land was purchased for preservation by Edward Warren in 1879. Since it has never been used for lumbering, many sycamores, beeches and maples in this forest are 125 feet tall with five-foot diameters. Located on the Galien River, Warren Woods has a 3 and 1/2 mile hiking trail. Spring bird watching and brilliant fall colors attract many visitors. Warren Woods is south of Warren Dunes and can be reached by exiting I-94 at exit 6 and heading east on Elm Valley Road; or following Red Arrow Highway south, past the entrance to Warren Dunes, to Warren Woods Road, then east on Warren Woods Road.

Grand Mere State Park is a 985-acre site that is also managed by Warren Dunes State Park. Located on Lake Michigan north of Warren Dunes, Grand Mere has three lakes that were formed by glacial action. Ancient dunes forested with oak, beech, sugar maple and hemlock separate these lakes from Lake Michigan.

Grand Mere is a relatively undeveloped park with few facilities other than parking lots. There are hiking trails, but they are ungroomed. However, many nature lovers are attracted by the park's rare and endangered plant communities which range from aquatic to terrestrial. The environment also exemplifies plant succession from open sand to forested hill. Bird watching is good at Grand Mere where hawks, veery, prairie and Canada warblers, Louisiana waterthrush, Acadian flycatchers and hooded warblers have been seen. Cross-country skiers also like this park. Grand Mere can be reached from I-94, exit 22, then east for a very short distance on John Beers Road to Thornton Road, south on Thornton to park entrance.

ADDRESS: Red Arrow Highway, Sawyer, MI 49125
TELEPHONE: 616-426-4013
HOURS: Daily, 8 a.m. to 10 p.m.
ADMISSION: Daily Michigan state park vehicle permit $3.00, non-resident $4.00, annual vehicle permit $15.00
FACILITIES: Warren Dunes: 4,705 acres of beaches and sand dunes; 197 modern campsites; picnic area; swimming; beach houses; hiking trails; hang gliding; cross-country skiing; Warren Woods: 311-acre nature area, hiking trails; picnic area; Grand Mere State Park: 985 acres on Lake Michigan, hiking, bird watching, fishing; cross-country skiing
LOCATION: On Lake Michigan, 16 miles north of the Indiana state line, southwest of Bridgman, about 54 miles from Chicago
BED & BREAKFASTS: The Pebble House, 15093 Lakeshore Road, PO Box 62, Lakeside 49116, 616-469-1416; The Inn at Union Pier, 9708 Berrien, P.O. Box 222, Union Pier 49129, 616-469-4700
HOTELS/MOTELS: Lazy V Motel, 9999 Red Arrow Highway, Bridgman 49106, 616-465-3187; Edgewood Motel, P.O. Box 293, New Buffalo 49117, 616-469-3345

CAMPING: Warren Dunes State Park, Red Arrow Highway, Sawyer, 49125, 616-426-4013; Weko Beach Park, Bridgman, 616-465-5144; Shamrock Park, 112 N. Cass Street, Berrien Springs 49103, 616-473-5691

DIRECTIONS: From Chicago, take the Dan Ryan Expressway, I-90/94, or the Tri-State Tollway, I-294, south to I-94 into Michigan, from I-94, use exit 16, Bridgman, and follow Red Arrow Highway south to the Warren Dunes State Park entrance

14. SOUTH HAVEN:
KAL-HAVEN TRAIL SESQUICENTENNIAL STATE PARK

A new state park, the Kal-Haven Trail has tremendous potential for stress-reducing get-away weekends. Exercise by hiking or biking on the nature trail, swim and sunbathe at Lake Michigan's beach in Van Buren State Park or South Haven's public beaches, and sleep in a cozy bed-and-breakfast or campground near the shore.

Kal-Haven is a 34-mile trail between Kalamazoo and South Haven that runs along the abandoned Penn Central Railroad line. It is jointly operated by the Michigan Department of Natural Resources and the Friends of the Kal-Haven Trail, a nonprofit organization.

The name of the park is derived from the towns at either end of the trail: Kalamazoo and South Haven. Sesquicentennial refers to the 150th anniversary of Michigan's statehood which was celebrated in 1987, the year the land along the railroad right-of-way was acquired.

The trail is intended for use by hikers, bikers, horseback riders and, in winter, snowmobilers. Plans call for three separate trails for hikers, cyclists and equestrians. Pets on 6-foot leashes are permitted. The trail passes through natural areas and a series of small towns that originally sprang up because of the railroad. Most of these small towns have food stores, restaurants, and restrooms. There are bicycle stores in Kalamazoo and Gobles.

ADDRESS: Van Buren State Park, 23960 Ruggles Road, South Haven, MI 49090
TELEPHONE: 616-637-4984, 616-637-2788
HOURS: Sunrise to 10 p.m.
ADMISSION: Individual daily pass $2.00, individual annual pass $10.00, family daily pass $5.00, family annual pass $25.00; passes are available at east and west trailheads and at Bloomingdale, South Haven, Van Buren State Park, Grand Junction, Gobles and Beehive Farm in Kendall
FACILITIES: 34-mile hike/bike trail; information centers
LOCATION: Kalamazoo and South Haven are located in southwestern Michigan, 34 to 40 miles north of the Michigan-Indiana border; South Haven is on Lake Michigan while Kalamazoo is about 40 miles east of Lake Michigan; the trail is approximately 120 miles from Chicago
BED & BREAKFASTS: Old Harbor Inn, 515 Williams St., South Haven 49090, 616-637-8480; Hall House B&B, 106 Thompson St., Kalamazoo 49007, 616-343-2500; Kalamazoo House, 447 W. South St., Kalamazoo 49007, 616-343-5426; Stuart Avenue Inn, 405 Stuart Avenue, Kalamazoo 49007, 616-342-0230; Kal-Haven B&B, 23491 Paulson Road, Gobles 49055, 616-628-4932; Bed and Breakfast Inns of South Haven, Rt. 5, Box 43, South Haven, MI 49090
HOTELS/MOTELS: Friendship Inn, 09817 MI 140, South Haven 49090, 616-637-5141, 800-345-4366, 800 527-9122 (in MI); Lake Bluff, 76658 11th Avenue, South Haven 49090, 616-637-8531
CAMPING: Van Buren State Park, 23960 Ruggles Road, South Haven 49090, 616-637-2788; Fun Valley Rec Area, 47508 Co.

Rd. 384, Grand Junction, 616-521-7571; Beehive Farm, Co.
Rd. 388, Kendall, 616-628-2854
DIRECTIONS: see Van Buren State Park (#15)

15. SOUTH HAVEN:
VAN BUREN STATE PARK

Located on the shore of Lake Michigan, Van Buren
State Park is a wooded, 320-acre site with a wide
beach, sand dunes, and a campground with over 200
campsites. Park features include a three-quarters-of-a-
mile beach, picnic areas with tables and grills, a concession building, changing areas, showers and toilets.
This popular park attracts both daily visitors and
campers

The campground has toilet and shower buildings,
and each campsite is equipped with electricity, a fire
circle and picnic table. Reservations, which may be
made by phone or in writing, are essential during the
summer months and must be for a minimum of two
nights. Campsite application forms can be obtained at
any Michigan state park or from the Department of
Natural Resources, P.O. Box 30028, Lansing, MI 48909.

South Haven, which is less than five miles north of
Van Buren State Park, has been a resort town for Chicagoans since the 1880s when city dwellers crossed
Lake Michigan on passenger steamboats. The town is
now known as a fruit-growing area, peaches and blue-
berries in particular. In season, many orchards allow
you to pick your own fruit, or you can purchase it at
one of the many farm stands. The National Blueberry
Festival is in July.

South Haven has two public beaches, public boat
launch facilities, charter boat fishing, marinas and pier

fishing. The Lake Michigan Maritime Museum, located at Dyckman Avenue at the Black River Bridge, is a floating museum with nautical exhibits that recall Lake Michigan's earlier shipping era: admission fee; P.O. Box 534, South Haven 49090, 616-637-8078.

The Liberty Hyde Bailey Memorial Museum is the restored birthplace of the noted botanist and horticulturist. A state historic site, the 1850s house contains Bailey's books, household articles and collections of Indian artifacts. Open Tuesday and Friday; free; 903 S. Bailey Avenue, South Haven 49090, 616-637-3251.

ADDRESS: 23960 Ruggles Road, South Haven, MI 49090
TELEPHONE: 616-637-2788
HOURS: Daily, 8 a.m. to 10 p.m. for day use; campgrounds open 24 hours a day
ADMISSION: Daily Michigan state park vehicle permit $3.00, annual vehicle permit $15.00; campground: $8.00 per night from April 15 to October 15, $6.00 per night rest of year
FACILITIES: Beach and dunes on Lake Michigan; picnic areas and picnic shelters; bathhouse and concession stands; campground with 220 campsites
LOCATION: In southwestern Michigan on Lake Michigan, a few miles south of South Haven, approximately 120 miles from Chicago
BED & BREAKFASTS: see Kal-Haven Trail Sesquicentennial State Park (#14)
HOTELS/MOTELS: see Kal-Haven Trail Sesquicentennial State Park (#14)
CAMPING: Van Buren State Park, 23960 Ruggles Road, South Haven 49090, 616-637-2788
DIRECTIONS: From Chicago, take the Dan Ryan Expressway, I-90/94, or the Tri-State Tollway, I-294, south into Indiana, continue on I-94 into Michigan, exit at I-196 near St. Joseph/Benton Harbor, I-196 to South Haven, exit 13, then west on 32nd St. to Blue Star Memorial Highway, north on Blue Star to Ruggles Road, west to park entrance

16. TIPTON:
HIDDEN LAKE GARDENS

Hidden Lake Gardens is a horticultural garden on 670-acres which was donated to Michigan State University in 1945. In a setting of rolling hills and forests, the landscaped arboretum contains over 2,500 woody plants, flowering trees including magnolias, cherries, and crab apples, and the Harper Collection of Dwarf and Rare Conifers. In the conservatory are displays of tropical, arid and temperate plants. You can drive through the gardens on 6 miles of roads or better yet, walk on five miles of hiking trails. A Visitor Center building has a gift shop, library, exhibits and classrooms.

ADDRESS: 6280 W. Munger Road (M-50), Tipton, MI 49287
TELEPHONE: 517-431-2060
HOURS: Daily, 8 a.m. to dusk
ADMISSION: From April through October, weekends and holidays $3.00 per person, weekdays $1.00 per person; November through March $1.00 per person
FACILITIES: 670 landscaped acres; conservatory; plant collections and displays; Visitor Center with gift shop and library; wheelchair accessible; hiking trails
LOCATION: In Irish Hills area of southeastern Michigan, on MI 50, just west of Tipton, 170 miles from Chicago, 50 miles west of Detroit
HOTELS/MOTELS: see W. J. Hayes State Park (#12)
CAMPING: W. J. Hayes State Park, 12220 Wampler's Lake Road, Onsted 49265, 517-467-7401
DIRECTIONS: Same as for W. J. Hayes State Park (#12) to Jackson, exit at U.S. 127 South, U.S. 127 to MI 50 South/East, gardens are on MI 50 just west of Tipton

PART 5:

Wisconsin

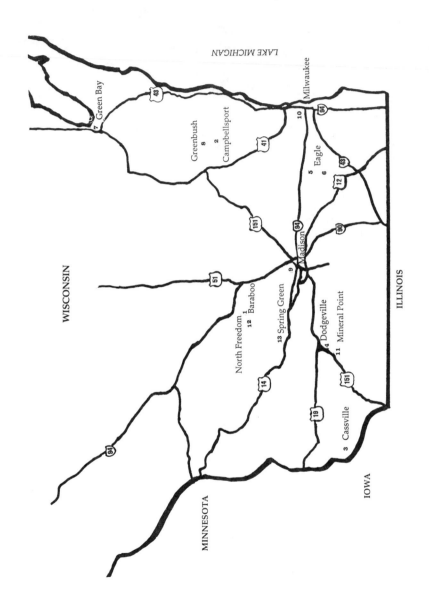

1. BARABOO:
CIRCUS WORLD MUSEUM

Have your children ever dragged you to a museum? They would if they heard about Circus World Museum where visiting is like a day at the circus. Located in Baraboo, it relates the history of the Ringling Brothers Circus not only through artifacts, but also by presenting professional circus acts in traditional performances.

Not to be missed is the circus show given at 11 a.m. and 3 p.m. in the circus tent, the Big Top. This one-ring circus features clowns, trained lions and tigers, dancing elephants, a band, acrobats on horseback, jugglers, aerial ballet and high-wire acts. Seats are close enough to the ring to get a good view of the heart-stopping trapeze artists and large caged animals.

The Mantle of Magic, presented at 1 p.m., is another fascinating show for kids and adults. Children can sit on the floor right in front of the stage to watch the magician perform incomprehensible stunts, including levitation.

Baraboo is the site of Circus World Museum because in this small Wisconsin town five brothers started a

---

Wisconsin

circus which grew into the world-famous Ringling Bros. and Barnum & Bailey Circus. The Ringlings of Baraboo set up their circus in 1884 and traveled with it each summer. In the winter they returned to Baraboo where, in 15 buildings on Water Street, they trained animals, repaired and built wagons and equipment, and practiced new acts. Baraboo was the winter home of the Ringling Bros. Circus until 1918.

Circus World Museum has a large collection of restored antique, hand-carved wooden circus wagons which are displayed in the W. W. Deppe Wagon Pavilion. This huge exhibit hall also displays circus photographs, some of which date as far back as the Civil War.

New to Circus World Museum, which is owned and operated by the State Historical Society of Wisconsin, is the Irvin Feld Exhibit Hall and Visitor Center. A large miniature Ringling Bros. Barnum and Bailey Circus, on a scale of three-quarter inch to one foot, is its focal point. The whole behind-the-scenes circus world of the 1930s has been recreated by Howard Tibbals, an engineer who worked on the project for 30 years.

The Ringling family exhibit provides the history of the Gus Ringling family and their five sons, Alf, Al, Charles, John and Otto. Each one's life and roles in the circus business is explored.

The museum has an extensive collection of lithographs used to advertise the coming of the circus. An 85-foot railroad car used by the Ringling Bros. and Barnum & Bailey Circus in the 1950s may be toured. Exhibits explain the role of advance men and posters in publicizing the arrival of the circus.

The subject of another exhibit is the freak show, which became a popular circus attraction. Photographs document the physical deformities that qualified these sad people as freaks. Clowns are another subject of circus history and their make-up and costumes are on exhibit.

A trolley leaving from Circus World will take visitors through Baraboo, pointing out the homes and buildings relating to the Ringling brothers and their famous circus.

ADDRESS: 426 Water Street, Baraboo, WI 53913

TELEPHONE: 608-356-0800, 608-356-8341

HOURS: Daily, 9 a.m. to 6 p.m. early May to mid-September, 9 a.m. to 9:30 p.m. from last week in July to third week in August

ADMISSION: Adults $8.95, seniors $7.95, children 3-12 $5.50; additional charges for carousel, pony and elephant rides, and trolley tour of Baraboo

FACILITIES: Circus show in Big Top; magic show; Exhibit Hall and Visitor Center; W. W. Deppe Wagon Pavilion; elephant rides; pony rides; carousel, petting menagerie; refreshment stands; trolley tours of Baraboo

LOCATION: In south central Wisconsin, 40 miles northwest of Madison, 175 miles northeast of Chicago

BED & BREAKFASTS: House of Seven Gables, 215 6th Street, Baraboo 53913, 608-356-8387; The Barrister's House, 226 9th Avenue, Baraboo 53913, 608-366-3344

HOTELS/MOTELS: Best Western Baraboo Inn, Hwy. 12, West Baraboo 53913, 608-356-1100; Campus Inn Motel, 750 West Pine Street, West Baraboo 53913, 608-356-8366; Spinning Wheel Motel, 809 8th Street, Hwy. 33, Baraboo 53913, 608-356-3933

CAMPING: Devil's Lake State Park, S5975 Park Road, Baraboo 53913, 608-356-6618; Mirror Lake State Park, E 10320 Fern Dell Road, Baraboo 53913, 608-254-2333; Double K-D Ranch, E 12442, Co. W, Baraboo 53913, 608-356-4622

DIRECTIONS: From Chicago, take the Northwest Tollway, I-90, to I-90/94 near Madison, continue on I-90/94 to exit 106, WI 33, west to Baraboo

2. CAMPBELLSPORT:

KETTLE MORAINE STATE FOREST—NORTHERN UNIT and ICE AGE NATIONAL SCIENTIFIC RESERVE

Over 27,000 acres of forest, lakes, hiking trails, scenic drives, campgrounds and glacial topography make Kettle Moraine State Forest one of Wisconsin's finest natural recreational facilities. Because the effects of continental glaciation are so clearly visible at Kettle Moraine, the state forest is a unit of the Ice Age National Scientific Reserve, a part of the National Park System. The National Park's Ice Age Visitor Center is located at Kettle Moraine.

The Ice Age National Scientific Reserve was established in 1971 to preserve select glacial landforms and landscapes created by the Wisconsinite glacier, which is thought to have begun 70,000 years ago and ended more than 10,000 years ago. Kettle Moraine North is the largest of the nine units which comprise the reserve. Five of the nine units, which total 40,000 acres, are currently operational. In addition to Kettle Moraine, Horican Marsh Wildlife Area, Devil's Lake State Park, Mill Bluff State Park and Interstate Park can be visited. Units that are not yet open to the public include Two Creeks Buried Forest, Campbellsport Drumlins, Cross Plains and Chippewa Moraine.

At Kettle Moraine two finger-like lobes of the glacier met, and billions of tons of sand, gravel and rock were deposited at their junction as the ice slowly melted. Called end moraines, these vestiges of the Wisconsinite glacier are clearly evident.

Ice sheets one mile thick covered the northern United States and Canada for over a million years. During that period, there were four major glacier stages: Nebraskan, Kansan, Illinoisan and Wisconsinite. The Wisconsinite glacier stage is so named because Wisconsin was the southern-most point reached by the glacier. Slowly moving south across the land, the gigantic glacial ice sheet incorporated soil and rock into its mass as it leveled hills and bluffs. Each glacial period erased the effects of the previous glacier on the terrain. Therefore, the landscape of the northern states today show the impact of the Wisconsinite glacier.

Units in the Ice Age National Scientific Reserve display a variety of significant features of glaciated landscapes. Visitors' centers at Kettle Moraine and Interstate have been opened by the National Park Service to aid visitors in understanding what they see. At the Henry S. Reuss Ice Age Visitor Center in the Kettle Moraine, an outstanding film about glaciers is shown in the theater. Exhibits explain glacial landscape features to watch for when hiking.

Glacial features at Kettle Moraine include kames, kettles and eskers. Kames are conical hills formed by debris deposited by meltwater flowing into funnel-shaped holes in the ice. Examples are Dundee Mountain, just south of the Long Lake Recreational Area, and a gumdrop-shaped kame to the south of Rt. F, east of Dundee. Kettles are surface depressions formed as sand and gravel settled over a melting ice block. Greenbush Kettle is about two miles north of WI 67 on the Kettle Moraine Scenic Drive. Eskers are serpentine ridges of gravel and sand, which probably mark stream channels under stagnant ice sheets. An example is Parnell Esker, at Butler Lake wayside, 1 and 1/2 miles east of Long Lake Recreation Area.

Hiking is the best way to observe the glacial landscape and enjoy the forest. Here you can see 60 species of trees, including white pine, paper birch, aspen, basswood, balsam, fir, sugar maple, shagbark hickory, white oak, red maple, and jack pine, the most common being the northern red oak. Shrubs, ferns, spring wildflowers and wildlife, including 40 mammal species, dozens of bird species, salamanders, frogs and turtles, are some of the other sights hikers will encounter.

Self-guided nature trails originate at the Ice Age Visitor Center, at Mauthe Lake, and Long Lake. Hiking trails include the Parnell Trail which is over four miles, the three-mile Butler Lake Trail, ten-mile Zillmer Trail, twelve-mile Greenbush Trail and three-mile Indoor Group Camp Trail. The 29-mile Glacial Trail, part of the Ice Age National Scenic Trail, has trailside shelters which must be reserved in advance. Horseback riding can be enjoyed on the 33-mile Kettle Moraine Bridle Trail. Naturalist-led hikes operate in the summer. Swimming beaches can be found at Mauthe Lake and Long Lake. Kettle Moraine Scenic Drive, which connects Southern and Northern units of the state forest, is especially beautiful in early and mid-October because of the fall color.

ADDRESS: Box 410, Campbellsport, WI 53010

TELEPHONE: 414-626-2116

HOURS: Daily, 6 a.m. to 11 p.m.; Henry S. Reuss Ice Age Visitor Center: 8:30 a.m. to 4 p.m. weekdays, and 9:30 a.m. to 5 p.m. weekends

ADMISSION: Wisconsin state park vehicle admission sticker: resident $14.00 annually, $3.50 daily; non-resident $30.00 annually, $6.00 daily

FACILITIES: 27,700 acres; Ice Age Reserve Unit; Visitor Center; 358 campsites; indoor and outdoor group camping; nature trails; 72 miles of hiking trails; lakes with beaches, bathhouses and lifeguards; boat-launching facilities; cross-country skiing; snowmobiling; horseback riding trails; horse-rider's camping; naturalist talks and hikes; Kettle Moraine Scenic Drive

LOCATION: In southeast Wisconsin, 20 miles west of Sheboygan, 140 miles north of Chicago

BED & BREAKFASTS: 52 Stafford, 52 Stafford Street, P.O. Box 565, Plymouth 53073, 414-893-0552; Yankee Hill B&B, 315 Collins St., Plymouth 53073, 414-892-2222; Mielke-Mauk House, 994 Rt. F, Kettle Moraine Lake, Campbellsport 53010, 414-533-8602

HOTELS/MOTELS: The American Club, Highland Dr., Kohler 53044, 414-457-8000, 800-344-2838; Budgetel Inn, 2932 Kohler Memorial Dr., Sheboygan 53081, 414-457-2321

CAMPING: Kettle Moraine State Forest—Northern Unit, Box 410, Campbellsport 53010, 414-626-2116

DIRECTIONS: From Chicago, take the Kennedy Expressway, I-90/94, or the Tri-State Tollway, I-294, north continuing on the Tri-State Tollway, I-94, north to Milwaukee, then, in Milwaukee, take I-43 north to WI 23 west near Sheboygan

3. CASSVILLE:

STONEFIELD and NELSON DEWEY STATE PARK

Stonefield was the name of a 2,000-acre farm along the Mississippi River owned by Nelson Dewey, Wisconsin's first governor. In the 1930s, Wisconsin purchased 700 acres of the original Dewey estate for a state park. Named Nelson Dewey State Park, it features the restored Nelson Dewey home, the State Agricultural Museum, and Stonefield Village, a re-creation of a rural 1890s Wisconsin crossroads village, operated by the State Historical Society.

A 35-building museum village, Stonefield is not a restoration but a facsimile of an 1890s village. Recently constructed buildings built in an 1890s style are filled with late-nineteenth-century furniture and artifacts from rural Wisconsin homes, stores, offices and other buildings. The idea was to simulate the appearance of a typical Wisconsin town and the lifestyle of its people.

A crossroads village both geographically and in terms of time, Stonefield emphasizes both the rural past and the industrial future of the United States. The earliest southern Wisconsin settlements revolved around mining and agriculture. Towns were business centers that also served settlers' social, religious and educational needs. The 1890s was a decade of rapid change brought about by the railroad, agricultural inventions and industrialization. Towns such as Stonefield either grew into larger urban areas or gradually died through depopulation.

Arranged around a town square nestled on the flat banks of the Mississippi River, Stonefield Village's turn-of-the-century retail businesses include a Drug Store, Barbershop, Harness & Hardware Store, Millinery Shop, Meat Market, General Store, Saloon, Photography Shop, Jewelry Store, Bookstore, Cheese Factory and Confectionery. Service-oriented concerns are the Post Office, Jail, Newspaper, Bank, Law Office, Doctor's Office, Undertaking Parlor, Telephone Exchange, Volunteer Fire Department, Livery Stable, School, Church, and Railroad Depot.

Craft demonstrations and special weekend activities provide insights into the daily lives of the townspeople and make the town come alive. Special activities include butter, cheese and ice cream making, ice harvesting and storing, harness making, horseshoeing, threshing, canning, cider pressing, and sauerkraut and sorghum making. Craft demonstrations are given in the Broom Factory and the Blacksmith Shop.

Agricultural history in Wisconsin is the focus of the State Agricultural Museum, which traces farming from Indian days to the 1930s. The museum was built on the stone foundation of Dewey's 1854 cattle barn which burned down in the early 1900s. Dewey was a large-scale farmer and agricultural experimenter. An outstanding collection of early farm machinery, including tractors and threshers, is exhibited. An audio-visual program is shown in the auditorium.

Unfortunately, the southern plantation home built by Dewey in 1867, at a cost of $100,000, burned down in 1873. This was but one in a series of heavy financial losses Dewey suffered. Dewey's story went from riches to rags. First governor of Wisconsin at age 35, owner of a 2,000-acre estate with a palatial mansion, Dewey died in poverty in 1889.

Rebuilt on the same foundation, the restored Dewey House is a considerably more modest, two-story brick building in Greek Revival style. Outbuildings from the original house include an 1860s limestone wine cellar and a smokehouse.

Nelson Dewey State Park's 750 scenic acres on the Mississippi River offer spectacular views from its blufftops. In addition to enjoying its beautiful location, visitors can picnic, fish, camp, look for Indian burial mounds, go for a hike, take a nature walk, or stroll through Dewey Heights Prairie.

STONEFIELD:
ADDRESS: Cassville WI 53806
TELEPHONE: 608-725-5210
HOURS: Daily, 9 a.m. to 5 p.m., Memorial Day through first week in October
ADMISSION: Adults $4.00, seniors $3.60, children $1.50, family $10.00; horse-drawn carriage rides $0.50 per person; state park vehicle sticker not required
FACILITIES: Re-created Wisconsin crossroads village; State Agricultural Museum; Nelson Dewey Home; Visitors Center; special events; craft demonstrations

NELSON DEWEY STATE PARK:
ADDRESS: Cassville, WI 53806
TELEPHONE: 608-725-5374
HOURS: Daily, 6 a.m. to 11 p.m.
ADMISSION: Wisconsin state park vehicle admission sticker: resident $14.00 annually, $3.50 daily; non-resident $30.00 annually, $6.00 daily
FACILITIES: 750 acres overlooking the Mississippi River; nature trail; hiking trail; picnic areas; fishing; campgrounds; Dewey Heights Prairie; campground is minimally accessible to handicapped

LOCATION: On the western border of southwestern Wisconsin, near the Mississippi River, 200 miles from Chicago, 30 miles from Dubuque, Iowa, two miles west of Cassville
BED & BREAKFASTS: Geiger House, 401 Denniston, Cassville 53806, 608-725-5419; The Parson's Inn B&B, Rock School Road, Glen Haven 53810, 608-794-2491; O'Reilly House, 7509 Stiger Rd., Potosi 53820, 608-763-2386
HOTELS/MOTELS: Brisbois Motor Inn, 533 N. Marquette Rd., Prairie du Chien 53821, 608-326-8404; Prairie Motel, 1616 S. Marquette Rd., Prairie du Chien 53821, 608-326-6461, 800-526-3776
CAMPING: Nelson Dewey State Park, Cassville 53806, 608-725-5374
DIRECTIONS: From Chicago, take the Northwest Tollway, I-90, to Rockford, at Rockford take U.S. 20 west to Dubuque, Iowa, there take U.S. 61 north into Wisconsin to Tennyson, then WI 133 west to Cassville

4. DODGEVILLE:
GOVERNOR DODGE STATE PARK

Over 5,000 acres of unique Midwestern scenery consisting of steep hills, sandstone bluffs and deep valleys makes Governor Dodge State Park a special place. A series of glaciers, which flattened hills and filled in valleys, accounts for most of the typical, flat Midwestern terrain, but for some little-understood geological reason, no glacier ever covered the southwestern section of Wisconsin. This region is called the Driftless Area, referring to the absence of drift, or the accumulated rock and soil left by retreating glaciers.

Towering sandstone bluffs were formed millions of years ago as sand from seas covering the area was deposited, layer on layer. When the seas retreated, wind and water carved the valleys. Archeological evidence indicates that Indians made their winter camps in the shelter of the bluffs some 8,000 years ago. In addition to hunting bison, these Native Americans discovered and mined the lead ore that lay near the surface of the earth. When white miners arrived in the 1820s, lured by the lead deposits, conflicts arose between the whites and the Winnebagos.

General Henry Dodge was an early settler in the area and was later appointed first territorial governor of Wisconsin. Wisconsin's second largest state park is named in his honor.

The park's two popular, man-made lakes were formed by earthen dams erected in 1958 and 1966. Cox Hollow Lake and Twin Valley Lake have beaches, picnic grounds, and boat launch areas. Fishermen catch bass and walleye in the lakes, trout in nearby streams, and muskie in Twin Valley Lake.

To enjoy the natural topography of the park, head for the hiking and cross-country trails. The 3 and ½ mile White Oak Trail and the two-mile White Pine Nature Trail are designated hiking trails. In addition, you can walk the cross-country ski trails, the almost seven-mile Meadow Valley Trail, the 8-mile Lost Canyon Trail, and the three-mile Mill Creek Trail. You'll pass through meadows of wildflowers, oak-hickory forests, and enjoy the views from pine-covered sandstone bluffs.

If you're lucky, you could spot some of the wildlife which makes Governor Dodge State Park its home. Inhabitants include white-tailed deer, wild turkeys, grouse, red and grey fox, beaver, wood-chucks and muskrats. Over 150 species of birds, including barred owls, woodpeckers, and hawks, have been seen in the park.

ADDRESS: Route 1, Box 42, Dodgeville, WI 53533
TELEPHONE: 608-935-2315
HOURS: June-August daily, 8 a.m. to 11 p.m.; May, September and October, Sunday-Thursday 8 a.m. to 4:30 p.m., weekends, 8 a.m. to 11 p.m.; November-April daily, 8 a.m. to 4:30 p.m.
ADMISSION: Wisconsin state park vehicle admission sticker: resident $14.00 annually, $3.50 daily; nonresident $28.00 annually, $6.00 daily
FACILITIES: 5,029 acres; three lakes; swimming; fishing; boating; hiking; picnic areas; boat and canoe rentals; 267 family campsites; group campsites accommodating 800; nature trail; hiking trails; cross-country skiing; horse trail; naturalist-led hikes; backpack camping; horseback riding; horse camping; concession stand; amphitheater; handicapped accessible facilities include two campsites, shelter buildings, picnic tables at beaches, fishing deck and amphitheater
LOCATION: In southwest Wisconsin, 40 miles west of Madison, 180 miles from Chicago
BED & BREAKFAST: see Pendarvis, Mineral Point (#11)
HOTELS/MOTELS: Don Q Inn, Hwy. 23 N, Box 199, Dodgeville 53533, 608-935-2321, 800-362-2950; Super 8 Motel, 1308 Johns St., Dodgeville 53533, 608-935-3888; New Concord Inn, Hwy. 23 N, Dodgeville 53533, 608-935-3770; Pine Ridge Motel, Hwy. YZ East, Dodgeville 53533, 608-935-3386; Rocks Motel, Hwy. 23 N, R. #1, Dodgeville 53533, 608-935-3304

CAMPING: Governor Dodge State Park, Rt. 1, Box 42, Dodgeville 53533, 608-935-2315

DIRECTIONS: From Chicago, take the Northwest Tollway, I-90, into Wisconsin, at Madison take exit 142, U.S. 12/18, west a short distance to U.S. 18/151, south/west to U.S. 18 West to Dodgeville, north on WI 23 to park

5. EAGLE:
KETTLE MORAINE STATE FOREST—SOUTHERN UNIT

Nineteen thousand acres of unusual glacial topography await young and old hikers, fishermen, bird watchers, nature lovers, campers and urban burnouts in the Southern Unit of the Kettle Moraine Forest. Formed thousands of years ago by the receding Wisconsinite glacier, the Kettle Moraine landscape exhibits a variety of glacial features including moraines, kettles, outwash plains, kames and eskers (see Northern Unit, #2). Even if this state forest's geological background was unknown, the natural beauty of the hills, lakes, forests and flowering meadows are lure enough for visitors.

The Southern, Northern and Lapham Peak Units of the Kettle Moraine State Forest share a common glacial history. The Wisconsinite Glacier divided into icy lobes, large, tongue-shaped projections from a glacier extending into lowlands, which were instrumental in the formation of the area. When the east flank of the Green Bay Lobe merged with the west flank of the Lake Michigan Lobe, a collection of landforms developed, now known as the Kettle Moraine.

Over the long period in which the two lobes were melting back, several interruptions occurred. During these stable periods, rock debris accumulated at the

edge of the ice sheet, forming moraine ridges visible in
the southern part of the Kettle Moraine. The conspicu-
ous sand plains in the southern part of the Kettle Moraine are the result of streams carrying meltwater and
rock debris from the melting ice. Sand plains were
usually bounded by the glacier on one side and by
older, higher remnants of sand plains or moraines on
the other side. Eventually large prairies developed on
the flat glacial outwash areas.

Much of the terrain in the Southern Unit formerly
consisted of prairies and oak openings. Though domi-
nated by oak, the forest in the Southern Unit also
contains black cherry, shagbark, hickory, white ash
and quaking aspen, along with small saplings and
shrubs such as gray dogwood, hazelnut, prickly ash,
blackberry and honeysuckle. In spring, woodland,
wetland, and prairie wildflowers abound including
prairie smoke, birdsfoot violet, blue-eyed grass,
downy phlox, golden alexander, puccoon, pasque
flowers, shooting star, prairie dock, compass plant,
gayfeather, prairie coneflower, rattle snakemaster,
round-lobed hepatica, may-apple, false solomon's
seal, yellow lady-slipper, bellwort, bloodroot, wild ge-
ranium and enchanter's nightshade.

Hiking is the best way to enjoy the geological and
natural bounty of the Kettle Moraine. There are four
self-guided and labeled nature trails a half-mile to a
mile in length, and four marked hiking trails two to
nine miles long. A 36-mile portion of the Ice Age Trail
runs through the forest. Over 40 miles of trail are open
for cross-country skiing. Horseback riders have 27
miles of trail.

Although handicapped individuals often encounter
difficulties at natural sites, Paradise Springs Nature
Area has been designed with them in mind. There is a
half-mile paved trail designed for use by people with

a mobility impairment. Tape recordings of nature labels along the trail are available at the Visitors Center, for visually impaired persons. A large flowing spring and a catch-and-release trout pond are found at Paradise Springs. The Gotten Cabin, a recently restored pioneer cabin, is across from Paradise Springs.

Swimming is available at Ottawa and Whitewater lakes, which have beaches and bathhouses. There are family campgrounds at Ottawa Lake, Pine Woods, La Grange and Whitewater. Backpack camping on the Ice Age Trail is by reservation only. The Visitor Center, located on WI 59, three miles west of Eagle, has a small natural history museum and an audio-visual program on the park's geology, plants and animals. Park naturalists conduct nature hikes and evening programs from April through October.

Although administered jointly, the three units of the Kettle Moraine State Forest, Northern, Southern and Lapham Peak, are separate recreational areas. The Southern section is closest to Chicago, and Lapham Peak, the smallest and still undeveloped unit of the state forest, is west of Milwaukee.

ADDRESS: S91 W39091 Highway 59, Eagle, WI 53119
TELEPHONE: 414-594-2135
HOURS: Daily, 6 a.m. to 11 p.m.; Visitor Center: 7:45 a.m. to 4:30 p.m. weekdays, 9 a.m. to 5 p.m. weekends
ADMISSION: Wisconsin state park vehicle admission sticker: resident $14.00 annually, $3.50 daily; non-resident $28.00 annually, $6.00 daily
FACILITIES: 19,000 acres; lakes with beaches and boat launches; 75 miles of hiking trails; nature trails; handicapped-accessible nature trail; Ice Age Trail; picnic areas; five campgrounds; 27 miles of horseback riding trails; swimming; fishing; snowmobiling, cross-country skiing; visitor center with audio-visual program

LOCATION: Southeastern Wisconsin, 35 miles southwest of downtown Milwaukee, 75 miles northwest of Chicago

BED & BREAKFAST: see Old World Wisconsin (#6)

HOTELS/MOTELS: see Old World Wisconsin (#6)

CAMPING: Kettle Moraine State Forest—Southern Unit, S91 W39091 Hwy. 59, Eagle 53119, 414-594-2135

DIRECTIONS: From Chicago, take the Tri-State Tollway, I-294, north to exit 44, Dempster/U.S. 12/14, take Dempster west a very short distance to U.S. 12/Rand Road, then follow U.S. 12 north and west into Wisconsin to WI 67 just north of Elkhorn, WI 67 north to Eagle; or take I-355, North-South Tollway, to exit at U.S. 12/Rand Road, and proceed as noted previously.

6. EAGLE:

OLD WORLD WISCONSIN

Old World Wisconsin looks better every time we visit. Wisconsin's ethnic architectural heritage, combined with the wooded glaciated landscape of the Kettle Moraine State Forest, make this Wisconsin State Historic Site a must-see destination. Carefully re-created farms, and the restored buildings of Wisconsin's European immigrants, provide visitors with a real sense of the lifestyle of these pioneers.

This outdoor museum exhibits original nineteenth-century rural architecture and artifacts of the European ethnic groups that settled the midwestern state. Rural buildings found throughout Wisconsin were moved to the museum where they were painstakingly restored and arranged into farmsteads, according to nationality. Extensive historical research on buildings and their owners has meant that each farm has been restored as if it were occupied by the owner's family in a particular year. Flower, herb and vegetable gardens are appropriate to the historic period, as are the cultivated fields and barnyard animals. Costumed interpreters at every farmstead tell stories about the former residents while performing chores, such as food preparation, in the manner of the time.

Farmsteads are very well spaced at the museum so each one seems like it is alone in the midwestern wilderness, a deliberate attempt to recreate the isolation experienced on the frontier. Newly arrived immigrants built their homes, barns and outbuildings in the style of the country they came from because it was the pattern with which they were most familiar. Thus, the German farmsteads resembled farms in Germany, the Finnish, farms in Finland. Gradually, changes and adaptations emerged in the new country.

The purpose of the museum is to preserve examples of European-style buildings built by the state's early settlers. Richard W. E. Perrin, an architect and expert on Wisconsin's historic buildings, spearheaded the movement to save the state's diverse rural architectural history. The concept of an outdoor museum, that is a site with a contiguous collection of original buildings which reflect an historical time and lifestyle, originated in Scandinavia and this was the model for Old World Wisconsin.

Buildings at Old World Wisconsin have been grouped into ten farm units depicting European ethnic groups. There is also a Yankee area and a multi-ethnic crossroads village. Rural ethnic groups include Germans, Finns, Danes, Norwegians and Poles. Yankees were Easterners who were usually of English extraction. Tours begin with an audio-visual program in the Visitor Center, the 1841 Ramsey Barn from Fort Atkinson. You can either walk or take the tram around the village and farms. Caution: Old World Wisconsin is a 576-acre site which it takes almost all day to see; trams are highly recommended to avoid the tired feet syndrome. Trams leave from the visitors' center and make frequent stops at each exhibit.

There are three farms in the German area. The 1880 Koepsell Farm has two barns, a machine shed and an outhouse, all of which were built between 1855 and 1880. The farm house is an example of German Fachwerk, half timbered architecture, built with hand-made bricks in 1858 in Jackson. The 1875 Schottler Farm has two barns, a smokehouse, a summer kitchen and a farm house in the German Blockbau style built in Germantown in 1847. The 1860 Schulz Farm has a traditional Pomeranian half-timbered house with a "black kitchen," an interior smoke house which turns black because of the smoke.

The Kruza House, a Polish house, has been recently added to the museum. This small, rectangular structure has two rooms, one for people and one for chickens. It is an example of stovewood architecture, in which stovewood-length logs are set in mortar.

The Norwegian area has two farms and a schoolhouse. The Fossebrekke House dates to 1841. On the Kvaale Farm is a dogtrot barn, the Sorbergshagen Barn, with one side built in 1872 and the other added in 1880. The Raspberry School was built by three Norwegian families in 1896 in Russell, Bayfield County. Named after Lake Superior's Raspberry Bay, this one-room country school, which served all eight grades, has been restored to its appearance in 1906.

The queen of Denmark traveled to Wisconsin in 1976 to dedicate the Danish area's Pederson House, built in 1872 in Luck and restored to its 1890 appearance. In the house are wooden shoes, similar to those made by Jens Jensen, the Dane who built the Jensen Barn.

There are two farms in the Finnish area, the 1897

Rankinen farm and the 1915 seven-structure Ketola Farm, which features a sauna built in 1919 in Maple County.

The Yankee area features the sophisticated Sanford House built in 1858 in La Grange. This Greek Revival house reflects the prosperity of a farmer from New York. On the first floor are well-decorated formal and informal parlors, an office, dining room and a modern kitchen of 1860. Sanford was a farmer and business-man who hired men to run his farm.

The Crossroads Village structures were erected by a variety of nationalities. The 1876 Harmony Town Hall was a Yankee institution from the East, where deci-sions were made at town meetings. The 1881 Wagon Shop was built by Andrew Peterson, a Norwegian; the Blacksmith Shop was built in 1886 by Henry Gro-telueschen, a German; the Shoe Shop and House was the work of Anton Sisel, a Bohemian, while the Haf-ford House, built in 1885, was occupied by Mary Haf-ford, an Irish widow. St. Peter's Catholic Church was built in Milwaukee in 1839. Also in the village is the Four-Mile House, a stagecoach inn from Rolling Prai-rie. Its bar-room is unique in that alcohol was not served, because the owners of the inn believed in tem-perance. Although guests entered on the first floor, their luggage was unloaded from the top of the coach onto the second floor porch.

Lunch is served in the Clausing Barn Restaurant and usually features an ethnic dish. There are also picnic areas.

ADDRESS: S103 W37894 Hwy. 67, Eagle, WI 53119
TELEPHONE: 414-594-2116
HOURS: 10 a.m. to 5 p.m. daily, July-August and weekends from May-October; 10 a.m. to 4 p.m. weekdays during May, June, September and October

ADMISSION: Adults $7.00, seniors $6.30, children 5-17 $3.00, family $20.00; tram rides: $1.00 per person

FACILITIES: Ethnic architecture museum; state historic site; ethnic farmsteads and crossroads village; 50 original, reconstructed nineteenth- and early-twentieth-century buildings on 576 acres in Kettle Moraine State Forest, southern unit; Clausing Barn Restaurant; gift and book shop; audio-visual presentation; picnic areas; special events; handicapped accessible

LOCATION: Southeastern Wisconsin, 35 miles southwest of downtown Milwaukee, 75 miles northwest of Chicago

BED & BREAKFASTS: Eagle Centre House, W370 S9590 Hwy. 67, Eagle 53119, 414-363-4700; The Greene House B&B, Rt. 2, Box 214, Hwy. 12, Whitewater 53190, 414-495-8771, 800-468-1959; Ye Olde Manor House, Rt. 5, Box 390, Elkhorn 53121, 414-742-2450

HOTELS/MOTELS: Comfort Inn Waukesha, 2111 E. Moreland Blvd,, Waukesha 53186, 414-547-7770; Fairfield Inn by Marriott, 20150 W. Blue Mound Rd., Waukesha 53186, 414-785-0500

CAMPING: Kettle Moraine State Forest—Southern Unit, Hwy. 59, Eagle 53119, 414-594-2135

DIRECTIONS: From Chicago, take the Tri-State Tollway, I-294, north to exit 44, Dempster/U.S. 12/14, take Dempster west a very short distance to U.S. 12/Rand Road, then follow U.S. 12 north and west into Wisconsin to WI 67 just north of Elkhorn, WI 67 north to Eagle; or take I-355, North-South Tollway, to exit at U.S. 12/Rand Road, and proceed as above

7. GREEN BAY:
HERITAGE HILL STATE PARK

Heritage Hill State Park, located in Green Bay, is a living history outdoor museum focused on the diverse history of northeastern Wisconsin. On a 40-acre site on

the banks of the Fox River, 25 historic or recreated
structures, filled with authentic furniture and artifacts,
are arranged to reflect four historical themes: Pioneer
Heritage, Military Heritage, Small Town, and Agricul-
tural/Ethnic Heritage.

Green Bay, the oldest settlement in Wisconsin, is
located at the southern tip of Green Bay, the second
largest bay on the Great Lakes. In the area claimed for
France by Jean Nicolet in 1634, it was called La Baye.
A French Jesuit mission was established there in 1669.
After explorers Marquette and Jolliet discovered a
water route to the Mississippi River from Lake Michigan, La Baye's strategic position made it an important
fur trading center. A frontier fort and trading post was
built on the site in 1684 and traders, trappers, Indians,
missionaries and French soldiers settled there.

During the first half of the eighteenth century, the
French were engaged in constant warfare with the Fox
Indians over hunting and trading rights. Fort La Baye,
a new fort built by the French in 1716, was destroyed
by the Indians in 1728, and rebuilt by the French in
1733. Abandoned by the French in the 1750s, Fort La
Baye was occupied by the British in 1763, after the
French and Indian War. Renamed Fort Edward Augus-
tus, the post was an active and prosperous fur trading
and farming community that remained under British
control until the War of 1812.

In 1816, the Americans took possession of Green
Bay, and built Fort Howard in the same location as the
earlier French and British forts. Control of fur trading
was taken over by John Jacob Astor's American Fur
Company. By the mid-nineteenth century, Green Bay
had developed into a lumber port, and a trade and
supply center for immigrants settling in northeastern
Wisconsin.

The Pioneer Heritage Area represents the period

from the mid-seventeenth century to the early nineteenth century. An authentic French fur trader's log cabin was built in the French Canadian piece sur piece style around 1800. This method of construction, piece on piece, consisted of a heavy timber framework filled in with light weight horizontal wall logs or planks. The French presence in Green Bay is also represented by the replica seventeenth-century Bark Chapel.

Wisconsin's territorial period is the subject of the Military Heritage Area which represents life in 1836 at the American military fort, Fort Howard. A mix of historical and replica buildings includes a hospital, officers' quarters, a barracks kitchen, and a post school.

The year 1871 is encountered in the Small Town Heritage Area which has homes and businesses found in Green Bay at that time. The Tank Cottage, built between 1775 and 1800, is one of Wisconsin's oldest houses. It was remodeled several times and is restored to its 1870s appearance.

European immigrants who came to Wisconsin to farm are represented at the Agricultural/Ethnic Area. Farm buildings owned by a Belgian family have been moved to Heritage Hill.

Docents at Heritage Hill include costumed interpreters who explain what you see, and role players who assume the parts of an actual characters. Kids especially enjoy the challenge of conversing with an eighteenth-century individual.

Heritage Hill conducts special events throughout the summer, ranging from Revolutionary War and French and Indian War encampments to fur trade rendezvous, to country fairs. Evening concerts are presented about half a dozen times during the summer.

While in Green Bay, you can visit the National Railroad Museum which exhibits steam locomotives, diesels and railroad cars; 2285 S. Broadway, 414-435-7245. Leave your Chicago Bears sweatshirt in the suitcase if you visit the Green Bay Packer Hall of Fame: Brown County Expo Centre, 855 Lombardi Ave., 414-499-4281.

It's a shame to come all the way to Green Bay and not visit Door County, which unfortunately is outside this book's 200-mile radius of Chicago. Door County, Wisconsin, is a little world of its own, in, but separate from, the rest of the state. Often compared to Cape Cod, it is an 85-mile-long peninsula with 250 miles of shoreline on Lake Michigan and Green Bay. Fishing villages dot its shore, yet it is home to farms, cherry orchards, art studios, summer cottages, four state parks, and a 15-mile segment of the Ice Age Trail. Art galleries, inns, fish boils, fishing boats, picturesque villages, fall color, great scenery and cool weather are some of its specialties. Highly recommended. Contact Door County Chamber of Commerce, Green Bay Road, Box 346, Sturgeon Bay 54235, 414-743-4456.

ADDRESS: 2640 S. Webster Avenue, Green Bay, WI 54301
TELEPHONE: 414-448-5150
HOURS: Memorial Day through Labor Day, 10 a.m. to 5 p.m., Tuesday-Sunday; May and September weekends, 10 a.m. to 5 p.m.; last week of November and first week of December, 10 a.m. to 5 p.m. daily; closed Mondays except Memorial and Labor Days
ADMISSION: Adult $5.00, senior $4.00, child 6-17 $2.75, family $12.75
FACILITIES: Outdoor museum with 25 buildings on 40-acre site; visitors center; special events; Christmas Festival; summer evening concerts
LOCATION: The city of Green Bay is in east central Wisconsin at the southern edge of Green Bay, 200 miles from Chicago; Heritage Hill is on the east side of the Fox River, just north of the intersection of Rt. 172 and Webster Avenue

HOTELS/MOTELS: Mariner Motel, 2222 Riverside Dr. (WI 57),
Green Bay 54301, 414-437-7107; Holiday Inn Airport
Holidome, 2580 S. Ashland Ave., (U.S. 41 Bus., WI 32 at U.S.
172), Green Bay 54304, 414-499-5121; Ramada Inn, 2750
Ramada Way, Green Bay 54304, 414-499-0631
CAMPING: Devils River Campers Park, 16612 Rt. R, Maribel
54227, 414-863-2812; Happy Hollow Campground, Rt. 3,
DePere 54115, 414-532-4386
DIRECTIONS: From Chicago, take the Kennedy Expressway,
I-90/94, or the Tri-State Tollway, I-294, north continuing on
the Tri-State Tollway, I-94, north to Milwaukee, in Milwau-
kee take I-43 north to Green Bay, then WI 172 west to
Webster Avenue

8. GREENBUSH:
OLD WADE HOUSE

A 27-room stagecoach inn in the tiny town of Greenbush was built for $300 by Sylvanus and Betsey Wade
in 1850. Designed by Charles Robinson, Wade House
served passengers who traveled over the plank road
between Sheboygan and Fond du Lac. The restored
building is now a Wisconsin State Historical Site.

Sylvanus Wade, born in Massachusetts, and his
wife, Betsey, from Pennsylvania, had lived in Illinois
and Ft. Atkinson, Wisconsin, for eight years before
they and their nine children moved to Greenbush in
1844. Mr. Wade was already a successful blacksmith
and farmer in addition to becoming an innkeeper.
Wade House was home to the large Wade family, as
well as an inn.

Guided tours of the Wade House, a three-story,
white-frame, Greek Revival building with green shutters, are given by authentically costumed guides.
Tours begin in the taproom where male customers

gathered for drinks and recreation. Females adjourned to the ladies' parlor as it was not considered proper for them to be in the taproom. The long table in the dining room was a busy spot. Customers ate quickly because so many were still waiting their turn. Food was cooked in the fireplace woodburning stove or dutch oven in the kitchen. The inn also had a summer kitchen, a room with doors on opposite sides which could be opened to get a breeze, with an interior well and a cast iron stove.

On the third floor were eight bedrooms to accommodate overnight guests. The rooms are simply furnished with rope beds, corn husk mattresses, and hooked rugs. All open onto a large central room heated by a cast iron stove, where town meetings and occasional dances were held.

Family rooms, which were on the second floor, consisted of a parlor, a bedroom for Sylvanus and his wife, along with children's bedrooms and servants' quarters. Much of the furniture and artifacts now in these rooms belonged to the Wade family.

The railroad made the stagecoach and its cumbersome plank road obsolete. Since the railroad bypassed Greenbush, the small settlement did not grow after 1865. Wade family descendants lived in the house until 1941. The inn was restored by Ruth De Young Kohler and the Kohler Foundation, and donated to the State Historical Society of Wisconsin in 1953.

Also on the site is the Charles Robinson House, the home of a Wade daughter, Julia Wade Robinson and her husband. Charles Robinson was one of the founding members of the Republican party. Built in 1855, the white-frame Greek Revival house, which was designed by Robinson, has a cupola, and butternut or white pine woodwork.

The Wesley W. Jung Carriage Museum houses more

than 120 horse- and hand-drawn 1870-1915 carriages and sleighs, many of which have been restored to like-new condition. The majority were manufactured by Jung Carriage Company, founded in 1855 by Jacob Jung, an immigrant from Baden, Germany. The thriving Sheboygan business operated for 60 years, until the automobile age.

Wesley W. Jung, Jacob Jung's grandson, began the collection by restoring sleds and wagons that had been made for the children in the family. In 1963, Wesley Jung donated over 100 carriages, wagons and sleighs, some of which were made by manufacturers other than Jung, to the Wade House site. There are hearses, a street sprinkler, fire engines, a dray wagon, a tobacco wagon, an omnibus, a Kingsbury beer wagon, a circus wagon, and a governess cart. The variety of sleighs attest to the long, snowy Wisconsin winters.

A reconstructed working blacksmith shop and the ruins of a saw mill are also on the site. The Wade House property is well-landscaped and has red brick sidewalks throughout. At the Stage Coach Inn Restaurant directly across the street from the blacksmith shop, they serve home-made potato chips with their hamburgers, and the best chicken dumpling soup ever.

The American Club (see Hotels/Motels) is a destination in itself. The Tudor-style hotel is in the renovated early nineteenth-century building used as a boarding-house for immigrant employees of a large plumbing manufacturer. In a wooded setting not far from Lake Michigan, the hotel is known for its fine restaurants and opulent bathrooms.

ADDRESS: Greenbush, WI 53026
TELEPHONE: 414-526-3271
HOURS: Daily, 9 a.m. to 5 p.m., May 1 to October 31

ADMISSION: Adults $5.00, seniors $4.50, children 5-17 $2.00, family $14.00; horse-drawn wagon rides: $1.00

FACILITIES: Restored stagecoach inn; Jung Carriage Museum; reception center with audio-visual presentation and gift shop; picnic area; special events; state historical site

LOCATION: Northeast Wisconsin, halfway between Fond du Lac and Sheboygan, 52 miles north of Milwaukee, 145 miles north of Chicago

BED & BREAKFASTS: 52 Stafford, 52 Stafford Street, P.O. Box 565, Plymouth 53073, 414-893-0552; Mielke-Mauk House, 994 Co. Hwy. F, Kettle Moraine Lake, Campbellsport 53010, 414-533-8602; Yankee Hill, 315 Collins, Plymouth 53073, 892-2222

HOTELS/MOTELS: The American Club, Highland Drive, Kohler 53044, 414-457-8000, 800-458-2562; AmericInn, 1708 Eastern Avenue, Plymouth 53073, 414-892-6644

CAMPING: Kettle Moraine State Forest—Northern Unit, Box 410, Campbellsport 53010, 414-626-2116

DIRECTIONS: From Chicago, take the Kennedy Expressway, I-90/94, to the Edens Expressway, I-94; or the Tri-State Tollway, I-294, north, continuing north on the Tri-State Tollway, I-94, into Wisconsin, at Milwaukee take I-43 north to Sheboygan, then WI 23 west for twenty miles to Greenbush

9. MADISON:
ICE AGE NATIONAL SCENIC TRAIL

Ray Zillmer dreamed no little dreams. In the 1950s, this Milwaukean proposed the formation of an Ice Age Glacier National Forest Park in Wisconsin, focusing on the end moraines of the state's last glacier. An avid hiker, Zillmer also advocated establishment of a 1,000-mile footpath along the entire length of the moraines. Although not all of Zillmer's ideas have been realized, he was taken seriously. In 1964, the National Park

System authorized the Ice Age National Scientific Reserve, consisting of nine separate units located across the state to protect significant features of continental glaciation left by the Wisconsinite glacier.

In 1980, Congress designated the Ice Age Trail as a National Scenic Trail which will eventually travel 1,000 miles across Wisconsin, following a chain of glacial landscape features. Four hundred miles are currently open, and trail development continues. When completed, the Ice Age Trail will join the ranks of other major national recreational trails like the Appalachian Trail.

A myriad of federal, state, county, civic and private organizations are involved in the maintenance and development of the trail, which lies on both private and public land. Camping facilities along the trail are also being developed. The sections of trail that are currently operational are not continuous, and tend to be on state lands. Although hiking is permitted on the entire trail, bicycling, horseback riding, cross-country skiing, snowshoeing, jogging, snowmobiling, fishing and hunting are permitted only on certain segments, as determined by local authorities.

Potawatomi State Park, on Green Bay in Door County, marks the eastern end point of the Ice Age National Scenic Trail. Trail segments within 200 miles of Chicago include the 29-mile Glacial Trail in Kettle Moraine State Forest—Northern Unit, a 36-mile trail in Kettle Moraine State Forest—Southern Unit, and Sugar River Trail which runs for over 23 miles between New Glarus and Brodhead in south central Wisconsin. Also a state bicycle trail, Sugar River State Park Trail has its headquarters at the New Glarus former Milwaukee Road Railroad depot.

ADDRESS: National Park Service, 7818 Big Sky Drive, Suite 117, Madison WI 53719

TELEPHONE: 608-833-2788

HOURS: Daily, 6 a.m. to 11 p.m.

ADMISSION: No hiking fees. Wisconsin state park vehicle admission sticker required for cars in state parks: resident $14.00 annually, $3.50 daily; nonresident $30.00 annually, $6.00 daily. Bike trail admission cards required for adult cyclists; Wisconsin resident $5.00 annually, $1.50 daily; nonresident $7.00 annually, $2.00 daily.

FACILITIES: 400 miles of hiking trails; bicycling; cross-country skiing; horseback riding; snowshoeing; jogging; snowmobiling; fishing and hunting allowed on portions of trail; Henry S. Reuss Ice Age Visitor Center in Kettle Moraine State Forest—Northern Unit

LOCATION: Trail, which is not continuous, originates in Door County, a peninsula on the northeastern edge of Wisconsin between Lake Michigan and Green Bay, and ends in northwestern Wisconsin.

BED & BREAKFAST: see Kettle Moraine State Forests (#2, 5)

HOTELS/MOTELS: see Kettle Moraine State Forests (#2, 5)

CAMPING: Potawatomi State Park, 3740 Park Dr., Sturgeon Bay 54235, 414-743-8869 or 8860; Kettle Moraine State Forest—Northern Unit, Box 410, Campbellsport 53010, 414-626-2116; Kettle Moraine State Forest—Southern Unit, Hwy. 59, Eagle 53119, 414-594-2135

DIRECTIONS: see Kettle Moraine State Forest, Northern and Southern Units (#2, 5)

10. MILWAUKEE

Flowers that bloom year round, a top-notch zoo, brewery tours and German food are good reasons for a trip to Milwaukee. The overlay of German gemutlichkeit is what separates this neighbor from other midwestern cities. Only 95 miles from Chicago,

Milwaukee offers a change of pace. Its special attractions are the seasonal flower shows at the Mitchell Park Horticultural Conservatory, the animals at the Milwaukee County Zoo, tours of the Miller and Pabst breweries and the opulent Pabst Mansion, and the exhibits of the Milwaukee Public Museum.

The Milwaukee County Zoo, founded in the late 1890s, is a 184-acre zoological park known for its updated natural outdoor exhibits. Animals, birds, reptiles and fish are grouped by continents in naturalistic settings. A unique feature is the presentation of animals in predator/prey outdoor exhibits separated by deep moats. Facilities include an aviary with a walkthrough tropical bird exhibit, a children's zoo, elephant, camel and pony rides, and dolphin and sea lion shows. You can see the zoo aboard a miniature train or by guided tours on the Zoomobile. 10001 W. Blue Mound Road, Milwaukee, 53226, 414-771-3040; open daily, 9 a.m. to 5 p.m.; adults $4.50, seniors $3.00, children $2.50. Wheelchair accessible.

Flower lovers beat a path to the well-known flower shows at the Mitchell Park Horticultural Conservatory. The Conservatory dates back to 1898 but the beehive-shape domes that Mitchell Park is known for were built in the 1960s. Three 140-foot wide and 85-foot high domes cover an area of 15,000 square feet. Displays in the Tropical Dome feature 1,200 species from five continents including fruits, nuts, spices and orchids found in tropical rain forests. The Arid Dome recreates a desert environment in which is displayed cacti, succulents, shrubs and land bulbs from the arid regions of the world.

Variety is found in the Show Dome's five shows each year: a fall show from the beginning of October through mid-November, a Christmas show from Thanksgiving to the first week in January, a winter show from late January to mid-March, a spring show in April and May, and a summer show from June through August. Elaborate themes form the background for the floral displays. A winter show, the English Woodlands, was designed like the garden of a large English estate with a profusion of azaleas, cyclamen, rhododendrons along woodland paths leading to a small thatched roof garden house.

In addition to the indoor displays, there is an outdoor sunken garden, acres of formal floral gardens, and a picnic area. 524 S. Layton Boulevard, Milwaukee 53215, 414-649-9800. Open daily, 9 a.m. to 5 p.m.; adults $2.50, children $1.00. Wheelchair accessible.

The Milwaukee Public Museum, a museum of natural and human history founded in 1882, presents its artifact collection in cultural settings including Asia, Africa, South America, and Europe. Space is also devoted to the geological and historical background of Wisconsin, and there is a re-creation of the shops in early Milwaukee.

Two of the most elaborate and popular exhibits are the Third Planet exhibit which includes a Metasequoia Swamp diorama with life-size dinosaurs, and the two-story tropical American rain forest complete with waterfall. The museum has a cafeteria, gift shops, and is wheelchair accessible. 800 W. Wells Street, Milwaukee 53233, 414-278-2702; open Tuesday-Sunday 9 a.m. to 5 p.m., Monday noon to 8 p.m.; adults $4.00, children $2.00, family $10.00.

German residents were in the brewery business in Milwaukee as early as the 1840s. Pabst, Miller, Blatz, Gettelman and Schlitz breweries were all founded by German immigrants who brought Old World brewing skills with them. The breweries played an important role in Milwaukee's economy, and the city became nationally known for beer. Free brewery tours are given at Miller Brewing Company Monday-Saturday, from May through September and Tuesday-Saturday, from October through April, 4251 W. State Street, Milwaukee, 414-931-2337. Pabst Brewing Company tours are given daily except holidays, 915 W. Juneau Avenue, Milwaukee, 414-223-3709, free.

The Pabst Mansion, designed by George Bowman Ferry in 1893, is in the Flemish Renaissance Revival-style. Its owner, Frederick Pabst, had been a captain on a Great Lakes ship before he became a partner in Phillip Best's brewing company in 1864. Pabst married Best's oldest daughter, became president of the brewery, and changed its name.

The 37 room Pabst Mansion has 12 baths, 14 fireplaces, and carved panels from a seventeenth-century Bavarian castle. Built at a cost of $255,000, the mansion on Grand Avenue, now Wisconsin Avenue, was located on a street lined with elegant homes. Now it is one of the few that remains. Most of the furnishings are original. 2000 W. Wisconsin Avenue, Milwaukee 53233, 414-931-0808; open mid-March through December, Monday-Saturday, 10 a.m. to 3:30 p.m., Sunday noon to 3:30 p.m., January to mid-March, Saturday 10 a.m. to 3:30 p.m. and Sunday noon to 3:30 p.m., admission.

Although Germans were just one of the European groups to settle in Milwaukee in the mid-nineteenth century, they were the most numerous, and had a strong cultural impact on the city. As late as 1940, twenty per cent of Milwaukee's residents were German speaking. Two restaurants, Mader's and Karl Ratzsch's, are musts for German food. Mader's German Restaurant, 1037-41 N. Old World Third Street, Milwaukee 53203, 414-271-3377; Karl Ratzsch's Old World Restaurant, 320 E. Mason Street, Milwaukee 53202, 414-276-2720. Purchases of sausages and wursts can be made at Usinger's sausage factory and shop, 1030 N. Old World Third Street, Milwaukee 53203, 414-276-9100.

For more information on Milwaukee sites, contact the Greater Milwaukee Convention and Visitors Bureau, Inc., 756 N. Milwaukee Street, Milwaukee 53202, 414-277-9833.

LOCATION: Milwaukee is in southeast Wisconsin, on the shore of Lake Michigan, 95 miles north of Chicago

BED & BREAKFASTS: Bed & Breakfast of Milwaukee, Inc., 320 E. Buffalo, Milwaukee WI 53202, 414-271-2337 (a reservation service)

MOTELS/HOTELS: The Pfister Hotel, 424 E. Wisconsin Avenue, Milwaukee 53202, 414-273-8222; Howard Johnson Plaza, 611 W. Wisconsin Avenue, Milwaukee 53203, 414-273-2950; Marc Plaza, 509 W. Wisconsin Avenue, Milwaukee 53203, 414-271-7250; Dillon Inn, 11111 W. North Avenue, Wauwatosa 53226, 414-778-0333; Best Western Midway Motor Lodge, 1005 S. Moorland Road, Brookfield 53005, 414-786-9540

CAMPING: Wisconsin State Fair RV Park, West Allis, WI 53214, 414-257-8844; Jellystone Park, 8425 Hwy. 38, Caledonia 53108, 414-835-2565, 800-558-2954

DIRECTIONS: From Chicago, take the Edens Expressway, I-94, or the Tri-State Tollway, I-294, north, continuing on I-94 North to Milwaukee

11. MINERAL POINT:
PENDARVIS

Pendarvis, a State Historical Site located in the town of Mineral Point, is a restored group of limestone cottages built in the 1830s by Cornish men. These migrants from Cornwall, England, were tin miners who came to Wisconsin when lead was discovered in the 1820s.

The lead boom which occurred in Mineral Point attracted prospectors from the East and South who did shallow mining, and the Cornish who were hard rock miners. By the mid-1830s, the population of the town was over 2,000. When Wisconsin became a territory in 1836, residents of Mineral Point tried unsuccessfully to have the territorial capital established there.

In addition to their mining abilities, the Cornish men were skilled stonemasons who built more than 30 limestone and log houses. Structures were built along a ravine, with limestone removed from quarries under the houses. Only the stones on the street side of the house were dressed or faced. Face stones were carefully cut so that they fit together neatly.

Houses had 18 inch-thick walls, interior end chimneys, oak floors and trim, handmade iron nails, and shingle roofs. They were located along Shake Rag Alley, named because miners' wives would shake rags to call their husbands, who were working in nearby mines, home to dinner.

Lead production declined after 1847 and miners either turned to farming or left for the California gold rush. Their houses gradually fell into disrepair and some were torn down. In 1935, Robert Neal and Edgar Hellum began restoring the remaining Cornish-style cottages. They began with a one-story cottage which they named Pendarvis, after a village in Cornwall. Other properties restored were Trelawny, a two-story stone structure; Polperro, a three-story stone and log house; and Tamblyn's Row, a three-unit rowhouse.

Owned and operated by the State Historical Society of Wisconsin since 1971, the cottages can be toured every half hour between 9 a.m. and 4 p.m., with costumed guides. Building interiors, which are furnished with mid-nineteenth-century furniture and artifacts, have small rooms and low ceilings, despite the fact that miners' families were often large. The simplicity and difficulty of the miners' lives is evident from the basic furnishings and crowded conditions.

During the restoration process, Neal and Hellum were surprised to discover a kiddlywink, a Cornish pub, on the lower level of Tamblyn's Row, that had been completely hidden by dirt. Used by the miners to enjoy hard-earned drinks and companionship, the charming pub has stone walls, a beamed ceiling, a fireplace, trestle tables and Windsor chairs.

Tours conclude in the Pendarvis Book and Gift Shop. A self-guided tour may be taken of the Merry Christmas Mine Hill across the street.

Even without Pendarvis, Mineral Point is an interesting weekend getaway. The terrain is hilly because it is in the driftless, or unglaciated part, of Wisconsin. The town is small and streets are laid out irregularly, following the miners' footpaths. Architecture is a mix of Cornish limestone cottages and mansions in various styles, including Greek and Gothic revival. Some are used as bed and breakfasts.

Cornish food like bread pudding, pasties (beef, potatoes and onions in a flaky crust), and figgyhobbin (a dessert pastry rolled up with raisins) are still served in many of the restaurants in town. The Chesterfield Inn, a former stagecoach stop that is now a Bed and Breakfast, also serves Cornish food in its Ovens of Brittany, antique-filled restaurant.

Mineral Point has attracted many artisans, and work by local weavers, potters, woodworkers, glass artists and painters is available in many of the shops. Antiquing is also good as there are more than half a dozen shops with a variety of merchandise in town. Antique shows are held on the second weekends of June and October.

ADDRESS: 114 Shake Rag Street, Mineral Point, WI 53565
TELEPHONE: 608-987-2122
HOURS: Daily, 9 a.m. to 5 p.m., May 1 to October 31
ADMISSION: Adults $4.00, seniors $3.60, children 5-17 $1.50
FACILITIES: Restored 1830s Cornish lead miners' houses; guided tours; Merry Christmas Mine Hill walk; book and gift shop; special events; state historical site; NR
LOCATION: Mineral Point is in south central Wisconsin, 175 miles northwest of Chicago, 54 miles southwest of Madison
BED & BREAKFASTS: Chesterfield Inn B&B, 20 Commerce Street, Mineral Point 53565, 608-987-3682; Chesterfield Inn on Shake Rag, Mineral Point 53565, 608-987-3682; The Duke House B&B, 618 Maiden Street, Mineral Point 53565, 608-987-2821; Wm. A. Jones House B&B, 215 Ridge St., P.O. Box 130, Mineral Point 53565, 608-987-2337
HOTELS/MOTELS: Redwood Motel, Hwy. 51 N, Mineral Point 53565, 608-987-2242
CAMPING: Governor Dodge State Park, Rt. 1, Box 42, Dodgeville 53533, 608-935-2315; Moe-Harding Camp Grounds, Hwy. 23, Mineral Point 53565, 608-987-3456
DIRECTIONS: From Chicago, take the Northwest Tollway, I-90, north into Wisconsin to the Madison area, then U.S. 12/18 West to U.S. 18/151 South (still in Madison area), to U.S. 151 South near Dodgeville, to Mineral Point

12. NORTH FREEDOM:
MID-CONTINENT RAILWAY

Near the tiny town of North Freedom, the Mid-Continent Railway, an early 1900s steam train, offers a nine-mile roundtrip ride on a branch line of the Chicago & North Western Railroad. Known as the Rattlesnake Line, the track was laid in 1903 to serve iron ore mines in the town of LaRue. After the mines closed, the train line served a quarry until 1962, and then was abandoned.

The Mid-Continent Railway Historical Society, formed in 1959, acquired the Rattlesnake Line, restored the track, and began purchasing both railroad equipment and buildings. Their goal was the preservation and re-creation of now-vanished early twentieth-century railroading. By 1963, the Historical Society was operating their first steam train and a railroad museum.

In the Coach Shed is a display of wooden passenger and freight cars, all beautifully restored. There is a first class coach built by the Pullman Company in 1905, a 1925 Great Northern caboose, a 1905 baggage/coach car, and a 1906 snowplow. A graphic explanation of the varieties of steam locomotives is displayed inside the 1886 Wisconsin Central Baggage Car no. 305.

The steam locomotives used to pull the excursion train are on the tracks outside. They include Chicago & North Western no. 1385, built in 1907; Dardanelle & Russellville no. 9, built in 1884; and Western Coal & Coke no. 1, built in 1913. Also outside, in the Depot Display Area, are cabooses, flat-cars, box-cars, tank cars, and a snowplow.

The restored train station, which serves as ticket office and gift shop, is a small frame depot built in 1894 at nearby Rock Springs. It was moved to North Freedom in 1963 and has a display of railroad lanterns, switch locks and keys, photographs and railway maps, in its waiting room.

The train ride itself is the greatest fun and seems to mesmerize children and adults alike. Conductors are in period uniforms. If you want air conditioning, you can open a window but don't be surprised if some cinders fly in. The scenery in the Baraboo River Valley is rural and wooded. Every time the train approaches a road, it blows its ear-shattering whistle.

If you're in the last car leaving the station, you'll be in the first car returning, as the train uses the same tracks in both directions. While waiting for the crew to prepare the train for our return trip, some not-so-little boy passengers put coins on the track to see what would happen when the train rolled over them. (They became unbelievably thin and flat.) The only complaint heard on the turn-of-century train was that the ride was too short.

A snow train complete with plow car is operated one week end in February. Call the historical society for information.

ADDRESS: North Freedom, WI 53951
TELEPHONE: 608-522-4261
HOURS: Museum: daily, 9:30 a.m. to 5 p.m., mid-May through Labor Day; weekends only September-October; train rides depart at 10:30 a.m., 12:30, 2, and 3:30 p.m.
ADMISSION: Adults $6.00, children 5-15 $3.00
FACILITIES: Steam train rides; railroad museum with restored railroad cars; gift shop; picnic area and playground; restored train station
LOCATION: In south central Wisconsin, seven miles west of Baraboo, 175 miles northeast of Chicago
BED & BREAKFAST: see Circus World Museum, Baraboo (#1)
HOTELS/MOTELS: see Circus World Museum, Baraboo (#1)
CAMPING: see Circus World Museum, Baraboo (#1)
DIRECTIONS: From Chicago, take the Northwest Tollway, I-90, to I-90/94 near Madison, continue north on I-90/94 to exit 92, U.S. 12, then south on U.S. 12 to WI 136, west on WI 136 to Co. Rt. PF, south on Co. Rt. PF to North Freedom; Mid-Continent is one-half mile west of the four-way stop in North Freedom

13. SPRING GREEN:
TALIESIN

Taliesin, Frank Lloyd Wright's Wisconsin home and architectural school, is in Jones Valley near the Wisconsin River. The setting is pastoral, its rolling hills dotted with trees and flowers. Wright's buildings enhance the beauty of the landscape. In his development of the valley, Wright protected the natural setting by running utility lines underground, preserving large trees and prohibiting road signs. Wright returned to his Welsh ancestors' New World home to find peace, and a sense of peacefulness still permeates the valley today.

Frank Lloyd Wright returned to Wisconsin, his native state, in 1911. After two decades of living and working in Oak Park, Illinois, (see Chicago and Suburbs #24), Wright had abandoned his wife, Catherine, their six children, and a thriving architectural business in 1909, when he went to Europe with his lover, Mamah Borthwich Cheney. Mamah Cheney was a neighbor and the wife of a client, Edwin Cheney, for whom Wright had built a house in Oak Park.

On his return from Europe, Wright begin building on a 200-acre site acquired from his mother in the Jones Valley, settled by, and named after, her Welsh ancestors. As a child, he had spent many summers in this area with his relatives. It was here that he chose to work and live with the now divorced Mamah. He named his house Taliesin, a Welsh word which means "shining brow," because Taliesin was built into the brow of a wooded slope overlooking the Wisconsin River. Its site reflected Wright's belief that buildings should form a natural part of a landscape, not perch on a landscape.

Wright intended Taliesin to be a self-contained site.

In addition to living space and working space, there was an icehouse, stables, a granary, and a power plant. The desire for self-sufficiency probably resulted from the general disapproval of Wright's unconventional lifestyle. Because of his prominence in architectural and social circles, Wright's personal relationships with women were well publicized by the press and created a great deal of scandal.

Wright and Mamah intended to live a private, happy life together in Spring Green but a tragedy ended their dream. On 14 August 1914, while Wright was in Chicago supervising a project, Mamah was having lunch with her two children and their friend and five Taliesin workmen. The Barbadian chef, Julian Carlston, locked the dining room door, set the house on fire, and axed to death the few who managed to escape the house. Seven people died, including Mamah and her son and daughter. No explanation was ever provided for the demented act, and a few days later Carlston committed suicide in jail. Much of Taliesin was destroyed in the fire, and was rebuilt by Wright.

Taliesin was not simply the architectural project of Frank Lloyd Wright; it was his home from 1911 until his death in 1959. It was the second of three homes Wright built for himself. The first was in Oak Park, Illinois, in 1889, and the third was a winter home in Scottsdale, Arizona, in 1938. At each site, Wright combined living quarters with his architectural studio and business.

Spring Green, in the Jones Valley, had been the site of the first building ever designed and built by Frank Lloyd Wright. The 20-year-old was commissioned to erect a school building for his aunts, Jane and Nell Lloyd Jones, who started a school in 1887, primarily for their many nieces and nephews. The teachers believed in nature study, outdoor work, individualized projects, spontaneity and close student-faculty relationships. In 1887, Wright designed the first Hillside Home School.

Hillside expanded into a coeducational boarding school. When success led it to outgrow its original facility, Wright was commissioned to build another school on the site. The 1902 Hillside Home School, called a prairie building because of its similarity to the Prairie Houses, was built of local timber and sandstone on a gently sloping site. Its spacious open interior reflected the educational philosophy of the school.

After the school closed in 1917, the building was neglected and vandalized. Wright inherited the Hillside property, located about a mile from Taliesin, in 1920 after both of his aunts died. In 1932, he and his third wife, Olgivanna, began Taliesin Fellowship, a combination of an arts and architecture school with a communal lifestyle. A hill village, Taliesin had several small apartments and other living quarters in which Fellowship members and Wright's relatives lived. One of the first projects assigned to the students was to remodel the Hillside Home School for their own use. The gymnasium was turned into a theater. Additions included a drafting room and a dormitory in 1934, and a dining room, a kitchen, galleries, and more sleeping quarters in 1939.

Visitors who pull off Highway 23 into Frank Lloyd Wright's Taliesin are actually at the Hillside Home School, now known as Taliesin Fellowship Buildings. The interior of the sandstone and native oak buildings may be seen on guided tours. During the summer, the complex is the home and studio of architecture students in the school begun by Wright. It also houses Taliesin Architects, the architecture firm that continues Wright's tradition.

Although the entire site in Spring Green is called Taliesin, that is the name given by Wright to his home. Formerly the interior of that house had only been open to sponsored groups, but plans are currently underway to open the house on a limited basis for individuals by reservation. The exterior of Taliesin may be seen on guided walking tours. One and one-half hour walking tours of the Taliesin property begin at Hillside Home School, go past several Wright structures, including the Romeo and Juliet Windmill which is being restored; Tany-deri, a home Wright built for his sister; Midway Farm, and into the gardens of Taliesin.

Taliesin, an impressive U-shaped, multi-story, stone-and-frame structure poised on the side of a hill overlooking the Wisconsin River, is a series of connecting wings, each zoned for a particular use. It features low, hipped roof sections with overhanging eaves, light colored walls, casement windows, and much stonework. Large Oriental urns and statues decorate the garden. It is called Taliesin III because the wings containing Wright's living quarters in both the first and second Taliesins burned and were rebuilt. Stone that survived the fires was incorporated into the new structures. Taliesin and Hillside Home School are owned and operated by the Frank Lloyd Wright Foundation.

While in Spring Green, you can have dinner in the Spring Green Restaurant, the only restaurant designed by Frank Lloyd Wright. It is located south of Spring Green, near the intersection of WI 23 and Co. Rt. C, just south of the Wisconsin River, 608-588-2571.

The American Players Theatre, a professional repertory theater devoted to the classics, performs on an outdoor stage from late June to early October. Their address is Box 819, Spring Green 53588, 608-588-7401; box office: 608-588-2361.

Also in Spring Green is a popular tourist attraction called the House on the Rock. This bizarre combination of fun house and museum, created by Alex Jordan, has room after room filled with huge displays of a mixture of antiques and reproductions. Featured are stained glass, music machines, carousel horses, doll houses, vast whiskey stills, and a 200-foot fiberglass whale. Open daily, April-October; WI 23, Spring Green 53588, 608-935-3639.

ADDRESS: Spring Green, Wisconsin 53588-9304
TELEPHONE: 608-588-2511
HOURS: Tours of Hillside Home School (also known as Taliesin Fellowship Buildings): daily, 9 a.m. to 4 p.m., May-October; Walking tours of Taliesin property (not including house interior): Monday-Saturday, 10:30 a.m., mid-June through September; call for dates and times of Taliesin interior tours
ADMISSION: Hillside School tour: adults $6.00, children 12 and under $3.00; Taliesin walking tour: $15.00
FACILITIES: Book and gift shop; guided tours; NHL
LOCATION: In southwestern Wisconsin, about 40 miles west of Madison, approximately 170 miles from Chicago
BED & BREAKFASTS: Wildwood Lodge, Upper Wyoming Rd., Spring Green 53588, 608-588-2514; Hill Street Bed & Breakfast, 353 Hill St., Spring Green 53588, 608-588-7751
HOTELS/MOTELS: Spring Green Motel, U.S. 14, Spring Green 53588, 608-588-2141; Round Barn Lodge, just west of jct. of U.S. 14 & WI 23S, Spring Green 53588, 608-588-2568; Prairie House Motel, Spring Green 53588, 608-588-2088
CAMPING: Tower Hill State Park, Rt. 3, Spring Green 53588, 608-588-2116; Governor Dodge State Park, Rt. 1, Box 42, Dodgeville 53533, 608-935-2315
DIRECTIONS: From Chicago, take the Northwest Tollway, I-90, north to Madison, Wisconsin, exit I-90 at U.S. 12/18, west to U.S. 12/14, U.S. 14 west to Spring Green, then WI 23 south to Hillside Home School

CHICAGO AREA HOTELS AND MOTELS

NEAR NORTH

Ambassador West
1300 N. State Parkway, Chicago 60610
312-787-7900, 800-621-8090

Barclay
166 E. Superior, Chicago 60611
312-787-6000, 800-621-8004

Best Western Inn of Chicago
162 E. Ohio Street, Chicago 60611
312-787-3100

Best Western River North
125 W. Ohio Street, Chicago 60610
312-467-0800

Claridge
1244 N. Dearborn Parkway, Chicago 60610
312-787-4980, 800-245-1258

Days Inn Lake Shore Drive
644 N. Lake Shore Drive, Chicago 60611
312-943-9200

The Drake
140 E. Walton Place, Chicago 60611
312-787-2200

Executive House
71 E. Wacker Drive, Chicago 60601
312-346-7100, 800-621-4005

Fairmont at Illinois Center
200 N. Columbus Drive, Chicago 60601
312-565-8000, 800-527-4727

Four Seasons
120 E. Delaware Place, Chicago 60611
312-280-8800

Holiday Inn-City Centre
300 E. Ohio Street, Chicago 60611
312-787-6100

Hotel Nikko Chicago
320 N. Dearborn, Chicago 60610
312-744-1900, 800-645-5687

Hotel 21 East
21 E. Bellevue Place, Chicago 60611
312-266-2100, 800-426-3135

Hyatt Regency
151 E. Wacker Drive, Chi-
   cago 60601
312-565-1234

Inter-Continental Chicago
505 N. Michigan Avenue,
   Chicago 60611
312-944-4100

Knickerbocker
163 E. Walton Place, Chicago
   60611
312-751-8100

Lenox House
616 N. Rush Street, Chicago
   60611
312-337-1000, 800-445-3669

Marriott
540 N. Michigan Avenue,
   Chicago 60611
312-836-0100

Mayfair Regent
181 E. Lake Shore Drive, Chicago 60611
312-787-8500, 800-545-4000

Omni Ambassador East
1301 N. State Parkway, Chicago 60610
312-787-7200

Park Hyatt on Water Tower
   Square
800 N. Michigan Avenue,
   Chicago 60611
312-280-2222

Raphael
201 E. Delaware, Chicago
   60611
312-943-5000; 800-821-5343

Richmont
162 E. Ontario, Chicago
   60611
312-787-3580

Ritz-Carlton
160 E. Pearson Street, Chicago 60611
312-266-1000, 800-621-6906

Sheraton-Plaza
160 E. Huron, Chicago 60611
312-787-2900

Swiss Grand
323 E. Wacker Drive, Chi-
   cago 60601
312-565-0565, 800-654-7263

Tremont
100 E. Chestnut, Chicago
   60611
312-751-1900, 800-621-8133

The Westin Hotel, Chicago
909 N. Michigan Avenue,
   Chicago 60611
312-943-7200

LOOP

Bismarck
171 W. Randolph Street, Chicago 60601
312-236-0123, 800-643-1500

Blackstone
636 S. Michigan Avenue, Chicago 60605
312-427-4300

Essex Inn
800 S. Michigan Avenue, Chicago 60605
312-939-2800, 800-621-6909

Hilton & Towers
720 S. Michigan Avenue, Chicago 60605
312-922-4400

Midland
172 W. Adams, Chicago 60603
312-332-1200, 800-621-2360

Omni Morton
500 S. Dearborn, Chicago 60605
312-663-3200

Palmer House
17 E. Monroe Street, Chicago 60690
312-726-7500

SOUTH SIDE

Hilton at Hyde Park
4900 S. Lake Shore Drive, Chicago 60615
312-288-5800

Holiday Inn-Midway Airport
7353 S. Cicero Avenue, Chicago 60629
312-581-5300

Mc Cormick Center
451 E. 23rd Street, Chicago 60616
312-791-1900

Midway Airport Inn
5400 S. Cicero Avenue, Chicago 60638
312-581-0500, 800-621-0127, 800-238-0638 (IL)

SUBURBS—NORTH

Holiday Inn
1501 Sherman Avenue, Evanston 60201
708-491-6400

Omni Orrington
1710 Orrington Avenue, Evanston 60201
708-866-8700

Budgetel Inn
1625 Milwaukee Avenue, Glenview 60025
708-635-8300

Courtyard by Marriott
1801 N. Milwaukee Avenue,
  Glenview 60025
708-803-2500

Radisson Suites
1400 Milwaukee Avenue,
  Glenview 60025
708-803-9800

Holiday Inn
6161 W. Grand Avenue,
  Gurnee 60031
708-336-6300

Courtyard by Marriott
1505 Lake Cook Road, Highland Park 60035
708-831-3338

Deer Path Inn
255 East Illinois Road, Lake
  Forest 60045
708-234-2280

Allgauer's
2855 N. Milwaukee Avenue,
  Northbrook 60062
708-480-7500, 800-328-6516

Sheraton-North Shore Inn
933 Skokie Blvd., North-
  brook 60062
708-498-6500

Holiday Inn
5300 W. Touhy Avenue,
  Skokie 60077
708-679-8900

Howard Johnson
9333 Skokie Boulevard,
  Skokie 60077
708-679-4200

SUBURBS—NORTHWEST

Dillon Inn
2120 S. Arlington Heights
  Road, Arlington Heights
  60005
708-593-9400

Radisson
75 W. Algonquin Road, Ar-
  lington Heights 60005
708-364-7600

Barrington Motor Lodge
405 W. Northwest Highway,
  Barrington 60010
708-381-2640

Holiday Inn
800 S. IL 31, Crystal Lake
  60014
815-477-7000

Comfort Inn
2175 E. Touhy Avenue, Des
  Plaines 60018
708-635-7572

Hampton Inn
100 Busse Road, Elk Grove
  Village 60007
708-593-8600

Stouffer Hamilton
400 Park Boulevard, Itasca
  60143
708-773-4000

Courtyard by Marriott
505 Milwaukee Avenue, Lincolnshire 60069
708-634-9555

Holiday Inn-O'Hare at Kennedy
5440 N. River Road, Rosemont 60018
708-671-6350

Hotel Sofitel Chicago at O'Hare
5550 N. River Road, Rosemont 60018
708-678-4488

Hyatt Regency O'Hare
9300 W. Bryn Mawr Avenue, Rosemont 60018
708-696-1234

The Westin Hotel, O'Hare
6100 River Road, Rosemont 60018
708-698-6000

Compri
800 N. State Parkway, Schaumburg 60173

SUBURBS—WEST

Days Inn
300 S. Frontage Road, Burr Ridge 60521
708-325-2900

Hampton Inn
6251 Joliet Road, Countryside 60525
708-354-5200

Dillon Inn
3031 Finley Road, Downers Grove 60515
708-810-9500

Marriott Suites
1500 Opus Place, Downers Grove 60515
708-852-1500

Radisson Suite Hotel
2111 Butterfield Road, Downers Grove 60515
708-971-2000

Holiday Inn
1250 Roosevelt Road, Glen Ellyn 60137
708-629-6000

Holiday Inn
4400 Frontage Road, Hillside 60162
708-544-9300

Holiday Inn
6201 Joliet Road, La Grange 60525
708-354-4200

Hilton Inn
3003 Corporate West, Lisle 60532
708-369-0900

Holiday Inn Crowne Plaza
3000 Warrenville Road, Lisle 60532
708-505-1000

Embassy Suites
7076 E. Butterfield Road,
  Lombard 60148
708-969-7500

Coutryard by Marriott
1155 Diehl Road, Naperville
  60566
708-961-1500

Exel Inn
1585 N. Naperville/Whea-
  ton Road, Naperville 60540
708-357-0022

Hampton Inn
1087 Diehl Road, Naperville
  60566
708-505-1400

Sheraton
1801 N. Naper Boulevard,
  Naperville 60540
708-369-1900

Drake
2301 S. York Road, Oak
  Brook 60521
708-574-5700, 800-334-9805

Oak Brook Hills
3500 Midwest Road, Oak
  Brook 60521
708-850-5555, 800-445-3315

Stouffer
2100 Spring Road, Oak
  Brook 60521
708-573-2800

Holiday Inn-Oak Brook Terrace
17W350 22nd Street, Oak-
  brook Terrace 60181
708-833-3600

Carleton
1110 Pleasant Street, Oak
  Park 60302
708-848-5000

The Wheaton Inn
301 West Roosevelt Road,
  Wheaton 60187
708-690-2600

Holiday Inn-Willowbrook
7800 S. Kingery Highway, IL
  83, Willowbrook 60521
708-325-6400

Red Roof Inn
7535 IL 83, Willowbrook
  60521
708-323-8811

SUBURBS—SOUTH

Days Inn
17220 S. Halsted Street, East
  Hazelcrest 60429
708-957-5900

Sheraton
17400 S. Halsted Street,
  Homewood 60430
708-957-1600

Hilton Inn of Oak Lawn
9333 S. Cicero Avenue, Oak
  Lawn 60453
708-425-7800

Holiday Inn-Oak Lawn
4140 W. 95th Street, Oak
    Lawn 60453
708-425-7900

Budgetel Inn
17225 Halsted Street, South
    Holland 60473
708-596-8700

TOLL-FREE 800 NUMBERS FOR HOTELS AND MOTELS

Best Western International,
    Inc.
800-528-1234

Budgetel Inns
800-4-BUDGET

Clarion Hotels
800-CLARION

Comfort Inns
800-228-5150

Courtyard by Marriott
800-321-2211

Days Inn
800-325-2525

Dillon Inn
800-253-7503

Embassy Suites
800-362-2779

Exel Inns of America
800-356-8013

Fairfield Inn by Marriott
800-228-2800

Fairmont Hotels
800-527-4727

Four Seasons Hotels
800-332-3442

Friendship Inns of America
    Int'l
800-453-4511

Hampton Inn
800-HAMPTON

Hilton Hotels Corp.
800-HILTONS

Holiday Inns
800-HOLIDAY

Howard Johnson
800-654-2000

Hyatt Corp.
800-228-9000

Imperial Inns
800-368-4400

La Quinta Motor Inns, Inc.
800-531-5900

Lexington Hotel Suites
800-53-SUITE

Loews Hotels
800-223-0888

Marriott Hotels
800-228-9290

Omni Hotels
800-843-6664

Park Inns Int'l
800-437-PARK

Pickett Suite Hotels
800-PICKETT

Quality Inns
800-228-5151

Radisson Hotel Corp.
800-333-3333

Ramada Inns
800-2-RAMADA

Red Carpet/Scottish Inns
800-251-1962

Red Roof Inns
800-843-7663

Regal 8 Inn
800-851-8888

Residence Inn by Marriott
800-331-3131

Ritz-Carlton
800-241-3333
800-621-6906 (Chicago)

Rodeway Inns International
800-228-2000

Sheraton Hotels & Inns
800-325-3535

Signature Inns
800-822-5252

Stouffer Hotels and Resorts
800-HOTELS-1

Super 8 Motels
800-843-1991

Susse Chalet Motor Lodges
  & Inns
800-258-1980

Travelodge International Inc.
800-255-3050

Treadway Inns Corp.
800-873-2392

Westin Hotels
800-228-3000

APPENDIX C:

STATE TOURIST INFORMATION

CHICAGO

Chicago Tourism Council
Historic Water Tower in-the-
Park, 806 N. Michigan Avenue, 60611
312-280-5740

Chicago Convention and
Visitors Bureau
312-567-8500

Chicago Transit Authority
and Regional Transporta-
tion Authority
312-836-7000

ILLINOIS

Illinois Travel Information
Center
310 S. Michigan Avenue,
Suite 108, Chicago 60604
312-793-2094

Illinois Office of Tourism
State of Illinois Center, 100
W. Randolph, Chicago
60601
312-917-4732
Illinois Office of Tourism
620 East Adams Street,
Springfield 62710

Illinois Travel Information
800-637-8560

Illinois Department of Conservation, State Park Division
524 S. Second Street, Springfield 62706

Illinois Historic Perservation
Agency
Old State Capitol, Spring-
field 62701

INDIANA

Indiana Department of Commerce, Tourism Develop-
ment Division
One N. Capitol Street, Suite
700, Indianapolis 46204
317-232-8860; 800-2-WAN-
DER

Indiana Department of Natural Resources, Division of
State Parks
616 State Office Building, Indianapolis 46204
317-232-4200; 800-622-4931

MICHIGAN

The Travel Bureau, Michigan
  Department of Commerce
Box 30226, Lansing 48909
517-373-1195; 800-543-2YES

Michigan Department of
  Natural Resources, Parks
  Division
Box 30028, Lansing 48909
517-373-1220; 517-373-1270

WISCONSIN

Wisconsin Division of Tourism
Box 7606, Madison 53707
608-266-2161; 800-ESCAPES

Wisconsin Tourist Information Center
123 W. Washington Avenue,
  Madison 53702
608-266-2161

Wisconsin Tourist Information Center
342 N. Michigan Avenue,
  Chicago, IL 60601
312-332-7274

Wisconsin Division of Natural Resources, Parks & Recreation
Box 7921, Madison 53707

State Historical Society of
  Wisconsin
816 State Street, Madison
  53706
608-262-9606

Index

Great Western Depot, 143-44
Green Bay Packer Hall of Fame, 243
Green Bay, WI
  Green Bay Packer Hall of Fame,
    243
  Heritage Hill State Park, 240-44
  National Railroad Museum, 242-43
Greenbush, WI
  Old Wade House, 244-47
Grosse Point Lighthouse Park, 66-68

Hackley & Hume Historic Site,
  205-6
Handicapped accessible sites
  Illinois
    Balzekas Museum of Lithuanian
      Culture, 23-25
    Brookfield Zoo, 15-18
    Chicago Academy of Sciences,
      18-20
    Chicago Botanic Garden, 68-70
    Chicago Historical Society, 20-22
    Clarke House, 36-39
    DuSable Museum of African
      American History, 25-26
    Field Museum of Natural
      History, 33-35
    Lincoln Park Zoo, 46-48
    Lincoln's New Salem State
      Historic Site, 136-42
    Museum of Science and
      Industry, 48-51
    Swedish American Museum
      Center, 29-30
  Indiana
    Children's Museum of
      Indianapolis, 165-68
  Michigan
    Gerald R. Ford Museum, 185-89
    Hart-Montague Bicycle Trail
      State Park, 199-200
    Hidden Lake Gardens, 218
    Michigan Historical Museum,
      196-98
  Wisconsin
    Governor Dodge State Park,
      230-32
    Milwaukee County Zoo, 250
    Milwaukee Public Museum, 251

Old World Wisconsin, 236-40
Handicapped facilities
  fishing pier, 156
  garden, 69
  nature trail, 147-48, 174, 234-35
Hang gliding
  Warren Dunes State Park, 210-14
Harrison, President Benjamin,
  Memorial Home, 168-70
Hart-Montague Bicycle Trail State
  Park, 199-200
Hastings, MI
  Charlton Park Village and
    Museum, 189-92
Heritage Hill State Park, 240-44
Hidden Lake Gardens, 218
Hiking trails
  Illinois
    Castle Rock State Park, 131-32
    Chain O'Lakes State Park, 147-48
    Fullersburg Woods Forest
      Preserve and Nature Center,
      78-81
    Goose Lake Prairie State Natural
      Area, 124-26
    Illinois Beach State Park, 156-59
    Illinois and Michigan Canal
      State Trail, 126-31
    Illinois Prairie Path, 92-94
    Little Red Schoolhouse Nature
      Center, 95-96
    Lowden State Park, 132-34
    Moraine Hills State Park, 121-23
    Ryerson, Edward L.,
      Conservation Area, 62-64
    Sand Ridge Nature Center, 86-88
    Starved Rock State Park, 148-52
    White Pines Forest State Park,
      134-36
  Indiana
    Indiana Dunes National
      Lakeshore, 175-79
    Indiana Dunes State Park, 175-79
    Pokagon State Park, 163-65
  Michigan
    Hart-Montague Bicycle Trail
      State Park, 199-200